1997

Towards justice and virtue challenges the rivalry between those who advocate only abstract universal principles of justice and those who commend only the particularities of virtuous lives. Onora O'Neill traces this impasse to defects in underlying conceptions of reasoning about action. She proposes and vindicates an alternative, more modest, account of ethical reasoning, a reasoned way of answering the question 'who counts?', and constructs a linked account of the principles which are basic for moving towards just institutions and virtuous lives.

TOWARDS JUSTICE AND VIRTUE

Terence Garvey
1915–1985
in fond and vivid memory

TOWARDS JUSTICE
AND VIRTUE

A constructive account of practical reasoning

ONORA O'NEILL

Newnham College, Cambridge

CAMBRIDGE
UNIVERSITY PRESS

Published by the Press Syndicate of the University of Cambridge
The Pitt Building, Trumpington Street, Cambridge CB2 1RP
40 West 20th Street, New York, NY 10011-4211, USA
10 Stamford Road, Oakleigh, Melbourne 3166, Australia

First published 1996

Printed in Great Britain at the University Press, Cambridge

A catalogue record for this book is available from the British Library

Library of Congress cataloguing in publication data
O'Neill, Onora, 1941–
Towards justice and virtue / Onora O'Neill.
p.   cm
Includes bibliographical references and index.
ISBN 0 521 48095 7 (hardback). – ISBN 0 521 48559 2 (paperback).
1. Justice (Philosophy). 2. Justice. 3. Virtue. 4. Virtues.
1. Title.
B105.J87O54   1996
170 – dc20   95–49161   CIP

ISBN 0 521 48095 7 hardback
ISBN 0 521 48559 2 paperback

Contents

Preface

This book has been part of my life for many years. Many of its claims and arguments have been explored in one form and another with varied audiences, and discussed with sceptical but patient friends. I am grateful and hope that I have learnt from them, as well as from many colleagues who have taken time to comment on drafts and articles in which stretches of the argument have been presented.

For long-drawn-out work it is not only the many audiences of each year, but sustaining institutions and friendships which matter most. Throughout the 1980s I was lucky enough to find at the University of Essex colleagues who took seriously my growing suspicions that much recent writing in ethics and political philosophy is disoriented, and that much that it presents as practical reasoning is neither practical nor reasoned. They also took seriously my stubborn refusal to assuage these suspicions by settling for relativist or postmodernist conclusions, or to concede that we must either advocate justice or befriend the virtues, but that we cannot coherently do both. I thank them for years of discussion, criticism and encouragement.

The leisure to start the book I owe to the Wissenschaftskolleg in Berlin, where I spent the memorable year 1989/90. In spite of the many distractions of those politically riveting months, this proved a good time and place for writing. I am grateful to the Rektor, Professor Wolf Lepenies, and to the Fellows who formed the *philosophischen Kreis*, for a rare opportunity to write intensively and talk companionably.

I left Berlin with a manuscript, and a large hole in its argument: the account of practical reasoning on which the whole endeavour builds had not yet been extracted from its Kantian origins and connected adequately to contemporary work in ethics and political philosophy. Much intervening time has been spent thinking and writing about conceptions of practical reason and making these connections.

It has taken me longer than it might to complete this task, in part because of energies spent moving to and into Cambridge. Once again I have been fortunate in my surroundings; I thank Cambridge colleagues for support and encouragement.

For many helpful, and a few exasperating, comments on later drafts of the book I must thank Jerry Schneewind, Rüdiger Bittner, Thomas Pogge, Nicholas Rengger, Jacob Nell and the readers for Cambridge University Press; its deficiencies are my own.

Newnham College, Cambridge   ONORA O'NEILL
August 1995

Introduction

Writing philosophically – like writing novels or history, like drawing or journalism, like taking photographs – presents countless choices about inclusions and exclusions which will enable the work to be read in one or another way, by one or another audience. How much should be said about the premisses of arguments, or about the context or history of a given discussion or position? How much should be allowed to fade into the background? How far should the detailed implications and ramifications of a position or an argument be developed?

Some difficult choices arise because philosophical writing aspires to sound argument. Is soundness of argument partly achieved, or at least buttressed, by careful commentary on kindred and on rival work? Does it help to discuss or defeat the strategies and arguments of work that has different starting points or different conclusions? Will 'engaging with the literature' be useful for maintaining convincing standards and strategies of argument? Or will it produce a cautiously and boringly 'professional' tone, put a lot of readers off, and camouflage the main lines of argument? Too much concentration on the failings of positions and lines of thought not taken might seem distracting and defensive; too cavalier a view of other work might seem arbitrary, dogmatic, and quite unprofessional.

In writing on justice and virtue I have repeatedly found these choices difficult. Nobody can write on justice or virtue without being aware of their importance in all our lives and of the centuries, indeed millennia, of thinking on both that lie behind us. Equally, nobody can look at contemporary writing on justice and on virtue without finding a certain disarray. In the event I decided that it might be useful to probe this disarray.

So the book begins with an *overview* of current work in ethics and political philosophy, and tries to make sense of the now widespread view that justice and virtue are the focus of rival rather than of complementary approaches to ethical and political concern. Nearly all contemporary work on justice is universalist: it advocates universal and abstract principles. Much contemporary writing on virtue is particularist: it criticizes both abstraction and universality, and interprets virtue as a matter of judging and responding to particular situations and relationships. Theories of justice argue for universal rights and obligations; virtues are seen as the time- and context-bound excellences of particular communities or lives.

Chapter 1 suggests that this rivalry between justice and virtue is historically anomalous and not well substantiated, and that the deepest sources of the supposed antagonism may lie in a range of questionable assumptions about action and reason. If these assumptions obstruct rather than help establish ethically and politically convincing and powerful thinking, discarding them may be productive. Or so I shall argue. However, discarding damaging or inadequate conceptions of action and reason will only paralyse reasoning about action if no more adequate conceptions of both can be found. Chapter 2 discusses reasoning about action, chapter 3 the role of principles of action in such reasoning.

In taking a view of reason and action I began with the thought that politics and ethics (whatever else they may be, however else they may be understood) are domains of *activity*. The reasoning that we bring to them must be *practical reasoning*, that is reasoning which we and others can use both in personal and in public life not merely to judge and appraise what is going on, not merely to assess what has been done, but to guide activity. The activities to be guided range from institution building and reform to the daily acts and attitudes of personal life. This demand has two aspects. The first is that some way or ways of guiding activity must be shown to have the sort of authority that would allow us to speak of them as *reasoned*, the second is that those ways of guiding action must be *practical*, in that they can help agents with quite limited and determinate capacities to live their lives.

The search for an adequate account of practical reason starts in chapter 2 with the thought that *abstraction*, far from being hard for agents with limited, non-ideal capacities to follow, or irrelevant for them, is unavoidable in all reasoning about action. Particularists have simply been wrong to claim that abstract thinking or reasoning is ethically damaging, or that it is avoidable. Universalists accept that abstraction is unavoidable, and some of them aim to combine abstraction with empirical claims and instrumental reasoning, and hope to reach substantive conclusions about justice, rights and obligations. I believe that by itself this universalist strategy does not work. It may show that certain sorts of action are *conditionally* required *if* certain ends are to be achieved, or certain preferences are to be satisfied; but it cannot show that ends or preferences are anything but arbitrary, hence cannot show that pursuit of one rather than another of them is reasoned.

Supposing that no metaphysically substantial accounts of the good can establish what the non-arbitrary 'ends of reason' would be, ethical reasoning would have to take some other, non-teleological form. One live possibility, which many friends of the virtues have endorsed, is to see the basic norms or commitments of a society, or of a life, as the bedrock for practical reasoning: authoritative practical reasoning for a given society or individual appeals to their constitutive norms, characters or senses of identity. This authority cannot be challenged because there is no way of going behind or below that which is most fundamental: 'ought' not only may but must be derived from 'is'. Yet this conception of practical reasoning has both ethical costs and theoretical limitations.

The only other live option is to use a conception of reason which can discriminate among courses of action, but does not simply endorse established norms or commitments, or existing traditions and senses of identity: such a conception of practical reason would be *critical*. If no critical account of practical reason can be *discovered*, either in the world or in human conceptions and identities, the only way in which it can be made available is if it can be *constructed*. The critical account of practical reason proposed here will be constructed from the demand that anything that is to count as reasoning must be followable by all relevant others. This demand articulates the thought that when reasons to adopt principles are given, those who do so must assume that those who receive them *could* adopt the recommended or prescribed principles. Practical reasoning begins with a minimal, modal, but authoritative demand: others cannot be given reasons for adopting principles which they cannot adopt.

This limited, modal account of practical reason applies to *principles of action*. Many proponents of virtue ethics will think that things have gone badly awry at this point, because they think that action on principles is ethically inadequate, and perhaps philo-sophically incoherent. Chapter 3 argues that, on the contrary, *action*, hence *principles of action*, indeed specifically *universal principles of action*, must be the *focus* of practical reasoning. However, universal principles have none of the features that have led most contemporary opponents of ethical universalism to fear and shun them. Universal principles are not empty; they do not prescribe rigidly uniform action or neglect of differences between cases; they do not dominate those who act on them; they do not undercut the importance of judgement.

However, a focus on universal principles cannot fix the *scope of ethical consideration*: it cannot show *who* falls within the domain of universal principles. Universality is in the first instance only the formal property of holding for all rather than only for some cases within a specified domain. If we cannot invoke the metaphysical certainties that were traditionally thought to underpin robust forms of perfectionism and of naturalism, on which many sorts of ethical universalism have been based, and in doing so establish who or what has moral standing, the proper scope of ethical consideration must be fixed by other considerations. Chapter 4 argues that the domain of ethical consideration relevant for a given context can be fixed by considering the assumptions agents make about the agency and the subjecthood of others whose lives they take to be connected to their own: what is assumed in action and in attitudes cannot be disowned for ethical purposes, so can be used to fix the proper scope of ethical consideration in a given context. The others for whom reasoned proposals are to be followable are all those whom agents already take for granted in acting.

This account of the *focus* and *scope* of ethical concern and con-sideration establishes the context in which ethical reasoning is undertaken. The character of that reasoning can then be outlined in three stages. Chapter 5 considers the *structure* of significant forms of ethical reasoning; chapters 6 and 7 turn to the *content* of central ethical requirements, and respectively move towards accounts of justice and of virtue.

The most significant *structures* of ethical concern can be expressed in linked webs of *requirements*, which are better articulated by beginning from the perspective of agents and their obligations rather than that of claimants and their rights. If obligations are accorded priority, both the connections and the differences between justice and many of the social virtues can be articulated.

Chapter 6 uses the conceptions of action and reason set out in earlier chapters to construct the elements of an account of *justice*. It argues that justice requires the *rejection of principles of injury*, hence the avoidance of action that injures either systematically or gratuitously. Since injury may be inflicted on others within the scope of ethical consideration either directly or indirectly (by damaging the social fabric and the natural and man-made environments on which others depend) justice will always require complex institutions and practices that can guide and constrain action and policy. Broadly speaking, just action aims to develop institutions and practices which effectively limit and prevent injury to all who fall within the scope of ethical consideration – on whichever side of various borders their lives are led. Although principles of justice do not provide a precise set of instructions, they set standards for building and maintaining *institutions* and *cultures*; their implications will differ in differing conditions.

The last chapter turns to ethical issues that lie beyond justice, and argues that some of these are nevertheless matters of requirement. In particular, certain social virtues are required rather than optional excellences. Their underlying principle requires the *rejection of indifference*, which (unlike injury) cannot be avoided in all action. These social virtues can therefore demand that systematic indifference be rejected, but not that gratuitous indifference be rejected. Like justice, these social virtues have implications not only for action that affects others directly, but for action that affects either the social fabric or the natural and man-made environments on which human lives depend. This account of required virtues does not show that all excellences are required: it allows for the thought that some supererogatory excellences go beyond duty, and that other optional excellences are not required and have no connection with universal principles of duty.

Throughout the book the constructive account of practical reasoning presented in chapter 2 provides the basic orientation. This account is meagre and modal; it makes no assumptions about motivation. It claims only that agents cannot offer others reasons for using one rather than another principle to guide their action unless they think that the recommended principle is a possibility for those others. Practical reasoning begins by requiring us to reject principles which we cannot view as principles for those for whom the reasoning is to count. This rather stringent conception of universalizability as the core of practical reasoning is the Kantian kernel of the book's argument.

It follows that the work has only limited affinity with most contemporary 'deontological' work on justice and rights, which mainly builds on empiricist accounts of motivation and instrumental accounts of rationality. Although this 'deontological' work is widely thought of as Kantian, not least by those who produce it, it in fact rejects most of the basic claims of Kant's practical philosophy, including in particular his conceptions of action, reason and freedom. The historical and exegetical claims that lie behind these rather brusque assertions about contemporary 'Kantianism' will not be explored or substantiated.[1] My intention in writing has not been to comment on the history of ethics, except in passing, but to show that justice and virtue need not be rivals, and that a rigorous conception of reasoning about action will allow us to construct substantive accounts of both without the need to establish any metaphysics of the person, or of the Good.

The results may, I hope, seem worth taking seriously both to those who think that human rights are the core of justice, but that there is nothing or little objective to be said about good lives, and to those who think that virtuous characters are the kernels of good lives, but that preoccupation with obligations and rights is ethically limited and even corrupting. I suspect that, on the contrary, failure to think about justice and virtue in tandem is likely to lead to blinkered and ungenerous, as well as implausible, visions of life, action and politics.

Although the argument of the book is continuous, it is inevitably much less than a detailed account of just societies or of virtuous lives. Some possible implications of rejecting injury and indifference in contemporary conditions are sketched, but much remains open. Principles of justice and of virtue will have differing implications in differing situations; institutions and practices that are just and feasible under one set of conditions may be neither in another; virtues that are vital in one social world may be obsolete or pointless in another.

---

[1] Some of them I discuss in 'Kant's Ethics and Kantian Ethics' forthcoming in *Bounds of Justice* (Cambridge University Press).

This is not the only way in which the account of justice and virtue is incomplete. Although the book engages sporadically with rival positions, it offers no systematic analysis and criticism of their favoured texts, or of the huge secondary literatures. There are enough footnotes to irritate some readers, and too few to satisfy others. I have neither tried to make every point that might be made on behalf of the accounts of practical reasoning, justice and virtue that I propose, nor to counter every point that might be made against them. The reasons that led me to these rather than other choices in writing have emerged gradually. If I was to articulate and illustrate the structure and sweep of a complex way of reasoning about ethics and politics in a relatively short book, much had to be left unsaid, and a good deal had to be stated with fewer qualifications and less detail, indeed with more ragged edges, than I would have liked. The book leads only *towards* an account of justice and *towards* an account of virtue; it does not offer a full account of either, but does show why a demand for a full yet context-free account of either is inappropriate.

There are further systematic omissions. One is the lack of an account of what is commonly called motivation, that is to say about the sources and psychology of action, rather than about its vindication. Unlike those contemporary accounts of justice and of the virtues that build (diverging) accounts of motivation into their very conceptions of practical reason, I have separated justification from motivation. 'Deontological' and consequentialist work on justice both often rely on *preferences* to orient reasoning; work on the virtues often relies on the *identities* of communities and individuals to do so. Both strategies seem to me misguided and self-defeating. In trying to build into their accounts of practical reasoning motivational elements such as preferences and identities, whose claims to be reasoned are minimal, these lines of thought limit and eventually undermine both their own claims about reason and the authority of their own conclusions. Both strategies also overlook the elementary point that a conception of practical reasoning will lack import for those for whom it is not followable. I did not return to the topic of motivation because it seems to me to be among the most confused and uncertain domains of philosophical inquiry at present.

In the background there are larger omissions. I offer only fleeting comments on realist metaphysics, on the vast variety of ethical positions that lay claim to the accolade 'realist' (with or

without metaphysical pretensions), or on the legions of perfectionist and naturalistic conceptions of universalism in ethics that have
traditionally claimed to sustain integrated accounts of justice and
of the virtues. Nor have I shown that no other convincing account of
practical reason can be given, or that there is no other way in which
links between justice and virtue might be restored. If a convincing
alternative could be found, some of the conclusions that I have
constructed might be reached by different and perhaps by easier
routes; others might be rebutted; conclusions that I have not
reached might be attainable.

Even those who sympathize with the constructive approach I
have taken may regret that it does not sustain or vindicate all the
ideals and visions which they cherish, and would hope that a full and
integrated account of justice and of virtue could establish. They
may find an account of justice that points to the construction of
institutions and practices, to the protection of capabilities and the
regulation of powers, rather than to a single, timeless check-list of
rights, or to a definitive answer to the question 'Equality of what?',
disappointing. They may perhaps feel that a better account of
global justice could have been be reached by swifter arguments, if
only a bolder view of the scope of ethical principles had been
asserted – or demonstrated – at the start. Or they may think that a
forthright adoption of less anthropocentric starting points would
have provided a better way of thinking about environmental justice
and green virtues. Others may be equally disappointed that I sketch
a wide but evidently incomplete account of the virtues, that I do not
show that virtue is the same for all time, or that the discussion of
judgement is not fuller. I hope that those who believe that these
further and stronger conclusions can be reached will show how it
might be done, using starting points which are available and
reasons which are convincing.

CHAPTER I

Overview: justice against virtue?

Justice was once celebrated as a virtue, indeed a cardinal virtue. Although few have shared the heady metaphysical vision that once led Plato to claim that virtue is enough and that good men need no laws, many have thought that justice is not simply one virtue among others, that good laws and good character complement one another and that politics and ethics are distinct but complementary spheres of practical reasoning. Accounts of justice – of good laws and institutions – have nearly always been allied with accounts of the virtues – of the characters of good men and women. For centuries both popular and philosophical writing accepted not only that good characters are vulnerable without good laws, but also that justice alone cannot guide human life, in which good laws must be buttressed by good characters.

Much contemporary writing on ethics and politics takes a different view. It depicts a focus on justice not only as distinct from but often as incompatible with serious concern for human virtue and excellence. Some leading advocates of justice now take pride in remaining 'agnostic about the Good for Man' and many more are carefully minimal about the good life. Staunch friends of the virtues claim that reliance on abstract principles of justice is inimical to virtue and so to good lives and good communities. Justice and virtue are now often discussed in quite different registers; they are depicted not as allies but as antagonists, whose philosophical champions skirmish over countless issues.

It is not obvious why concerns that were formerly seen as distinct but complementary are now depicted as incompatible. Even if justice constrains states, laws and institutions, while virtue informs the characters of men and women and the ethos of communities, might they not be compatible, indeed complementary, as earlier writers supposed? Even if the social and institutional

9

transformations of modernity require us to distinguish good institutions from good characters more sharply than seemed necessary in some traditional societies, do we not still need ethical standards for both domains of life? Or are recent writers right to depict justice and the virtues as fundamentally incompatible, and to argue that one provides an ethically sound and the other an ethically inadequate orientation to human life? If so, why has the vast majority of past writers on ethics and politics overlooked this fundamental incompatibility?

I shall argue that concern for justice and for the virtues can be compatible, indeed that they are mutually supporting, but I begin with some challenges to this view. For unless claims of incompatibility can be refuted there is no point in asking how justice and virtue might be connected. This sketchy review of positions proposed by recent partisans of justice and of virtue, and of the longer and older traditions which allied them, will omit a great deal. Positions will be presented schematically and without extensive textual attribution; certain contrasts will be heightened, others flattened or neglected. These liberties are taken in order to map some – but only some – of the salient features of contemporary debates. A map that locates some achievements, some failures and some gaps in these debates may help reveal whether and how an integrated account of justice and of virtue could be constructed. Later chapters will take on that constructive task.

This chapter begins with a sketch (section 1.1) of the ancient origins of a distinction between universalist and particularist conceptions of ethics. It then considers (in section 1.2) the current deployment of this distinction to distinguish the supposedly *universalist* claims of justice from the supposedly *particularist* claims of virtue, which underpins many claims that these are incompatible orientations to life. Section 1.3 discusses some stories that are commonly told to explain this alignment of universalist views with justice and of particularist views with virtue. I suggest that these stories are unconvincing and that there are no good reasons to suppose that thought about justice must be universalist and thought about the virtues particularist, nor consequently to think that the two orientations to life are incompatible. Section 1.4 tells some alternative, and no more speculative, stories that present a rather different account of the divergence between justice and the virtues.

1.1 UNIVERSALISTS AND PARTICULARISTS: ANCIENT ORIGINS

Ancient thinking about justice and about virtue did not see them as incompatible, but rather as closely linked. However, classical writings can be read as making some of the distinctions now often used to separate thought about the two domains. Among the most significant of these distinctions is that between *universalist* and *particularist* accounts of reasoning about action.

Broadly speaking, *universalists* orient ethical reasoning and judgement partly by appeal to certain universal principles that are to hold for all lives and across all situations. The most elementary thought of universalists is formal: there are certain ethical principles or standards which hold for all, and not merely for some cases. This claim about *form* is often closely linked to a second claim about the *scope* of universal principles, which universalists generally think is more-or-less cosmopolitan, at least for some basic principles.[1] Although universalists generally think that many subordinate ethical principles are formulated for *restricted* domains, they think that some basic ethical principles have *inclusive* scope.[2]

To sustain their claims about the form and scope, as well as about the content of ethical principles many earlier and more recent universalists have relied on metaphysically and epistemologically strenuous positions. Plato's account of the virtues, including justice, provides a classic and explicit example of universal ethical claims which are framed and supported by an account of the objectively good which transcends the empirical world, and is backed by a demanding metaphysics and epistemology. Good lives were to be guided by an ideal which Plato identified with the Form of the Good, and which other universalists who have been committed to a transcendent account of the good have variously identified with the Summum Bonum, the Glory of God and other ideals. Other universalists who have identified the good with inherent rather than transcendent values have also often been committed to

---

[1] The fact that many universalists have in practice narrowed the scope of their principles to exclude certain others – barbarians, women, slaves, the heathen, foreigners – shows that the principles by which they actually lived have far-less-than cosmopolitan scope.

[2] How this scope is to be fixed is a difficult and contentious matter; it will be discussed in chapter 4. Meanwhile the term 'more-or-less cosmopolitan' can be used as a filler for the sorts of views universalists take of the *inclusive* scope of basic ethical principles.

realist positions which are metaphysically and epistemologically demanding.

Many contemporary universalists claim that they do not rely on or need to vindicate metaphysically and epistemologically strenuous ideals. Both universalists who are labelled 'deontologists' (whose work is loosely described as 'Kantian'),[3] and those who are consequentialists hope to sustain universal claims without needing (much) metaphysical support. Even writers who see their work as continuing the Natural Law tradition aspire to minimize their reliance on metaphysical and religious certainties.[4] Yet elements of the metaphysical positions contemporary universalists claim to reject often seem to linger in the background of their arguments for universal principles. Some of them appeal to ideals of motivation and reason, or to ideals of the person or of impartiality, others assume exigent accounts of rational choosing which incorporate extravagant epistemological claims. It is an open question whether universalists who invoke these sorts of ideals can substantiate the principles for which they variously argue without establishing accounts of the metaphysics of the person, or certain conceptions of the good for man, or other metaphysically demanding claims. Many of their critics think that they cannot, and that they consequently leave large gaps in their defence of universal principles.

Contemporary *particularists*, whose work is often loosely described as 'Aristotelian' or 'Wittgensteinian',[5] view ethics quite differently.

---

[3] A list of some prominent 'Kantian' universalists and some of the works for which they are best known would include John Rawls, *A Theory of Justice* (Cambridge, Mass., Harvard University Press, 1971) and *Political Liberalism* (New York, Columbia University Press, 1993); Ronald Dworkin, *Taking Rights Seriously* (London, Duckworth, 1977); Thomas Nagel, *Equality and Impartiality* (Oxford University Press, 1991); Alan Gewirth, *Human Rights: Essays on Justification and Applications* (University of Chicago Press, 1982). There are countless others who have contributed to the huge literature on justice and rights, some of them consequentialists rather than 'Kantians'. In the German-speaking world prominent 'Kantian' writers include Jürgen Habermas and Karl-Otto Apel.

[4] See many of the essays in Robert P. George, ed., *Natural Law Theory: Contemporary Essays* (Oxford, Clarendon Press, 1992).

[5] 'Aristotelian' critics of universalist ethics include, for example, Charles Taylor, in *Philosophy and the Human Sciences: Philosophical Papers*, vol. II (Cambridge University Press, 1985); Alasdair MacIntyre, especially in *After Virtue: A Study in Moral Theory* (London, Duckworth, 1981); Michael J. Sandel, *Liberalism and the Limits of Justice* (Cambridge University Press, 1982); and (in part) Bernard Williams, especially in *Ethics and the Limits of Philosophy* (London, Fontana, 1985), as well as numerous others who have contributed to the huge literature on communitarianism and virtue ethics. 'Wittgensteinian' critics of universalist ethics include Peter Winch, *Ethics and Action* (London, Routledge and Kegan Paul, 1972); D. Z. Phillips and H. O. Mounce, *Moral Practices* (London, Routledge and

They hope to orient ethical reasoning without appeal to universal principles of inclusive scope, or more generally without claims about what would be good, or right, or obligatory for all human lives, or about ideals that are relevant for all. For the most part they seek to anchor ethical claims by appeal to the actual practices or traditions or patterns of judgement of particular communities or, more radically, without looking beyond the particular sensibilities, attachments or judgements of individuals in particular situations. Some radical particularists doubt whether there are or could be ethical principles either of wide or of narrow scope, hence whether there can be ethical principles of any sort; other historicizing particularists allow that there can be ethical principles, and indeed that these principles can be of universal *form*, but insist that none of them are inclusive, i.e. that none has more-or-less cosmopolitan scope.

Disputes between universalists and particularists are ancient. Plato not only advocates a classic form of universalism, but presents an explicit version of particularism, which he puts into Meno's arrogant mouth. When Meno is asked what virtue is, he confidently replies:

First of all, if it is manly virtue you are after, it is easy to see that the virtue of a man consists of managing the city's affairs capably, and so that he will help his friends and injure his foes while taking care to come to no harm himself. Or if you want a woman's virtue, that is easily described. She must be a good housewife, careful with her stores and obedient to her husband. Then there is another virtue for a child, male or female, and another for an old man, free or slave as you like; and a great many more kinds of virtue ... For every act and for every time of life, with reference to each separate function, there is a virtue for each one of us ... [6]

Kegan Paul, 1970) and D. Z. Phillips and Peter Winch, eds., *Wittgenstein: Attending to the Particular* (London, Macmillan, 1989); Sabina Lovibond, *Realism and Imagination in Ethics* (Oxford, Blackwell, 1983), Cora Diamond in the papers on ethics in her *The Realistic Spirit: Wittgenstein, Philosophy, and the Mind* (Cambridge, Mass., MIT Press., 1991); and many others. In the German-speaking world prominent critics of universalist positions include Odo Marquand and Hermann Lübbe.

[6] Plato, Meno in *Protagoras and Meno* , trans. W. K. C. Guthrie (Harmondsworth, Middlesex, Penguin, 1956), 71E. Meno's position is, of course, *formally* universalist: but his standards of virtue are to hold universally only across particularly small domains. His position, and many later ones that resemble it, are more easily seen as particularist than as universalist because the *scope* of their claims is so-far-from cosmopolitan. For discussion of more radical particularists who repudiate universal form as well as more-or-less cosmopolitan scope, so deny that ethics can appeal to principles of *any* sort, see below and also chapter 3.

Plato presents Meno's position only to dispute it. He insisted against Meno's particularism, which identified virtue with rather local norms and practices, whose scope is restricted to certain stages and statuses in life, that there must be an inner unity to human excellence, whose inclusive, universal principles do not vary with place, time or status. All virtuous action adheres to these inclusive universal standards: it manifests the inner harmony of a soul that is oriented towards the Form of the Good itself. More specifically it displays what came later to be known as the four cardinal virtues: wisdom, courage, temperance and justice. The several virtues are all aspects of one virtue. On Plato's vastly influential form of universalism, human characters rather than social institutions provide the primary embodiment of the Good, justice is itself a virtue, and the justice of cities is derivative from that of human souls. In this classical version of ethical universalism justice and other virtues make universal claims which are intended to hold for all humans for all time.

Although Aristotle denied both the unity and the transcendence of the good, traditional interpretations read him too as universalist rather than particularist. The Aristotle of tradition was committed to an historically invariant account of proper human functioning, hence of the Good for Man, and hence of the inclusive standards both of virtue and of justice, whose observance would constitute that good. Stoic and Christian thinkers could appropriate and adapt a universalist reading of Aristotle, in which a perfectionist account of the Good oriented not only good character (hence virtue) but the Natural Law (hence justice). Once again virtue and justice could be discussed in parallel terms. Accounts both of justice and of the (other) virtues could be integrated with the three divinely ordained theological virtues: for Aquinas faith, hope and above all charity frame inclusive accounts both of good character and of just institutions. A common reading of this premodern universalism in ethics is that much of the ethical thinking of classical antiquity and of Christian Europe took the category of the Good (variously understood) as fundamental, and set itself the task of discerning the inclusive universal claims that this implied and of showing how they were to be realized in actual lives and polities. A realist metaphysics was to ground a substantive morality whose inclusive universal principles were to be expressed both in more restricted principles that were appropriate to restricted spheres of life and ultimately in good characters and good laws.

A historicist reading of some of the same writings, more retrospective than contemporary, argues that the Aristotelian legacy belongs in particularist rather than universalist hands. The life of virtue is not to be thought of as a life that achieves any timeless Good for Man, but as a life guided by the good judgement of the *phronimos*, the 'man of practical wisdom', and the *phronimos* inhabits a particular time and place, whose practical wisdom his judging articulates.[7] Hence the virtuous community draws on good judgement and good traditions rather than on metaphysical certainties. The robust continuity between classical, Christian and contemporary ethics can then be interpreted not as entailed by abiding metaphysical truths, from which inclusive universal ethical principles can be derived, but as evidence of the historical continuity of traditions of life, thought and community. In this way a particularist (perhaps historicist, or even relativist) background theory can support a simulacrum of inclusive universal ethical principles, which it presents as reflecting actual social and ethical continuities rather than timeless truths.

Yet other contemporary interpreters impute a more radical particularism to Aristotle, by emphasizing his claim that 'in the end practical wisdom is concerned with the ultimate particular, which is the object . . . of perception'[8] rather than the thought that

---

[7] This influential reading of Aristotle is invoked by many contemporary writers whose broader aim is to argue for historicist or more specifically for communitarian positions, or for various forms of virtue ethics, or for all of these. See Hans-Georg Gadamer, *Truth and Method*, trans. Anon. (London, Sheed and Ward, 1975) and *Reason in the Age of Science*, trans. Frederick G. Lawrence (Cambridge, Mass., MIT Press, 1981), cf. p 82: 'Practice does not rely solely upon an abstract consciousness of norms, but challenges to a critique of prejudice. We are always dominated by convention'; MacIntyre, *After Virtue*; Nancy Sherman, *The Fabric of Character: Aristotle's Theory of Virtue* (Oxford, Clarendon Press, 1991). For comments on MacIntyre's reading of Aristotle and his historicism see also John Horton and Susan Mendus, eds., *After MacIntyre: Critical Perspectives on the Work of Alasdair MacIntyre* (Cambridge, Polity Press, 1994), especially the papers by Robert Stern and Janet Coleman. For an introduction to contemporary virtue ethics see Gregory Trianosky, 'What is Virtue Ethics All About?', *American Philosophical Quarterly*, 27 (1990), 335–44, which has a useful bibliography, and for more recent work see Roger Crisp, ed., *How Should One Live?* (Oxford University Press, 1996).

[8] Aristotle, *Nichomachean Ethics*, trans. W. D. Ross, in *The Basic Works of Aristotle*, ed. Richard McKeon (New York, Random House, 1941),1142a25. For a more radically particularist reading of Aristotle see in particular David Wiggins 'Deliberation and Practical Reason', originally in *The Proceedings of the Aristotelian Society*, 76 (1975–6), reprinted in revised version in his *Needs, Values and Truth: Essays in the Philosophy of Value*, Aristotelian Society Series 6 (Oxford, Blackwell, 1987).

the one who judges inhabits and is formed by a certain time and place. On this account, the central feature of 'Aristotelian', as of 'Wittgensteinian', ethical thought will be attention to, or appropriate perception of, salient features of particular situations, yielding (it is supposed) a form of internal or this-worldly realism which supposedly neither needs metaphysical backing nor places any marked emphasis on the social position or formation of those who attend or perceive.

I.2 UNIVERSALISTS AND PARTICULARISTS: CURRENT CONFRONTATIONS

The universalist and particularist views found in these contemporary readings of ancient ethics ostensibly contrast *two ways of looking at the whole of ethics*. Yet their proponents often seem content to *relegate* whichever domain of ethics fits less happily with their preferred view. Particularists not only reject universalist positions, but often seem content to say little about justice; universalists not only reject particularist positions, but often seem to accept that they cannot offer much of an account of the virtues. Contemporary universalists and particularists converge in the conclusion that concern for justice and for the virtues must be antithetical.

More specifically, certain contemporary writers on justice argue for inclusive universal principles, which define a range of human rights and obligations, and a conception of respect for persons, but accept that nothing, or rather little, or nothing objective, can be established either about good lives or about virtue.[9] In pluralist societies we will find ourselves confronted beyond the domain of justice only by a plurality of subjective 'conceptions of the good', between which we cannot hope to arbitrate rationally.[10] A just society or state will be neutral between the various conceptions of

---

[9] See in particular Rawls, *A Theory of Justice*, esp. section 60 ff, and *Political Liberalism*; Dworkin, *Taking Rights Seriously*. Most of the vast 'deontological' literature on justice takes a similarly guarded view of virtue. Perfectionists and utilitarians do not: they have the intellectual resources to offer an integrated account of justice and of virtue. Their 'deontologist' critics think that perfectionists do so at unacceptable metaphysical cost and utilitarians do so at the expense of paying inadequate attention to rights and to the separateness of persons, hence at the expense of a flawed conception of justice.

[10] The phrase is Rawls's, who in a recent clarification states forthrightly: 'the capacity for a conception of the good is the capacity to form, to revise, and rationally to pursue a conception of one's own rational advantage or good', *Political Liberalism*, p 19.

the good to which its citizens may adhere.[11] The only virtues which writers on justice who discuss *conceptions of the good* rather than *the good* are likely to emphasize are those which are corollaries of the theories of justice which they hope to establish (such as civic virtue, toleration and autonomy). However, some universalists think that this is not enough, that neutrality about the good is implausible, and that at least a limited form of perfectionism must also be established.

Contemporary friends of the virtues are even more varied than the contemporary advocates of justice; some of this variety reflects the rival appropriations of Aristotle discussed in the last section. Most of the new 'Aristotelians' espouse historicist forms of particularism, and hope to anchor the claims of virtue in judgements about the shared particularities of tradition, practice and community.[12] Others are more radical particularists, who seek to root ethical judgement in responses to particular situations that reflect individual sensibilities, attachments, commitments and senses of integrity.[13] Both sorts of particularist hold that ethical judgement

[11] Liberal theories of justice agree that the *state* must be neutral as between citizens who pursue various conceptions of the good life. However, it is inaccurate to think that all liberals, or even all liberals who are neither perfectionists nor utilitarians, hold that nothing objective can be said about morality or virtue. Most are emphatic that *some* account of morality, of the good, indeed of virtue, can be given. Their particularist critics can nevertheless object that their accounts of the good are too thin, or too closely tied to preferences (and so are merely subjective conceptions of the good) – or that the tally of liberal virtues is too limited. For liberal views on morality and virtue see, for example Stuart Hampshire, ed., *Public and Private Morality* (Cambridge University Press, 1978); Rawls, *A Theory of Justice*, esp. sections 60–6; Nancy L. Rosenblum, ed., *Liberalism and the Moral Life* (Cambridge, Mass., Harvard University Press, 1989); Stephen Macedo, *Liberal Virtues* (Oxford, Clarendon Press, 1990); David Strauss, 'The Liberal Virtues' in John W. Chapman and William A. Galston, eds., *Virtue* (*Nomos*, 34) (New York University Press, 1992).

[12] These particularists include communitarians, many virtue ethicists and certain 'radical' feminist writers who use closely parallel arguments. See the works cited in notes 5 and 7, and in particular Sandel, *Liberalism and the Limits of Justice* and Taylor, *Philosophy and the Human Sciences*, vol. II. For the issues that divide liberals and communitarians see Stephen Mulhall and Adam Swift, *Liberals and Communitarians* (Oxford, Blackwell, 1992). For some comparable particularist feminist positions see Carol McMillan, *Women, Reason and Nature* (London, Routledge and Kegan Paul, 1982); Carol Gilligan, *In a Different Voice: Psychological Theory and Women's Dependence*, 2nd edition (Cambridge, Mass., Harvard University Press, 1993); Eva Feders Kittay and Diane Meyers, *Women and Moral Theory* (Totowa, NJ, Rowman and Littlefield, 1987). Seyla Benhabib and Drucilla Cornell, eds. *Feminism as Critique* (Cambridge, Polity Press, 1987).

[13] Contemporary radical particularists are more often influenced by certain readings of Wittgenstein than of Aristotle. See note 8 and also Winch, *Ethics and Action*; John McDowell, 'Virtue and Reason', *Monist*, 62 (1979), 331–50 reworked in Steven Holtzman

should not, indeed cannot, appeal to inclusively universal principles or to any 'external' or universally available vantage point from which the judgements around which ethical life revolves can be criticized. They share a deep suspicion of contemporary universalist accounts of justice, which they condemn as ethically shallow and philosophically inadequate. The accusations they level against universalist thinking combine ethical and philosophical charges.

The main ethical failing with which particularists charge theories of justice, and in general what some of them term 'modern moral philosophy' is its very preoccupation with inclusively universal principles or rules, and in particular with principles of obligation.[14] This, it is said, has disastrous consequences: theories of justice which prescribe universally depend on *abstract* thinking and they prescribe *uniform* treatment or action. In order to formulate inclusively universal principles or rules, theories of justice first assume an inadequate, abstract (sometimes: 'atomistic' or 'deontological') view of the human agent, whose social relations and 'situatedness' (also: 'embeddedness', 'specificity', 'concrete reality') are not just overlooked, but denied. Secondly, and consequently, the inclusive universal principles or rules which they endorse, and above all the principles of obligation for which they argue, prescribe rigidly uniform action, and so countenance (or even demand) an oppressive lack of sensitivity or concern for the

---

and Christopher Leach, eds., *Wittgenstein: To Follow a Rule* (London, Routledge and Kegan Paul, 1981); the papers on ethics in Phillips and Winch, eds., *Wittgenstein: Attending to the Particular*. Certain passages in Bernard Williams, *Ethics and the Limits of Philosophy* and *Moral Luck: Philosophical Essays 1973–80* (Cambridge University Press, 1981) also emphasize attention to the particular. Some of these writings are discussed in chapter 3. Particularists speak of attention to particular situations, variously as 'perceiving', 'appreciating', 'attending to', 'responding to', 'appraising', 'intuiting' or to 'picking out salient moral features'.

[14] Many of them may have in mind G. E. M. Anscombe's influential paper 'Modern Moral Philosophy' in *The Collected Philosophical Papers of G. E. M. Anscombe*, vol. III, *Ethics, Religion and Politics* (Oxford, Blackwell, 1981), pp. 26–42, which was first published in 1958. Pejorative use of this and similarly vague terms – 'our contemporary ethical theories', 'our ethical theories', 'our moral theorists' – to refer to 'Kantian' and utilitarian positions can be found in varied writing that is hostile not only to utilitarianism and to rules, but more generally to justice, to rights, to obligations and to principles. See also Michael Stocker *Plural and Conflicting Values* (Oxford, Clarendon Press, 1990); L. W. Blum *Friendship, Altruism and Morality* (London, Routledge and Kegan Paul, 1980); Phillips and Winch, eds., *Wittgenstein: Attending to the Particular*; Diamond, *The Realistic Spirit: Wittgenstein, Philosophy, and the Mind*.

numerous differences between the persons and situations from which they have abstracted.[15]

The most fundamental philosophical failing of theories of justice, expressed in varying vocabularies by differing particularists, is that their purported vindications of universal, inclusive principles without appeal to metaphysical foundations fails. In substituting supposedly minimal appeals to reason for stronger metaphysical claims they provide inadequate foundations.[16] This fundamental flaw is said to be evident from the fact that theories of justice covertly draw on demanding assumptions about self, action or reason for which they need but do not provide adequate (meta-physical) backing.

Supporters of justice, whether 'Kantian' or conseqentialist, are equally eager to charge the friends of the virtues both with ethical and with philosophical failings. The range of ethical failings they claim to detect is large. The most evident difficulty they see in the writings of historicizing particularists is that by itself an appeal to local practices and traditions (however venerable, however passionately maintained) cannot but endorse evil practices and traditions, indeed vices.[17] A further glaring deficiency is that particularists do not offer an account of justice that is adequate to the contemporary world. Modern societies have and need powerful and complex political and economic systems, whose influence cannot be confined within state or other boundaries, and whose construction and regulation must answer to standards that have more than local or traditional backing. The vindication and legitimation of such standards is inevitably a search for inclusive universal principles of justice, for principles of more-or-less

---

[15] For further discussion of the significance of abstraction and its lack of connection with uniform prescription see section 3.1.

[16] This point is made forthrightly by Anscombe, but the foundational criticism comes less easily for most particularists, who are not themselves in the business of supplying foundations. For discussion of the varying conceptions of practical reason deployed by universalists and particularists and of their possible vindications see section 2.3.

[17] Cf. Alan Gewirth's criticism of MacIntyre: 'The crucial difficulty of MacIntyre's whole doctrine, then, is that he has removed from his account of virtues their morally necessary grounding in human rights', 'Rights and Virtues', *Analyse und Kritik*, 6 (1984), 28–48, p. 47; also in *Review of Metaphysics*, 38 (1985), 739–62. For a trenchant romp through twenty particularist mistakes about liberal, and more generally about universalist, thinking see Stephen Holmes, 'The Permanent Structure of Antiliberal Thought' in Nancy L. Rosenblum, ed. *Liberalism and the Moral Life* (Cambridge, Mass., Harvard University Press, 1989), pp. 225–53.

cosmopolitan scope, and for their vindication. In our world any attempt to do without an account of justice that addresses global as well as local issues may prove ethically disastrous.

This ethical disaster shows in the difficulty that many particularist positions have in making sense of ethical discourse or dialogue with 'outsiders', who supposedly do not share the same categories or sensibilities. Historicizing particularisms use categories and canons of judgement that have authority only within some tradition; more individualistic particularisms appeal to even more restricted sensibilities, commitments and attachments. These limitations will not always create immediate practical problems: both traditions and narrower commitments may define how 'outsiders' should be treated (e.g. oppressively or tolerantly, with the aim of assimilation or of exclusion).

However, in our world an inability to account for cross-cultural reasoning ultimately has fierce practical consequences. Many contemporary societies are culturally plural; nearly all have significant and varied relations with other, differing societies. A particularist account of ethical relations and reasoning that might have been practically adequate in a world of homogeneous, closed societies will almost certainly prove practically inadequate in a world marked by cultural pluralism within states, vastly intricate interregional, international and transnational relationships, and constantly shifting patterns of integration and connection between different spheres of life and different social groups. Far from being sensitive to the ethical pluralism of modernity, particularists are largely blind to it, since they see ethical life as encapsulated in distinct domains by rigid grids of categories and sensibilities.

From the perspective of their critics, particularists who ground restricted ethical principles in 'our' traditions indulge a cosy but dangerous nostalgia for a world now lost, and refuse to engage with the world we actually inhabit. More radical particularists, who ground ethics on individual sensibility or perception, may bravely do without the nostalgia, but will still have little of use to say about interaction with those whose sensibility differs.

However, the most fundamental objection that contemporary theorists of justice make against contemporary accounts of the virtues mirrors the most fundamental criticism made against them. It is that, even if appeal to particular, established standards, practices and commitments or sensibilities could resolve (an adequate range of) ethical questions and conflicts, still no good reasons would have been given for thinking that the resolutions proposed are ethically authoritative, important or even adequate. The most common argument advanced in favour of treating the particular practices and traditions of communities, or the particular sensibilities and attachments of individuals, as the bedrock for ethical justification is that they are constitutive of the identity either of a community or of an individual, so that there supposedly is no way for a community or for an individual to 'go behind' this level of justification. These norms and practices, these perceptions and preferences define what 'we' are; nothing more basic is available: 'ought' can and must be derived from 'is'; far from needing metaphysical backing, ethical realism is simply a matter of attending to what is the case.[18]

Those who look for inclusive universal principles are unconvinced. Fundamentally they see particularist claims as arbitrary, as lacking warrant. They think that there can be reasonable objections even to established norms and practices, even to passionately felt sensibilities and attachments. It is false that one cannot 'go behind' responses that are constitutive of identities, since identities are not fixed for all time; 'ought' still cannot be derived from 'is'. Critics of particularism also insist that a consensus may still be iniquitous and that social traditions and personal commitments may manifest corruption as readily as virtue. (Of course, in making such criticisms they must show how the standards they invoke could be met.)

Contemporary friends of the virtues frequently attempt to meet such charges of arbitrariness by pointing out that social traditions and personal orientations always include tenets and practices for debating and criticizing, for reflecting on and revising, their own

---

[18] This thought is variously expressed. For example, communitarians suggest that questioning identities destroys the locus and premisses for ethical reasoning; Winch and certain other Wittgensteinian writers stress that certain personal commitments are 'not a matter for decision', but rather a matter of noting 'what we do want to say', *Ethics and Action*; Bernard Williams suggests that those who try to give reasons for identity-constituting commitments have 'one thought too many', 'Persons, Character and Morality', *Moral Luck*, p. 18. Once ethical claims have been anchored in identities and commitments, the claim to 'realism' comes easily: nothing is more *real* than that which is the bedrock of our being. Of course, this sort of internal realism is based on a quite different view of what is real from that of traditional, metaphysical forms of realism. Cf. Hilary Putnam, *Realism and Reason: Philosophical Papers*, vol. III (Cambridge University Press, 1983).

standards, practices and judgements. 'Internal' critique of actual norms and commitments and reflexive self-criticism, rather than timeless appeals to fixed identities, are then taken as the bottom line in particularist practical reasoning.[19] However, this move does not meet all the objections made by those who take universalist approaches to ethics. First, since the 'internal' critical standards of traditions and the self-criticism of individuals also vary, the problems posed by conceptual differences and categorial incommensurability will recur at many junctures and frontiers where ethical questions are urgent. For example, 'internal' criticism is unlikely to resolve problems of international justice, or of gender and justice, where the very boundaries and categories of justice are at issue.[20] Second, appeals to 'internal' critique are themselves ultimately no less arbitrary than the traditions and sensibilities to which they are internal. For example, some traditions and some sensibilities devalue and demean certain sorts of agents, whose standing, achievements and communications they systematically disregard or belittle. Their procedures and practices for self-criticism will probably also devalue and demean those agents. Discrimination and oppression may not only be embedded in superficial, ostensibly revisable aspects of life, but also rooted in ways of interpretation and adjudication, so will form and limit the critical potential internal to those traditions and sensibilities. These factors may in part account for the difficulty of discerning, challenging, let alone overcoming, well-entrenched practices, such as class discrimination and deference, racism, sexism and statism by internal criticism.[21] The possibility of 'internal' critique and

---

[19] See for example MacIntyre, *After Virtue*; Michael Walzer, *Interpretation and Social Criticism* (Cambridge, Mass., Harvard University Press, 1987).

[20] For more detailed argument on some of these issues see Onora O'Neill, 'Justice, Gender, and International Boundaries' in Martha Nussbaum and Amartya Sen, eds., *Quality of Life* (Oxford, Clarendon Press, 1993), pp. 303–23 and 'Ethical Reasoning and Ideological Pluralism', *Ethics*, 98 (1988), 705–22.

[21] Even the victims of oppressive ways of thought and life have difficulty revising their self-denigrating views. For some writing that suggests how deeply a sense of blemished identity may be internalized and how well insulated from the resources of internal critique it may remain consider, for example, Erving Goffman, *Stigma: Notes on the Management of Spoiled Identity* (Englewood Cliffs, NJ, Prentice Hall, 1963); Richard Sennett and Jonathan Cobb, *The Hidden Injuries of Class* (Cambridge University Press, 1972); Axel Honneth *The Critique of Power: reflective stages in a critical social theory*, trans. Kenneth Baynes (Cambridge, Mass., MIT Press, 1991); Charles Taylor et al., *Multiculturalism and 'The Politics of Recognition'* (Princeton University Press, 1992).

correction cannot show that particularist judgements are anything but arbitrary.

Despite all these antagonisms, contemporary proponents of justice and of the virtues also share some ground. One part of this common ground is that both conclude that, for the reasons just sketched, we may be forced to choose between a commitment to justice and to the virtues. We must choose between abstract conceptions of inclusive universal principles and careful judgement of actual cases. We must choose between an abstract ('atomistic', 'deontological') conception of human agents, and a situated ('concrete', 'embedded') account of human beings. We must see our lives either in terms of principles and obligations or in terms of traditions, commitments or responsiveness to others.

Although the two camps may patch up certain differences in practice, for example, by concentrating on forms of particularism that arise within liberal communities, whose particular practices are infused with universal ethical claims, or by reminding us that subjective or localized conceptions of the good are not intrinsically envious or selfish, these cheering but blinkered assumptions cannot resolve the deeper or more general differences. Protagonists of both orientations are left looking back on ethical and political writings from antiquity until the recent past, in which commitment to justice and to virtue were so often coupled, without any general strategy that could overcome the supposedly unbridgeable antithesis they now see between inclusive universal principles of justice and virtuous concern for actual communities, lives and commitments.

1.3 MODERNITY, UNIVERSALISTS AND PARTICULARISTS: SOME POPULAR STORIES

How did the current identification of universalist thinking with concern for justice, rights and obligations and of particularist thinking with concern for virtue and sensitivity, relationships and commitments, come about? Why have proponents of universalist ethical reasoning come to think that they can say nothing, or at most very little, about the virtues? Why have some proponents of particularist ethical thought so little to say about justice, and least

of all about justice beyond borders? Why do universalists and
particularists often agree that neither can provide accounts both of
justice and of virtue?

The evident divergences between the contemporary proponents
of universalist accounts of justice and of particularist views of virtue
(and at most of 'local' justice) are often construed as a response to
the intellectual and social challenges of modernity. Yet it is not
evident why the *intellectual* challenges of modernity should not have
had *parallel* rather than *divergent* effects on what had been closely
related, and in general universalist, ways of thinking about justice
and virtue. Moreover, it is evident that many of the *social* changes
of modernity were quite adequately accommodated within that
universalist pattern of thought without fundamental change, let
alone systematic divergence between thinking about justice and
about virtue.

Consider first the foundational, intellectual issues. The deepest
intellectual challenge posed both to conceptions of justice and to
conceptions of virtue in the modern period, and above all in (early)
modern Europe, has been a rising suspicion about the religious and
metaphysical certainties, without which (it was feared) ethical
claims of all sorts might turn out to be arbitrary, a challenge
summarized in the slogan that 'if God is dead everything is
permitted'. One and the same intellectual crisis was brewing for
both domains of ethical thought. If both classical and Christian
accounts both of justice and of the virtues were based on varieties
of realist metaphysics (bolstered as needed by religious faith), any
threats to these foundations should have threatened both domains
of ethical thought equally.

This picture of a shared predicament is confirmed by the fact
that for generations fundamental challenge to conceptions of
justice and of virtue was kept at bay by a similar range of *ad hoc*
strategies. Attentive reading of early and not-so-early modern
ethical and political writing repeatedly reveals continued reliance if
not on overt, then on a more-or-less tacit background realism; if not
on avowed, then on latent theism; if not on flamboyant, then still on
subliminal perfectionism, which allowed a continued affirmation
of *universalist accounts both of justice and of virtue.* Nietzsche may
not have exaggerated when he hazarded that news of the Death
of God would take a thousand years to penetrate the caves of

men.[22] The intellectual crisis may gradually have diluted the authority of claims both about justice and about virtue, but dilution is not divergence: a shared intellectual crisis does not show why thinking about justice and about virtue has *diverged*.

Alternatively, consider the thought that the real sources of divergence were social rather than intellectual. It is once again unclear how numerous social changes of the most varied sorts can explain *systematic divergence* between conceptions of justice and of the virtues. Many social changes in the last four centuries have raised ethical challenges, but these challenges and the responses to them have often been piecemeal rather than systematic. Some changes have been rather readily accommodated within traditional, mainly universalist ethical thinking, by revaluing particular values, by adjusting or repudiating conceptions of the importance or the writ of one or another virtue or of justice, rather than by concluding that the thought about justice and about virtue must be fundamentally distinct.

Some of the questions that arose were quite specific, as a selective and anachronistic sample can suggest. Should princes live by, or should they merely simulate the traditional virtues of Christian princes? Were the time-honoured feudal virtues of courage and chivalry really just aristocratic vices? Was toleration perhaps a virtue and enforcing orthodoxy no virtue, even a vice?[23] Was greed, once a deadly sin, perhaps the motor of industry and wealth, and even a quasi virtue? Could Christian societies tolerate dissent and admire commerce?[24] Was charity, once the greatest of Christian virtues, no more than cold, optional philanthropy?[25]

---

[22] Nietzsche, *The Gay Science*, trans. Walter Kaufmann (New York, Vintage Press, 1974), # 108, # 125; as well as numerous passages in *Thus Spoke Zarathustra*, trans. R. J. Hollingdale (Harmondsworth, Middlesex, Penguin Books, 1961).

[23] These topics are themes for some of the most celebrated writers of the early modern period: consider Machiavelli on the virtues of princes; Cervantes on feudal virtues; Milton and Voltaire on toleration; the list could go on.

[24] The latter two revaluations of values are uncomfortably accommodated in the adage that private vices can be public virtues. See Albert O. Hirschmann, *The Passions and the Interests: Political Arguments for Capitalism before Its Triumph* (Princeton University Press, 1977); J. G. A. Pocock, *Virtue, Commerce and History* (Cambridge University Press, 1985).

[25] Alan Buchanan, 'Justice and Charity', *Ethics*, 97 (1987), 558–75; Onora O'Neill 'The Great Maxims of Justice and of Charity' in *Constructions of Reason: Explorations of Kant's Political Philosophy* (Cambridge University Press, 1989); Ellen Frankel Paul, et al., eds., *Philanthropy and the Public Good* (Oxford, Blackwell, 1987).

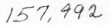

Should national loyalty count as virtue or as vice?[26] Do liberal
societies foster or need any but individualist virtues such as
autonomy, authenticity or sincerity?[27] Such questions about aspects
of traditional conceptions of justice and of virtue, and the
heterogeneous adaptations of life and thought by which they were
accommodated, can be read as a variety of partial adaptations to
specific social changes. It seems unlikely that these sorts of
challenges and the varied adaptations they led to can explain
why conceptions of justice and of virtue should have *diverged
systematically*.

Neither a crisis of shared foundations which has rumbled on
through centuries, nor an account of social changes, can show why
universalist accounts of justice are now preferred and universalist
accounts of virtue are not. Should not thought about the two
domains of ethics have changed in parallel ways? Would one not
expect even a limited background acceptance of a realist metaphysics, to support (or seem to support) an objective account of the
good, that could continue to anchor universalist conceptions both of
justice and of virtue? Would one not expect substantive moral
change, diversity and conflict in both domains to be interpreted
either as permissible local variation or as moral decline in both
domains, as calling for reform (or reformation) rather than for
fundamental theoretical reconstruction or differentiation of the
two domains? Would one not expect the full recognition of a crisis
of foundations to have led to similar revisions in thought about
justice and virtue?

The supposed *divergence* of thinking about justice and virtue
seems to need quite a different sort of explanation. One quasi-
Hegelian explanation has been put forward by Alasdair MacIntyre,
who surmises in *After Virtue* that the changes we associate with
modernity disrupted a once-coherent moral order that had revolved
around the particular claims of traditions of virtue, among whose
ruins our present lives are led. MacIntyre's explanation starts from
the controversial assumption that traditional thinking about the
good life and virtue had been particularist. He then aims to explain

---

[26] Alasdair MacIntyre, *Is Patriotism a Virtue?*, Lindley Lecture, Department of Philosophy,
University of Kansas, 1984; Isaiah Berlin, *The Crooked Timber of Humanity* (London, John
Murray, 1990); Yael Tamir, *Liberal Nationalism* (Princeton University Press, 1993).
[27] Lionel Trilling, *Sincerity and Authenticity* (Oxford University Press, 1972); Macedo *Liberal
Virtues*; Rosenblum, ed., *Liberalism and the Moral Life*; Strauss, 'The Liberal Virtues'.

divergence between justice and virtue by pointing to social changes that undermined particularist understandings of ethics. He depicts the emergence of what he sees as the hollow pretensions of universal accounts of justice – for example, of human rights – as a result of a loss of grasp of particular traditions of virtue. Measured against the standard of a supposed lost but virtuous past, whose thought was particularist, coherent and provided adequate ethical direction, a nostalgic longing for restored or renewed communities and their particular virtues can seem in place,[28] and a preoccupation with upstart notions of abstract universal justice groundless and useless. On this account it is universalist rather than particularist thinking that is the newcomer.

MacIntyre offers an account of the divergence of virtue and justice; but not a particularly convincing account. In the first place, he requires us to read premodern ethical thinking as solidly particularist, although the evidence is, to say the least, quite mixed. Much here depends on insisting on a particularist reading of Aristotle[29] and on playing down the degree to which Christian and post-Christian culture and life has been suffused with the universalist claims of Christian and post-Christian doctrine. Secondly, by neglecting the continuities of universalist thinking it casts a rather feeble light on the *reasons* why thinking about justice has been transformed. Justice has acquired new importance in modern societies because its *scope* and *tasks* expanded and changed with the emergence of strong states and with the increasing differentiation of Church from state, of state from society, and of society from economy. Justice could no longer be seen as one virtue among others, nor statecraft as one human activity among others. The sphere of justice became that of the state, later also that of a wider range of political and economic systems, even that of the system of states. Contemporary debate is increasingly about global justice. Controversies about the scope of justice become controversies about the ways in which exercises of state power, economic power

---

[28] The line of thought behind this nostalgia is questionable. The very historicism which this type of particularism insists upon puts the possibility of claiming that their views of past ethical traditions can be accurate in question; so more straightforwardly does the historical record, on which see Derek L. Phillips, *Looking Backward: A Critical Appraisal of Communitarian Thought* (Princeton University Press, 1993).

[29] See above section 1.1 and Horton and Mendus, eds., *After MacIntyre*, especially papers by Janet Coleman and Peter Johnson.

or of other social power should be subject to the demands of justice.[30]

No doubt some of these increases in the scope and tasks of justice have reduced the scope and tasks of certain virtues, whose capacity to regulate certain domains of life they challenge. But a change in the tasks and scope of justice and of virtue is not a fundamental divergence in thought about them. The social changes of modernity do not require us to think of justice as changing in *form*, as well as in its *scope* and hence in its tasks. As the scope and tasks of justice widened, it still required principles of universal form. Some of these would have to be inclusive principles of rather-closer-to-cosmopolitan scope; others might be more restricted principles whose scope was fixed by new institutional realities. These considerations suggest why writing on justice in the modern period has not wilted, but rather grown confident, fertile and expansive. Its achievements range from Social Contract Theory to contemporary work on human rights, democracy and constitutionalism; they include the intellectual origins of reform movements whose ambitions and successes range from the abolition of slavery to the building of democracy, from the creation of trade unions to the emancipation of women. It has left its mark on a gamut of social sciences. Visions of justice are among the strongest intellectual currents that emerged in the course of rethinking ethics and politics in a modernizing world.

Early modern and subsequent accounts of justice are less a mindless rejection of particularism than a confident reaffirmation and extension of the universalism which older accounts of justice and of virtue had deployed. What was new was largely the expanded and revised understanding of the *scope* of universal principles of justice. Particularist thinking would, in any case, have been notably unhelpful for those who sought an account of justice fit for modern circumstances.[31] Supposed accounts of justice which drew only on

---

[30] Even when the locus of justice is seen as enlarged, it has often been seen as having boundaries which exempt certain activities from the demands of justice. For example: patriarchal conceptions of justice exempt domestic and gender relations from the demands of justice; absolutist conceptions of just internal sovereignty exempt acts of state; 'realist' positions in international relations exempt the external exercise of state power.

[31] The upsurge of communitarian thinking about virtue and (in small measure) about justice in the 1980s fits oddly with the reality that economic and political structures were and are becoming increasingly cosmopolitan. Might it reflect the fact that cosmopolitan claims

particular beliefs, traditions or preferences, let alone on the judgement and perception of particular individuals, would have failed to
address acute problems in a world of ethical plurality, changing
beliefs and shifting boundaries. In a world where local communities
were being incorporated into modern states, in which Catholics and
Protestants had to tolerate one another, and in which Europeans
were colonizing others' ancestral lands, it would often have been
useless for *practical* purposes to ground justice on appeals to
particular practices or traditions, to particular beliefs or preferences, or to particular judgements and perceptions.

So it is hardly surprising that few early modern writers discuss,
let alone defend, particularist conceptions of justice. Those who
depict such conceptions of justice, often intend them only to serve
as ironic mirrors on European failings and foibles, so implicitly rely
on rather than repudiate universal standards. (Without implicit
reference to universal standards *Gulliver, Candide* and *The Persian
Letters* must be read simply as travellers' tales.) Even writers on
justice towards the end of the eighteenth century, whose consciousness of human differences and of the particularities of traditions is
apparent, do not repudiate universal standards of justice. Burke's
appeal to the particularities of tradition nests within a wider appeal
to more inclusive universal claims. Hegel embeds the stages of
particularity in the history of more inclusive universal reason.
Particularism and the relativist or locally bounded conceptions of
justice in which it can be expressed have rarely proved convincing
or attractive in the modern world.

None of this is surprising. Particularist ways of thought fail to
address quite *practical* problems wherever those with differing
traditions interact. Even those who might happily view *others'*
conceptions of justice as reflecting *their* social order (feudal justice,
bourgeois justice, 'oriental' justice) run aground when they try
to defend their own concern with justice by appeal to particular
considerations. Particularist accounts of ethics fit more happily into
an explanatory than into a practical approach: their appeal to
sociologists and historians does not make them useful in daily or in

are no longer advantageous to elites, as they perhaps were or were thought to be in the
recently past era of imperialism? In a post-imperial world, cosmopolitan arrangements
threaten rich states with uncontrolled economic forces and immigration and demands for
aid for the poor of the world, and autocratic states with demands that human rights be
guaranteed across boundaries.

institutional life. Despite the numerous shifts in discussions of justice over the last three centuries, it is hardly surprising that they remain firmly and in general fairly inclusively universalistic, or that the continuity of debates about justice since the seventeenth century is so marked.[32]

Those who thought of justice as having an enlarged scope and tasks often also retained an inclusively universal conception of the virtues, which were to provide an account of good character that was relevant for all. There is little evidence among early and not-so-early modern writers either of an instant or of a general divergence between universalist concern with justice and particularist concern with the virtues. If the foundations for an inclusively universalist conception of justice were available, why should they not also serve to ground an inclusively universal account of the virtues? Those who questioned and revised conceptions of justice in the seventeenth and eighteenth centuries, and more recently, have not usually thought that a revised concern with justice would cost them their concern with the virtues.[33] The popularity of particularist conceptions of virtue appears to be a much more recent phenomenon.

Neither the intellectual crisis of foundations, nor the social changes of the early modern period, nor a Hegelian story about the stages of particularity, provides a clue to the reasons for contemporary insistence that virtue and justice must be thought of in divergent ways. Even if the traditional metaphysical foundations of universalism were being slowly eroded, even if piecemeal adjustments were needed, even if the scope of justice was widened, still the superstructure of ethical thinking concern seemed to need repair and maintenance rather than radical overhaul. No general appeal either to the intellectual crisis or the social changes of modernity can explain the present systematic divergence between conceptions of the form and scope of justice and of virtue.

---

[32] The continuities are not always visible on the surface. Current work has little to say about the State of Nature, Constitutional Monarchy or the Natural Law; and a lot to say about the cross-cutting divergences between liberal and socialist conceptions of justice and between economic (consequentialist) and legal (principled) conceptions of practical reasoning. Nevertheless much current writing on justice can be and commonly is read as extending early modern discussions of the nature and vindication of just constitutions, laws, rights and the demands of international justice.

[33] See J. B. Schneewind 'The Misfortunes of Virtue', *Ethics*, 101 (1990), 42–63.

1.4 MODERNITY, UNIVERSALISTS AND PARTICULARISTS: SOME ALTERNATIVE STORIES

None of the schematic stories discussed in the last section offers an adequate account of the divergence between present conceptions of justice and of virtue. *At most* they suggest reasons why their *scope* could come to differ. If we are to understand what has driven a deeper wedge between ways of thinking about justice and about the virtues, so that they are now discussed in quite different registers, it may help to return to the problem posed by the gradual erosion of metaphysical foundations. For the one mutual accusation which the partisans of justice and of virtue make against one another is that proponents of the other position cannot justify their claims. Both contend that the other side repeatedly advances ethical claims which, if they cannot rest their case on traditional metaphysical foundations, are ultimately arbitrary. Both accusations may be right.

Much that I shall suggest in this section is speculation rather than argument: given the fact that metaphysical assumptions linger half-articulated in the background of ethical writing long after they are explicitly disowned it is extraordinarily hard to do better. Yet the speculation has a serious purpose. It offers an account of current discussions of justice and of virtue which provides a picture both of the sources and of the costs of divergence.

Broadly speaking my suggestion is that much early modern writing on justice and other virtues accommodates, or at least postpones, the intellectual crises of modernity by seeking a surrogate or supplement for metaphysical and religious certainties in naturalistic conceptions of the human passions and human reason. If this intellectual strategy had worked, inclusively universal ethical claims could be supported by appeal to a foreground account of human reason and human passions, to which all are subject, and which was discreetly backed by traditional metaphysical foundations and religious certainties.

One tempting belt-and-braces strategy for achieving this objective is to present the Science of Man itself as founded on the metaphysical certainties, for which it can then provide a more accessible and congenial surrogate.[34] If it can be shown, for

---

[34] Even Hutcheson uses this belt-and-braces strategy: in the foreground the moral sense; in the background the Deity implanting 'kind affections'. See Frances Hutcheson (1728),

example, that human desires are generally beneficent, or that the moral sense discerns the good, or that happiness is the measure of all value, then the foundations for a universalist position will be secure. Once one has a belt, it may be tempting to discard the braces – particularly if one fails to notice that only the braces are keeping the belt securely in position. At some point (but not anywhere one could pinpoint) the old metaphysical and religious certainties are no longer invoked to provide the foundation for a conception of human nature, which is then supposed to support ethical thinking without independent backing.

At that point the emperor's clothes may fall away. In place of an account of the *objective* good, a *subjective* conception of the good may be called on to provide the basis for ethical thinking. For example, in many utilitarian hands happiness is seen as subjective good, and further proof of its goodness is not required, or at any rate not offered. Just institutions are those which will do most to secure human happiness; virtues are psychological propensities that tend to maximize happiness. A revised universal account of justice and virtue can then be defended as derivable from claims about human desires and happiness, *provided that a subjective conception of the good is accepted*. A new Science of Man will supposedly serve when the old Metaphysics of the Good fails.[35] However, if no Science of Man can be established to replace metaphysical and religious certainties, or if the goodness of human happiness, or of other conceptions of natural or even of primary goods, can be called in question then inclusive universal ethical principles – of justice as well as of virtue – will be put in question. The smouldering intellectual crisis, which had been ingeniously postponed, would then threaten both justice and virtue. If this speculative story is closer to the truth than a particularist tale about lost traditions of virtue, the results might well be unstable. For on such an account, the robust theories of human nature which could anchor accounts of the (subjective) good, on which universal accounts both of justice and of virtue could

Illustrations upon the Moral Sense, ed. Bernard Peach (Cambridge, Mass., Harvard University Press, 1971).

[35] The view is highly contestable for many reasons: in naturalizing the basis of action and ethics, conceptions of action, reason and freedom are all metamorphosed, and many conclusions which were thought to be reached by relying on the earlier conceptions may prove inaccessible or lack analogues.

depend, seemingly with little need for metaphysical or religious certainties, might come under double assault.

One assault on naturalistic accounts of the good has been *external*. The emergence of historicized conceptions of the human subject challenged any universalism based on the assumption of invariant laws of human nature.[36] Virtue and justice might then vary when subjects varied, and if subjects were held to vary sufficiently at different times and in different societies, justice and virtue would do so too. A slide from robust naturalism to historicized conceptions of the human subject readily leads from inclusively universalist to particularist conceptions *of the whole of ethics*. It is this historicist move which underlies both the thought that particular virtues can best be construed as the fruit and proud possession of particular historical communities rather than as inclusively universal demands, and the thought that justice too can best be seen as an achievement of a particular community at a particular time.[37]

The particularist friends of the virtues, whether Aristotelian or Wittgensteinian, communitarian or feminist, have lost confidence in the plausibility of any robust Science of Man, and also in the prospect for a robust universal account of the subjectively good, on which parallel accounts of justice or of virtue might be built. However, by itself uneasiness about robust forms of naturalism provides no insight into the *divergence* of thinking about justice and about virtue.

A second sort of assault on robustly naturalist positions, which is less discussed, has in a way called all forms of naturalism in question. In place of a robustly empirical account of human desires and action, and their connection, many contemporary writers, both in ethics and in the social sciences, prefer a more guarded, interpretive account of 'revealed preferences'. The phrase 'revealed preference' misleads, since the point of the approach is that *preferences are not revealed*. In speaking of 'revealed preferences' the claim is only that actual behaviour can be interpreted *as if* it were

---

36 On which see, above all, Charles Taylor, *Sources of the Self* (Cambridge, Mass., Harvard University Press, 1989).

37 A thought that is found not only in communitarian work but in some of John Rawls's later writing. For examples of the two lines of thought see Michael Walzer, *Spheres of Justice: A Defence of Pluralism and Equality* (Oxford, Martin Robertson, 1983), ch. 1; John Rawls, 'Justice as Fairness: Political not Metaphysical', *Philosophy and Public Affairs*, 14 (1985), 223–51.

the product of a certain preference ordering. A revealed preference interpretation of human action (however elaborate the assumptions it makes about the structure of preferences) undercuts at least the more obvious and traditional reasons for supposing that satisfaction of preferences can define the subjectively good and so provide a basis for accounts either of justice or of virtue.

'Revealed' interpretations of preferences create difficulty for any simple identification of satisfaction of preferences with happiness (*a fortiori* with the subjectively good), because they *ascribe* preferences to agents inferentially on the basis of their action, assuming certain accounts of rationality, of the transitive ordering of preferences, of their connection and measurability, and of the coherence and accuracy of agents' beliefs. On such a view all action *must* inevitably aim at preference satisfaction, and further reasons would be needed to show why the satisfaction of any particular preferences was ethically desirable. In using the vocabulary of 'revealed preference' simply as a way of talking about the relations between different elements of behaviour we undercut traditional reasons for identifying the satisfaction of preferences with happiness and so with the (subjectively) good, so making it obscure why institutions or practices that conduce to preference satisfaction should be thought just, or why dispositions that do so should be thought virtuous.

This perhaps suggests why so little work on justice or the virtues is squarely and openly based on 'revealed', interpretive conceptions of the relation of preference to action. An account of justice based on valuing the satisfaction of 'revealed' preferences need not be empty, for it can propose ways in which the 'revealed' preferences of various agents are to be accommodated or aggregated – though the vindication of these proposals may be hard. However, an account of virtue that started by valuing the satisfaction of 'revealed' preferences would be empty indeed: it would lead to the thought that virtuous lives are those which satisfy, or satisfy most deeply – whatever 'preferences' they happen to express.[38] An

---

[38] See Amartya Sen, 'Behavior and the Concept of Preference', *Economica*, 40 (1973), 241–59 and 'Rational Fools: A Critique of the Behavioral Foundations of Economic Theory', *Philosophy and Public Affairs*, 6 (1977), 317–44, both of them reprinted in his *Choice, Welfare and Measurement* (Oxford, Blackwell, 1982); Onora O'Neill, 'Autonomy, Coherence and Independence' in *Liberalism, Autonomy and Citizenship*, ed. David Milligan and William Watts-Muller (London, Avebury, 1992), pp. 202–29.

interpretive conception of the relation of preference to action can then perhaps allow for highly individualistic, radically particularist conceptions of virtue. But at worst it allows for a misappropriation of the vocabulary of virtue, by which the pursuit of mere, sheer preference is fraudulently dignified.

Whereas historicist accounts of human subjects and action can accommodate robust, particularist conceptions of virtue, the theoretical economy of interpretive conceptions of human action offers only minimal footholds even for a radically particularist account of virtue. What neither of these approaches can offer is the basis for a universalist account of the virtues that continues the ambitions of positions that were supposedly based on traditional metaphysical or religious certainties, or even of positions that relied on their robustly naturalistic successors.

The first stage in the retreat from metaphysical certainty towards naturalism in writing on ethics had evident strengths and advantages. A naturalistic construal of the good can support accounts both of justice and of virtue. It can rely on those well-worked empiricist accounts of the relation of desire and action that presuppose only a slender negative freedom, so do not need to tangle with a stronger and more controversial conception of human freedom. By this strategy a universalist account of justice and virtue might, as the classical utilitarians supposed, be based on empirically confirmed accounts of human action, freedom and motivation.

Later stages in the movement away from metaphysical certainty lose these strengths and advantages. Different as they are, both historicist and revealed preference accounts of human motivation can leave room *only* for particularist conceptions of ethical standards, and can vindicate the standards for which they leave room only in limited ways. Historicists can give reasons for valuing the particular virtues prized in particular traditions, but only in terms of those particular traditions: vindication like critique has to be internal. Revealed preference theory, and the forms of existentialist and postmodern thinking with which it has under-explored affinities, can leave room only for minimal, particularist conceptions of virtue, and for vindications which amount to little more than endorsements of the pursuit of preference, of individuals' decisions and choices, or of their various life-projects. This uncomfortable situation is quite often masked by appeal to soothing examples of action that traditional conceptions of virtue would have vindicated with weightier reasons.[39] Other, more testing, examples would highlight the disconcerting ease with which both historicizing forms of particularism and positions which rely on 'revealed' preference theory, or more generally that stress the importance of decisions, projects and choices, can be used to sanitize what many would think vicious and to reclassify it as virtuous.

These considerations suggest some limitations of the various forms of particularism which dominate current discussions of virtue. Actual norms and traditions, actual preferences, attachments, and commitments can indeed guide action: but why should we conclude that they guide it virtuously? It may seem more honest to take a more self-consciously postmodern view, and conclude that practical reasoning that starts from the particularities of actual situations need point neither to justice nor to virtue, and that there are no reasons why it should not point to nihilism, egoism, or aestheticized modes of self-realization, or to ways of life traditionally seen as vicious. Particularist arguments do not rule out a contingent convergence of shared norms and traditions, or of individual preferences, attachments and commitments, with values and virtues that others think receive endorsement from deeper sources. Equally they offer no reason to think that any society's particular norms and traditions, or any individual's preferences, attachments or commitments, will disclose values that have objective standing or wider (let alone inclusive) import. Thinking along particularist lines we may in the end be driven to think of all values, of justice as well as virtue, as no more than received views or personal preferences or decisions in dignifying disguise.

If these alternative stories are at all plausible, the common fate

---

[39] Consider Sartre's celebrated discussion of a young man torn between joining the Free French or staying with and caring for his mother in *Existentialism is a Humanism* in W. Kaufmann ed., *Existentialism from Dostoevsky to Sartre* (Cleveland, World Publishing, 1956), pp 287–311. Sartre pits patriotic against filial duty. The sharpness of this 'existential' dilemma derives from its implicit reference to *rather traditional standards which would have to be established by arguments Sartre fails to provide* (contrast the 'dilemma' of patriotic duty versus a trip to the fair). Or consider discussions, by Bernard Williams and others, of the example of rescuing one's drowning wife, which has been used to suggest that identity-constituting attachments and life-projects are not to be challenged, so need not be underwritten by ethical justification. The claim might be true, but needs testing against examples of equally popular but less conventionally admired or respectable life-projects, such as revenge, domination or greed.

of discussions of justice and of virtue has been a loss of those supposed metaphysical or religious certainties on which the whole of ethics had been overtly or tacitly based. The unexplained divergence in the way the two domains of ethics are now discussed may reflect the mere reality that neither is firmly anchored. It has been tempting to continue to think of justice in universalist terms, because the broad scope and close-to-cosmopolitan tasks of justice are so important in the modern world. It has been tempting to think of virtue in particularistic terms because other approaches seem not merely unavailable but questionable in a culturally diverse world. If the crisis of foundations is to be taken seriously, there is little to be said for succumbing to either temptation. There is little to be said on behalf of inclusively universal principles, including those of justice, unless they can be based on convincing practical reasoning, which either sustains or replaces justifications once based on metaphysical or religious certainties. There is little to be said on behalf of particularist conceptions of the virtues unless convincing reasons can be found, which show why appeals to shared traditions or to individual sensibilities justify ethical claims.

In the end the *divergence* between justice and the virtues can best be seen neither solely as entailed by a shared crisis of foundations nor solely as a response to social change, but as alternative ways of reacting to a shared intellectual crisis. Most writing on justice has remained faithful to universalist and to increasingly cosmopolitan aspirations – but has hoped to jump ship when the metaphysical certainties foundered and to load old principles firmly on to minimal appeals to reason. Most writing on virtue has repudiated universalist ambitions, yet continues to use the old ethical vocabulary that relied on supposed metaphysical or religious certainties to endorse received habits, conventional excellences and prized commitments. The divergence of justice from virtue is not a matter of demonstrated difference: it has arisen because both are unanchored, and the two have drifted apart. Ultimately accounts of both domains of practical reasoning need to answer charges of arbitrariness.

CHAPTER 2

Practical reason: abstraction and construction

It is one thing to suggest that discussions of justice and of virtue have diverged because different responses to a crisis in their supposed shared foundations have proved easier for the two domains of ethics, another to imagine how the crisis might be overcome. What methods or approaches can ethical reasoning use if it starts neither from a conception of the objectively good (whether transcendent or inherent) nor from a naturalistic conception of subjective good that supposedly supplants objective conceptions, nor from the 'deep' particularities of common or of individual life? How else could we identify either convincing premises or sound methods for ethical reasoning?

One step towards sound starting points for ethical reasoning would be simply to filter out and reject any which need but lack metaphysical or empirical backing. Insisting on true premises is a reputable enough move. Although some of the crucial assumptions used both by universalists and by particularists are surely contestable, there are also surely many well-established empirical truths about human life and action which might provide acceptable starting points for practical reasoning.

So a first move may be to discard those claims which look implausible, and to abstract a minimal range of convincing starting points. Many contemporary universalists,[1] including most recent writers on justice and rights, follow this strategy. They have sought true but minimal, and (so they hope) uncontentious, claims about action, reason and motivation as starting points for justifying ethical claims. Their abstract approach has been rejected as ethically damaging and philosophically unconvincing by many particularists. So I begin by considering some disputes about the value and the

---

[1] See chapter 1, note 3 for a selection of prominent universalists.

dangers of relying on abstract and minimal starting points for ethical reasoning. I conclude that abstraction, properly understood, need not damage, but that by itself it is not likely to provide enough.

An adequate account of ethics will need not only convincing starting points but convincing ways of proceeding from those starting points, that is to say an adequate conception of practical reasoning. Ethical judgement may rest not on *discovering* ethical features in (or beyond) the world, but on *constructing* ethical principles. If it does, no selection of true starting points, abstract or less abstract, however well established, will provide enough: an adequate account of practical reasoning will also be needed. In this chapter I shall suggest how an account of practical reason might be constructed, and in later ones how it might be used to help build an account of ethics that will link justice and virtue.

The claims of many approaches which I neglect – in particular of many forms of ethical realism[2] or context-sensitive particularism – may seem overwhelming to some readers. However, a defensive account of the constructive approach for which I shall argue, that repeatedly skirmished with all rival approaches, would come to the point too slowly. In this chapter I take the first step towards constructing an account of justice and of virtue by discussing the contributions that abstraction and a constructive conception of practical reason can make to sound ethical reasoning.

2.1 ABSTRACTION AND IDEALIZATION

When universalists seek to justify ethical claims by relying on abstract and minimal starting points they see their strategy as innocuous and uncontroversial. Their hope is that by pruning away assumptions whose truth cannot be ascertained, and relying on a

---

[2] *Which kinds of realism* various readers will support is pretty open. In general, it will not be the distinctive, hard-edged metaphysical realism whose structure underpins (many readings of) classical and Christian ethics. It is more likely to be some more 'human kind of realism', or 'internal realism' or 'empirical realism' (terms used by Putnam, *Realism and Reason*, vol. III). Unfortunately, or fortunately, once metaphysical realism is set aside, the use of the term *realism* becomes so promiscuous that I can see little advantage either in laying claim to it or in hoping to refute its appropriation for other positions. Virtually all the types of ethical positions discussed in this book, including most forms of particularism, are hailed as forms of realism by some of their proponents. Rather than spend time trying to show who has the better claim to the term, I have simply offered reasons for accepting or questioning various positions.

meagre and parsimonious set of plausible assumptions, they will lend credibility to their conclusions, which more extravagant starting points would forfeit.[3] Their particularist critics think the hope forlorn, and that an abstract conception of the human subject or of action can lead only to an abstract view of ethical principles and to an impoverished ethical vision that concentrates on rights, obligations and blame.[4]

However, the objections many particularists raise in condemning abstraction are not strictly to premisses which *abstract* from known truths, but to the ungrounded introduction of *idealized* premisses. The distinction is fundamental, and frequently overlooked.[5] Abstraction, taken straightforwardly, is a matter of *bracketing*, but not of *denying*, predicates that are true of the matter under discussion. Abstraction *in this strict sense* is theoretically and practically unavoidable, and often ethically important. All uses of language must be more or less abstract; so must all reasoning. Even the most contextual ethical reasoning is abstract in this sense. Particularists, who may make much of the point that justice differs in Athens and in Sparta,[6] and conclude that abstract accounts of justice mislead, take for granted that the principles of Athenian or Spartan justice apply to many varying cases, from some of whose differences jury or judge must abstract. Reasoning that abstracts from a predicate makes claims that do not depend on that predicate holding, *or* on its not holding. The important merit of abstraction *in this strict sense* is that it never arbitrarily augments a given starting point, so will not lead one validly from a truth to a falsehood.[7]

---

[3] For example, John Rawls describes his theory of justice as one that 'generalizes and carries to a higher level of abstraction the traditional conception of the social contract', Rawls, *A Theory of Justice*, p. 3.

[4] For complaints about abstraction in ethics see Taylor, 'Atomism', pp. 187–210, as well as the works by Alasdair MacIntyre, Michael Sandel and Bernard Williams cited in chapter 1.

[5] For more detailed discussion of some ethical implications of differences between abstraction and idealization, see Onora O'Neill, 'Abstraction, Idealization and Ideology' in J. D. G. Evans, ed., *Moral Philosophy and Contemporary Problems* (RIP Series) (Cambridge University Press, 1988), pp. 55–69 and 'Justice, Gender and International Boundaries', pp. 303–23.

[6] The example chosen by an uncompromising universalist to illustrate his claim that justice does not differ with time or place: Cicero, *De Republica* III, 33. The section is included in Cicero, *On Government*, trans. Michael Grant (Harmondsworth, Middlesex, Penguin Books, 1993).

[7] Of course, abstracting can help mislead, as when somebody brackets central and salient elements of a situation and then makes the further, unjustified assumption that features

Idealization is another matter: it can easily lead to falsehood. An assumption, and derivatively a theory, idealizes when it ascribes predicates – often seen as enhanced, 'ideal' predicates – that are false of the case in hand, and so denies predicates that are true of that case. For example, if human beings are assumed to have capacities and capabilities[8] for rational choice or self-sufficiency or independence from others that are evidently not achieved by many or even by any actual human beings, the result is not mere abstraction; it is idealization. Insofar as contemporary theories of justice start by assuming 'ideal' conceptions of persons, rationality or independence they not merely abstract. They assume rather than establish specific ideals. If they then do not offer reasons for starting from these idealizing assumptions – which might require demanding metaphysical arguments – their theories will, strictly speaking, be inapplicable to the human case.

Of course, idealized models of choice and action may often have a point. For example, we learn something interesting about economic behaviour by considering 'idealized' consumers and 'perfect' markets.[9] But if as economic actors we assume that consumers and markets live up to these idealizing fictions we will fail to adjust our action to actual circumstances, and may pay, or exact, a heavy price. Practical reasoning that assumes that 'ideal' predicates are satisfied will not reach conclusions safely and soundly for cases where they are not satisfied.

The differing implications of idealizing strategies for theoretical and for practical reasoning are also often overlooked. Idealizations are not only important but may be indispensable for theoretical purposes (frictionless motion, ideal gases, perfect vacuum). In the natural sciences, and in general when explanation is sought,

not mentioned were missing, or allows or even encourages others to assume that they were missing. The fault in such cases lies in the second move.

[8] Here and hereafter I follow Amartya Sen in distinguishing individual *capacities* (e.g. traits of character, talents, physical abilities) from socially effective *capabilities*, whose exercise relies on effective institutional structures as well as individual capacities. I shall also generally speak of absent capabilities as *vulnerabilities*. See Jean Drèze and Amartya Sen, *Hunger and Public Action* (Oxford, Clarendon Press, 1989) for a clear explication of Sen's terms and references to the numerous works in which his thinking about capabilities has been developed.

[9] We may also fail to learn some interesting things about consumers and markets if we rely solely on idealizing theories. See Mary Douglas and Baron Isherwood, *The World of Goods* (Harmondsworth, Penguin, 1979), as well as the discussion of poverty in Drèze and Sen, *Hunger and Public Action*.

theories and hypotheses can be assessed for the accuracy with which they fit the world. If they introduce idealizations that are too wide of the mark, ordinary processes of confirmation and testing are likely to detect and reject them. Idealizations are far more dangerous in practical reasoning, because it aims at guidance rather than explanation. Practical reasoning seeks to guide action whose aim is to fit the world (in some measure) to its recommendations, rather than its conclusions to the world. If the world is to be adapted to fit the conclusions of practical reasoning, and these assume certain idealizations, the world rather than the reasoning may be judged at fault. More concretely, agents and institutions who fail to measure up to supposed ideals may be blamed for the misfit.[10]

Particularists have often, and rightly, criticized universalists for tacitly assuming various 'ideals' which they speak of as mere abstractions, and fail to vindicate. Communitarians complain that universalists variously assume 'ideals' of rationality, of mutual disinterestedness, of impartiality, of autonomy, and of the person.[11] They also complain about an allegedly more widespread assumption that human identities are given independently of their ends and their social relationships. Many of these complaints are aggregated in Taylor's strictures on 'atomism' and in Sandel's figure of the 'deontological self'[12] which he imputes to contemporary liberals. Feminist writers sometimes complain along parallel lines that liberal political theory covertly assumes and does not vindicate gendered, specifically 'male' ideals, while claiming to rely on abstract, gender-neutral conceptions of the human agent.[13] Particularists are not the only ones to complain about appeals to illusory ideals. Writing in bioethics – most of it universalist – often complains that exaggerated conceptions of autonomy or of

---

[10] Evidently there is a lot more to be said about the similarities and differences between abstraction and idealization in scientific and in ethical reasoning; but this is not the place to say it.

[11] Some complain specifically about Rawls's use of the 'Kantian ideal of the person', see John Rawls, 'Kantian Constructivism in Moral Theory' *Journal of Philosophy*, 77 (1980), pp. 515–72, revised version in his *Political Liberalism* (New York, Columbia University Press, 1993). For some commentary on these assumptions see D. O. Brink, 'Rawlsian Constructivism in Moral Theory', *Canadian Journal of Philosophy*, 17 (1987), 71–90; O'Neill, 'Constructivisms in Ethics' in *Constructions of Reason*, pp. 206–18, and see section 2.2 below.

[12] Sandel, *Liberalism and the Limits of Justice*.

[13] Carol Pateman, *The Sexual Contract* (Cambridge, Polity Press 1988); Susan Okin, 'Justice and Gender', *Philosophy and Public Affairs*, 16 (1987), 42–72.

'fully informed consent' are bandied about as if they were mere abstractions from human realities.

The lack of justification for starting with such 'ideal' conceptions of persons, reason or autonomy provides good reasons for querying these positions, but no reason for being suspicious about mere abstraction. Writers who start by assuming 'ideals' cannot justify them as mere abstractions, and need to supply appropriate justifications: this may be uphill work if they hope to reject metaphysical certainties that might ground demanding conceptions of the objectively good, or of the person. Insofar as critics of contemporary writing on justice identify and complain of covert and unargued idealizations lurking in its most basic premises, their criticisms are convincing – but they are not criticisms of abstraction.

However, because they fail to distinguish idealization from abstraction, many particularist critics of contemporary ethical universalism make a far more radical claim. They assume that if universalists fail to establish metaphysical certainties that will vindicate an account of the objectively good, they must not only do without metaphysics and idealized starting points, but forego abstraction. Since they doubt that metaphysical certainties can be established, they conclude that there is no acceptable option but to reject abstraction, and with it the very possibility of universal principles. They then see this as one reason for looking to the particularities of traditions or of personal life, rather than to abstract principles, yet often do not note that these particularist ways of thinking about ethics do not avoid abstraction in the strict sense – even if they successfully avoid assuming unvindicated ideals.[14] The many convincing criticisms of the idealized conceptions of persons, reason and action, on which one or another ethical universalist has in fact relied, while claiming only to abstract, do not show that there is anything wrong with abstraction, or provide reasons for adopting some form of particularism. To draw those conclusions we would also have to show that approaches that abstract, but do *not* invoke unvindicated ideals, cannot establish ethical principles. The fact that universalist writing has a penchant for abstraction creates no general problems.

---

[14] Some particularists in fact introduce their own unvindicated ideals, such as idealized conceptions of shared citizenship or of community, or idealized conceptions of attachment or of personal bonds.

A penchant for unvindicated idealizations is another matter. If the varying advocates of justice and the varying friends of the virtues *both* place exaggerated weight on contentious starting points, their disputes may amount largely to a phony, if rather noisy, war. There is little to choose between appeals to idealized but unvindicated conceptions of rationality, consent, autonomy, agency and the like, and equally unvindicated appeals to idealized versions of the categories and practices of traditions, or the actual sensibilities and commitments of individuals. If these strategies of justification were the only possibilities for ethics there would be little to do except to hunt doggedly for the missing vindications – or to lapse exhausted into unvindicated postmodern celebration or nihilist lament over mere, sheer difference. However, there is in principle no reason why abstract accounts of matters that can be established with at least adequate accuracy should not provide starting points for ethical, as for other sorts of reasoning. The problem may be just that the available starting points are too minimal to enable one to get very far. If they are, everything will depend on how much of the remaining task can be carried by a plausible conception of practical reason.

2.2 CONSTRUCTIVISM IN ETHICS: RAWLSIAN MODELS

Starting points are not enough. We also need a vindicable conception of how to proceed. How are action-guiding conclusions to be constructed on the basis of strictly abstract starting points? One account is given by John Rawls, to whom we owe the contemporary use of the term 'constructivism' as a label for a range of approaches to ethics. The several stages of Rawls's work provide an instructive illustration of several conceptions of the task of construction.

In *A Theory of Justice* he used the term *constructive* very broadly, to cover any moral theory which offered a procedure for answering ethical problems. Constructive methods in ethics are there contrasted with positions such as 'intuitionism', which Rawls characterizes (using a traditional but non-standard understanding of the term) as providing only a plurality of unranked principles, hence no procedure for resolving ethical problems. On this understanding of the term, many positions offer constructive criteria for ethics, including utilitarianism.[15] Rawls describes the specific constructive ethics that he worked out in *A Theory of Justice* as 'Contractarian', alluding once again to the claim that he carries 'to a higher level of abstraction the familiar theory of the social contract as found, say, in Locke, Rousseau, and Kant'.[16]

In later papers and in the 1980 Dewey lectures[17] Rawls took a stronger view of 'constructivism', and proposed that principles of justice be understood as principles which reasonable 'agents of construction' can work out (rather than discover) by following certain justifiable *procedures* of 'construction'. He hopes in this way to provide a 'procedural interpretation' of Kant's account of justice which can then be 'detached from its background in transcendental idealism'.[18] Constructivism in ethics, or specifically about justice, is in the first instance the claim that their principles are not established by metaphysical arguments, or discovered in the world, but that they must be constructed on the basis of plausible, no doubt abstract, assumptions.

Rawls's approach throughout this period has been criticized for relying on claims which when looked at more closely not merely abstract from established truths about human beings and human situations, but introduce various ideals and idealized conceptions of the human person as starting points for his construction of justice. For example, in *A Theory of Justice* the veil of ignorance, that constitutes the original position and forms part of the procedure for identifying principles of justice, is defined by reference to an *ideal* of fairness that requires mutual independence between the preferences of distinct agents, and assumes that there is a restricted set of primary goods of which agents always prefer more to less. Neither assumption is merely an abstraction from our

---

[15] Rawls, *A Theory of Justice*, pp. 34, 39–40, 49, 52.

[16] Rawls, *A Theory of Justice*, p. 11.

[17] John Rawls, 'The Basic Structure as Subject', *American Philosophical Quarterly*, 14 (1977), 159–65 and 'Kantian Constructivism in Moral Theory', *Journal of Philosophy*, 77, 1980, 515–72 (The Dewey Lectures). An extensively revised version of the Dewey Lectures appears in *Political Liberalism* (New York, Columbia University Press, 1993). In the revised work the essay 'Political Constructivism' (pp. 89–129) distinguishes *moral* from *political* constructivism, endorses only the latter and notes ways in which Rawls's position consequently differs not only from Kant's but also from that of others who have advanced constructivist approaches to the whole of ethics.

[18] Rawls 'The Basic Structure as Subject', p. 165; cf. *Political Liberalism*, p. 100. For discussion of some ways in which Rawls sees his position as differing from (a metaphysical reading of) Kant see also *A Theory of Justice*, pp 256–70.

world. The corresponding abstractions would be that it may or may not be the case that the preferences of distinct agents interlock, that it may or may not be the case that agents prefer more to less of primary goods.[19]

In the Dewey lectures Rawls introduces additional idealizations, in that he conceives of agents of construction as beings who are 'moved solely by their highest-order interests in their moral powers and by their concern to advance their determinate but unknown final ends'.[20] Here he explicitly does not describe his approach merely as abstracting, but rather takes an approach that 'specifies a particular conception of the person as an element in a reasonable procedure of construction, the outcome of which determines the content of the first principles of justice'.[21] This conception of the person is the 'Kantian ideal of the moral subject'. Yet Rawls offers little to explain what it is that vindicates taking this rather than another possible ideal of the subject or person as part of the procedure of construction, giving rise to the charge that, at least at that time, his constructivism was marked by latent metaphysical presuppositions.[22]

Rawls's later work has adjusted this emphasis by stressing that the ideals that may be taken as elements for the construction of principles of justice are justified because they are embedded in the particular culture of actual liberal democratic societies: the vindication of justice as fairness is to be seen as political, not metaphysical.[23] The imputation of latent reliance on metaphysical claims was thereby refuted at the cost of appearing to endorse a particularism with liberal content. This shift in Rawls's work can be read as a response to particularist, specifically communitarian, questions raised about his earlier approach: liberal principles are indeed maintained, but in his recent work their

---

[19] For comments on Rawlsian constructivism see also Arthur Ripstein, 'Foundationalism in Political Theory', *Philosophy and Public Affairs*, 16 (1987), pp. 115–37; Thomas E. Hill, Jr, 'Kantian Constructivism in Ethics' in his *Dignity and Practical Reason* (Ithaca, Cornell University Press, 1992); O'Neill 'Constructivisms in Ethics' in *Constructions of Reason*, pp. 206–18.

[20] Rawls, 'Kantian Constructivism in Moral Theory', p. 528, cf. 547, 568.

[21] Rawls, 'Kantian Constructivism in Moral Theory', pp. 516 ff.

[22] See esp. Brink, 'Rawlsian Constructivism in Moral Theory'; see also the other articles cited in note 19.

[23] Beginning with Rawls, 'Justice as Fairness: Political not Metaphysical'.

vindication, hence their relevance, is said to be internal to liberal societies.[24]

It is striking that some of the ideals and idealizations that Rawls introduced at various stages in developing his constructive account of justice are integral to his conceptions of practical reason. Two conceptions of practical reason are particularly important for his work. In the Original Position self-interested agents, under the idealized conditions imposed by an artfully woven 'veil of ignorance', use instrumental reasoning to choose among possible principles for organizing their society. The construction of the Original Position evidently assumes certain streamlined, idealized conceptions. However, Rawls offers a justification of these idealizations. The Original Position is to be seen as a 'device of representation' whose use can be vindicated by Reflective Equilibrium. Can a process of Reflective Equilibrium, which tests proposed principles of justice (chosen in the Original Position) against 'our considered moral judgements', or (in the later work) against those of a liberal democratic society, offer a justification which does not appeal to idealized conceptions of the human subject, of reason, or of action?

Much of the effort of Rawls's complex construction of justice is needed in order to retrieve his intuitive idea of justice as fairness which is jeopardized by his – perhaps idealized – assumption that human reasoning is governed by self-interest, whose adjustment behind a veil of ignorance can be justified by reference to the actual norms embodied in the 'considered moral judgements' of a liberal democratic society. The entire device of the original position is instituted in order to baffle the unfortunate results of imputed rational self-interest. If a preference-oriented conception of action, governed by a rather idealized conception of self-interest, had not been built into the original position, the task of identifying principles of justice might have relied less on idealizations. Equally, if 'considered moral judgements', or the norms of a society informed by liberal democratic structures and ideals, had not been built into the method of vindicating those principles, the vindication too might have been less open to question.

---

[24] For a view of this shift as a problem see Chandran Kukathas and Philip Pettit, *Rawls: 'A Theory of Justice' and its Critics* (Cambridge, Polity, 1990); Rawls's own view is that this shift is the solution to certain problems in his earlier formulations.

Still, scepticism is very much in order here. No method of construction can convince unless it shows just *which* constraints may legitimately govern a constructive procedure. Despite the difficulties of the sophisticated Rawlsian strategy of combining a somewhat idealized conception of instrumental reason (in the construction of the original position) and backing it with a some-what idealized conception of norm-oriented practical reason (in the wider framework of Reflective Equilibrium in liberal societies) the costs of doing without these idealizations might be paralysing. Once preference-oriented models of action are put aside, maximin reasoning will be no more available than maximizing reasoning is available when full-blooded utilitarianism is put aside; once norm-governed reasoning is put aside, neither a process of Reflective Equilibrium nor appeal to the actual ideals and norms of liberal democratic or other societies will retain authority.

The more guarded constructivism that I shall outline follows Rawls in that it does not look for the vindication of ethical principles in metaphysical argument, or in discoveries about the world. It differs from the one Rawls has developed in two ways. In the first place it assumes only an abstract, hence non-idealizing and banal, account of agents and of conditions of action. Secondly, it aims to articulate and to vindicate a conception of practical reasoning without appeal either to unvindicated ideals or to unvindicated particularities.

2.3 CONSTRUCTING PRACTICAL REASON

The task of vindicating an account of reason can seem impossible. Standards and principles of reason, if there are any, are to provide the most fundamental discipline for structuring and orienting thinking and acting. If there are no such standards or principles we would appeal to an illusory authority in speaking of beliefs or action as reasonable. Yet it seems that any vindication of the principles or standards of reason itself must fail: either it would draw on reasoned standards, so be circular, hence unreasoned, hence fail to vindicate; or else it would fail to draw on reasoned standards, so once again fail to vindicate. But if the authority of reason cannot be vindicated, vindications of action that appeal to reason will be at best conditional. Escher's marvellous drawing of a hand that draws another hand that draws the first hand illustrates the seeming impossibility of vindicating reason, either for practical or for theoretical use.

Conceptions of practical reasoning may be divided into two broad types. *Teleological conceptions of practical reasoning* seek to vindicate action, policies and characters as reasoned by showing that they are constitutive of or instrumental to certain ends. These ends may either be identified, as by 'Platonists', perfectionists and by metaphysical realists of various sorts, with certain objective goods (e.g. transcendent ideals or real moral properties) whose content, vindication, and cognitive accessibility remain traditional, if elusive, metaphysical goals. Or they may be identified, as by those universalists (not only consequentialists, but many 'deontologists') who hope to get by with nothing but an instrumental conception of reason, with the satisfaction of subjective ends, whose ethical significance is open to question.

Action-oriented conceptions of practical reasoning seek to vindicate action, policies and characters as reasoned not by showing that they are constitutive of or instrumental towards ends of any sort, but, more directly, by showing that they embody certain types or principles of action, described with varying degrees of specificity or abstraction. Those particularists who are historicists or communitarians, as well as many virtue ethicists, locate the source of practical reason in the (supposedly) *actual* norms or commitments of a given time or place; more radical particularists locate it in the (supposedly) *actual* sensibilities and attachments of a particular life. Yet it is not obvious *why* any particularities should be seen as constitutive of practical reason, or *how* appeals to particularities can show that certain ethical standards are justified as reasonable.

These conceptions of practical reason can be laid out in a simple diagram (see p. 50), which leaves space for a further, distinctive act-oriented conception of practical reason, which, I shall argue, we have reason to take extremely seriously. Despite the difficulty of vindicating any conception of practical reason, the proponents of both teleological conceptions of either type, and of the many varying conceptions of particularist reasoning, are not reticent in suggesting how their own accounts of reason might be vindicated. Yet the none of the more common vindications looks very promising. Some *'Platonist'* and perfectionist conceptions of reasoned action see it as drawn to or oriented by the objectively good, such as transcendent ideals or real moral properties, which

CONCEPTIONS OF PRACTICAL REASONING

End-oriented reasoning	Act-oriented reasoning
'Platonist':	*'Kantian' or Critical:*
reasoned action is oriented by by objective ends, such as real moral properties or meta- physically grounded moral ideals	reasoned action is informed by principles all in the relevant domain can follow
Instrumental:	*'Particularist':*
reasoned action is oriented by subjective ends, such as subjective conceptions of the good, preferences, desires, assisted by means ends reasoning	reasoned action is informed by actual norms and commitments

are the 'ends of reason', hence as vindicable *only* if the metaphysical and epistemological basis for such an account of the objectively Good can be sustained. *Instrumental* conceptions of practical reason-ing may be secure enough,[25] but (as legions of critics have pointed out) they provide no more than conditional reasons, which remain without force unless there are also reasons to pursue certain ends, which no instrumental conception of practical reason purports to offer. The varied *particularist* conceptions of practical reason may have local and limited force, but seemingly fail to explain why appeals to actual traditions, norms or practices, or to actual sensi-bilities and preferences, even to those that are constitutive of identities, should be held to vindicate principles or legitimate action, or identify excellences, rather than beg questions.

Moreover, these well-known ways of organizing practical thought and deliberation share a simpler deficiency, which shows why none

---

[25] Instrumental reasoning that is taken to conform to highly articulated models of rational choice will remain highly contentious. What is uncontentious is only a much more general conception of instrumental rationality, such as the claim that those who seek some end must, if rational, seek or take what they believe to be a means that contributes to that end. An uncontentious conception of instrumental reasoning must avoid exaggerated, idealizing assumptions about causal knowledge, so cannot (for example) mandate maximal efficiency.

of them can constitute a complete account of practical reasoning. For anything to count as practical reasoning it should, presumably, meet *at least* certain quite simple standards. It should, in particular, *at least aim to be followable by others for whom it is to count as reasoning*. Ways of organizing action or thinking about action that are expected to fail this minimal standard can hardly count as reasoned. Those who organize action and thinking about action in ways which they take not to be followable by some of those who are to follow, even be convinced by, their claims offer those others no reasons. What they say or do will appear arbitrary to those others.

Yet each of the three conceptions of practical reason discussed so far fails this elementary standard. Appeals to practical reasoning that is (supposedly) oriented by some conception of the objectively good will be arbitrary unless the necessary metaphysics that establishes that objective good and knowledge of it is available: those who do not accept the appropriate metaphysical and other arguments and positions may find proposals that depend on invoking them at worst incomprehensible and at best conditionally reasoned. Appeals to merely instrumental practical reasoning that subserves subjective ends are barefacedly arbitrary: they will seem at worst incomprehensible and at best conditionally reasoned to those who do not share those ends, or do not think them of value. The conditional rationality of action necessary as means to or as constitutive of some end cannot be metamorphosed into the unconditional rationality of seeking that end: unless an end is demonstrably objective, the fact that it is urgently desired, widely preferred or psychologically compelling, will make action that (helps) produce that end no less arbitrary than the end. Equally, appeals to the actual norms of a society or tradition, or to the actual sensibilities, attachments or commitments of individuals will seem at worst incomprehensible to those who do not grasp those norms and commitments and at best merely conditionally reasoned to those who grasp but do not share them; in either case they will seem arbitrary.

If these conceptions of practical reason are inadequate, can any conception be adequate? The mere requirement that practical reasoning be *followable by* those for whom it is to count as reasoning, although it is evidently not always met, looks too meagre to be action-guiding. It may be a necessary feature of any conception of practical reasoning that it be followable by relevant others, but it hardly seems likely that this demand could provide a robust or adequate conception of practical reasoning. Could such an apparently minimal demand be all that there is to practical reasoning, or even be an important element of such reasoning? Could it guide deliberation and action? Could action be viewed as reasoned merely by virtue of being based on principles that are followable by others?

Many apparently kindred attempts to provide an account of practical reason have failed to convince. For example, attempts to locate the authority of practical reason in actual discourse (or in the conditions for possible discourse), in actual agreement (or in the conditions for possible agreement) have seemingly failed.[26] What I shall propose, however, is not a further dialogical account of the authority of (practical) reason, as that notion is usually understood, but a more limitedly and strictly modal Kantian account, which identifies it with reliance on principles which (it is judged) *can* be principles for all, where the scope of 'all' is taken to vary with context.

Any Kantian account of the authority of (practical) reason, which identifies it with reliance on followable principles of action, must answer two demanding questions. The first asks 'By whom must practical reasoning be followable?' and the second 'What does it take for practical reasoning to be followable?'. The first question asks for an account of the *scope* of reasoning; the second for an account of *what makes attempted reasoning followable* by those who fall within a given scope.

Different stretches of (practical) reasoning may be aimed at or relevant for distinct and differing audiences, who may find different principles of thought or action followable. This is part of the thought behind, and part of the appeal of, particularist reasoning. The failings of particularist conceptions of (practical) reasoning lie not, I suggest, in their focus on rather specifically described action, nor in their attentiveness to conditions for being followable by

---

[26] Such attempts can be found, for example, in the work of Jürgen Habermas and Karl-Otto Apel. I believe that on inspection some dialogical accounts of reason turn out to be particularist, in that they hinge (for example) on *actual* agreement, while others are likely to need metaphysical backing because, for example, they refer to agreement achieved under supposedly ideal conditions, whose status needs vindicating.

some audiences, but in their assumption that reasoning need be followable only by a restricted audience who already share quite specific norms or practices, sensibilities or commitments.

Although particularist reasoning can allow for the revisability of norms or commitments across time, in the light of other norms and commitments (as argued in section 1.2: it is not, contrary to some critics, intrinsically conservative), it cannot allow for the thought that one stretch of practical reasoning may have multiple and differing audiences. Particularist reasoning is intrinsically 'insiders'' reasoning. Depending on context, it might be said to be ethnocentric (more flatteringly: communitarian) or simply egocentric (more flatteringly: authentic). Vindication of action is taken not to work across whatever borders there may be between 'insiders' and 'outsiders': it is reasoning for those who have internalized a given way of thought or life and its norms or traditions, its sensibilities, attachments or commitments.

Although it is plausible enough that *some* stretches of practical reasoning have a *restricted* scope, in the sense that they are taken to be followable only by a restricted and homogeneous audience, so are 'insiders'' reasoning, not all practical reasoning can have such restricted scope. In the first place practical reasoning has to be followable not only by those directly addressed on a given occasion, but by wider groups. In reasoning, in justifying what we do, in criticizing what others do, we constantly appeal to a wider group, of whose boundaries we usually lack any very definite conception. Secondly, we do not think that all those for whom thought or action is to be cogent will be closely similar to one another.

The wide scope and varied reception assumed for thinking and discussing action can be better understood either by considering individual lives from the inside, or by considering the interconnection of lives and societies. Considered from the point of view of any individual life, there is always a need for some ways of connecting claims that are internal to, and perhaps cogent for, one aspect of life or practice or activity to others that are internal to, and perhaps cogent for, other aspects of life or practices or activities: no life can be pre-compartmentalized into wholly watertight compartments. Considered from a wider, external point of view, some thinking about and justifications of action must be presentable, hence followable and exchangeable, not merely among an immediate group of participants, or of those present, or of the like-minded, or even among fellow-citizens, but among more diverse and often more dispersed others, whose exact boundaries cannot be readily defined.

This is borne out in ordinary experience. Reasons for action are often presented and sometimes accepted not only within a restricted set of the like-minded, but among more inclusive sets that comprise differing groups and individuals. Although the outer boundaries of *inclusive practical reasoning* cannot be set with any precision, they must be capacious in a world of multiple and diverse audiences who are linked rather than separated by porous state and regional boundaries, global telecommunications and interlocking and overlapping practices and polities. In such a world, those who aim to reason look for ways of structuring some of their thought and action so that it will be followable by multiple, differing and often dispersed audiences.[27] They do not, and perhaps cannot, aim to live wholly by reasoning which is restricted in its scope and authority, so does not reach beyond those who are (say) on the same side of family, village, national or wider feuds or boundaries; they cannot premise all their reasoning on categories, beliefs, desires or norms that are confined to such restricted groups of 'insiders'. Those whose action and plans of action constantly assume the intelligent cooperation and interaction of many others, who differ in diverse ways, will also expect some at least of their reasoning to be followable by those others.[28]

Once the scope relevant for a given stretch of thinking about action, whether inclusive or restricted, is fixed, it will (in a trivial sense) make sense to speak of it as having to be followable by *all* others within that inclusive or restricted domain. Unless it is followable by those others, it cannot be used to offer them reasons of any sort. This formally universal specification of the scope of anything that is to count as reasoned is not in itself informative; its import depends wholly on the specification of the inclusive or restricted domains within which that stretch of thinking about action is to be followable.

---

[27] For more detailed discussion of issues relevant to settling questions of scope see the discussion of the scope of ethical consideration in chapter 4.

[28] Are some others excluded? This is wholly possible with action and reason that is intended to reach only a restricted range of others, and wholly implausible in other cases, where much effort is put into justifying even trivial claims and action in ways that are intended to be cogent even to others who are very distant or different.

Although the extent of the more inclusive domains of practical reasoning which agents take themselves to address cannot be precisely fixed, it is evidently very wide. Chapter 4 will argue that virtually any agent in the contemporary world takes the *scope of ethical consideration* to be more-or-less cosmopolitan for some matters; Chapters 6 and 7 will offer reasons for thinking that those whose ethical consideration must be more-or-less cosmopolitan for some matters cannot express it *solely* by means of a mosaic of restricted ethical principles and commitments for dealing with restricted domains of life, but rather must adopt at least some basic ethical principles whose scope is much more inclusive, perhaps more-or-less cosmopolitan. There may be many different spheres of life, but each is connected to others, hence each agent needs to adopt at least some principles of inclusive scope. Those who are committed to some inclusive ethical principles will have to take a comparably inclusive view of the range of others to whom they might give reasons for those principles. Taken together these considerations can fix the required domain of practical reasoning for a given context. *Some* practical reasoning will need to have a relatively inclusive scope; some can have a relatively restricted scope. In either case anything that is to count as practical reasoning must be *followable by all others within the relevant scope*.

If some practical reasoning is to be inclusively followable by all within a wide (but not precisely determined) scope, its authority may be used to assess that of other stretches of practical reasoning that are intended to be followable only by those within some more restricted portion of that wider domain, and to connect restricted stretches of practical reasoning to one another. When it does, the claims and authority of relatively restricted reasoning may, in some cases, be *aufgehoben*, that is picked up and incorporated within stretches of more inclusive reasoning and so made followable by more inclusive audiences. For example, the conditional claims of particularist reasoning that has its place in a restricted context might gain sense and authority in the eyes of a far wider audience not because – as it happens – all those in the more inclusive domain came to hold the relevant restricted beliefs or norms, but because wider reasons could be given for viewing the actual beliefs and norms of that more restricted context as ethically significant. Universalist practical reasoning can sometimes show why the claims of some restricted reasoning should be taken seriously, even endorsed or denounced, beyond its immediate and appropriate contexts.[29]

Once the varying scope of different stretches of practical reasoning is explicitly noted, it is possible to state in outline what it will take for practical reasoning to be made followable by those with differing starting points. Reasoning that is to be inclusively followable by others who differ widely can assume nothing too specific about the actual capacities and capabilities of those by whom it is to be followable. It can assume only a rather abstract account of the ordinary capacities and capabilities and the routine forms of vulnerability that can be taken for granted in all others for whom the reasoning is to count. The specific categories, beliefs or desires, or specific cognitive or social skills of a restricted group, which various stretches of restricted particularist reasoning can rely on, cannot be assumed in practical reasoning that is to count more widely. For the same reason, inclusive practical reasoning cannot be based on claims that particular others will at a given moment have or lack the skill or the will, either temporarily or permanently, to act on a certain stretch of reasoning.

This conception of practical reasoning as having inclusive or restricted scope, and assuming correspondingly abstract or specific accounts of others' capacities, capabilities and vulnerabilities, can be surprisingly demanding. In inclusive contexts it amounts to a certain interpretation of the 'Kantian' requirement that reason and action be done on principles that can be principles for all, where the boundaries of 'all' are variable, and at their most inclusive are capacious, although not precisely defined.[30] Like particularist conceptions of practical reason, the 'Kantian' conception is act-oriented. However, although it focuses on principles of action rather than on ends, it does not treat the particularities of the current norms of societies or of the current identity-constituting attachments and commitments of individuals, or their actual

---

[29] Cf. in a rather different idiom, Alan Gewirth, 'Ethical Universalism and Particularism', *Journal of Philosophy*, 85 (1988), 283–302.

[30] Kant's best-known formulation of this doubly modal demand is the Formula of Universal Law version of the Categorical Imperative: *Act only on that maxim through which you can at the same time will that it be a universal law.* Immanuel Kant, *Groundwork of the Metaphysic of Morals*, trans. H. J. Paton (London, Hutchinson, 1953), p. 421 (Prussian Academy pagination). Kant's position has been the target of equally classical criticisms. Past debates, even recurrent debates, are only of tangential relevance here; however, subsequent chapters will comment sporadically on some of these criticisms and their success or failure.

perceptions or sensitivities, as elements of practical reason. It *demands* that practical reasoning follow principles that are thought of as *adoptable* or *followable* by all for whom it is to count as reasoning. This account of practical reason is *fundamentally and doubly modal*: reasons for action *must* be held *capable* of being followed or adopted by others. The first modal element states that reason sets *requirements*: what we deem reasoned *must* meet certain requirements; what we view as reason sets standards and claims authority. The second modal element explicates these requirements: those who act for reasons must (to the best of their belief) act on principles that *are followable or adoptable by* others for whom they take their reasons to count.

This account of the scope of practical reason, and of the implications which that scope has for its structure, provide the material for answering the second question, 'What does it take for practical reasoning to be followable?'. There are two parts to the answer. The first part is that for a principle to be followable by others is a matter of its being *followable in thought*. Here the demand is for *intelligibility*. I do not reason with others if the ways in which I structure my attempted communication or interaction are ones which I hold to be unfollowable in thought, hence unintelligible, in general or specifically for those others who are to follow the reasoning. Many advocates of particularist practical reasoning would concur: they insist that practical, like theoretical, reasoning must be intelligible to those to who are to follow it. That is their reason for stressing thick concepts and socially determinate norms. The account of practical reason proposed here concurs with this first requirement for followability, while noting that abstract as well as determinate categories and principles are followable in thought. Audiences for reasoning are multiple and diverse, so if the scope of some practical reasoning is to be inclusive, it must be followable on the basis of minimal assumptions about the characteristics of those for whom it is to be followable.

The second element of an answer to the question 'What does it take for a principle to be followable?' goes beyond intelligibility. Practical reasoning cannot aim only at intelligibility, which is the proper object of theoretical understanding. It must *also* aim to recommend or prescribe action, to warn against or proscribe action: it must be action guiding. Proposals for action will therefore not be reasoned unless they are not only intelligible, but real possibilities

for those who are to be offered reasons for certain recommendations or prescriptions, warnings or proscriptions. When reasons
for and against action on certain principles are given, those
principles are presented as ones which those who are to follow the
reasoning could adopt. What we recommend or prescribe is action
on principles that we think others *could* (in certain circumstances)
make part of their lives, and perhaps express in overt action, in
attitudes and in their responsiveness and sensitivities (although
they may not seek to do so). What we warn others against or
proscribe must be action on principles that we think they *could*
adopt (in some circumstances), perhaps even *could* find tempting,
could see as principles by which they *could* seek to live and to express
not only in overt action but in their attitudes and sensitivities. We
cannot give others reason for adopting principles which we do not
think they could adopt. If the demands of practical reason are
intrinsically *modal*, they will not require reasoners to conform to
what actually holds, or to what would hold in a hypothetical, or
ideal, or transcendent world; but they will demand that any
reasoned proposal for action be one that the proposer thinks *could*
be adopted by others for whom the reasoning is to count.

   This account of the doubly modal structure of practical reasoning
is formulated *from the reasoner's point of view*. In offering reasons for
action agents endorse principles that are *thought by the agent* to be
possible principles for all others in some domain. The demands of
reason are demands on reasoners. Reasoning is defective when
reasoners misjudge or misrepresent what others can follow. For
example, one of the many uses of idealized conceptions of the person
is to obscure the realities and vulnerabilities of others, and so obscure
the fact that purported reasoning is simply inaccessible to some for
whom it is disingenuously said to provide reasons for action (cf.
section 4.3). Of course, the reasoning may also fail in some of its
purposes when those to whom it is addressed, even if they can
follow a given stretch of practical reasoning, pay no attention, or do
not understand, or do not act on it as proposed: but in these cases
the failure is not that the proposals were unreasoned. Practical
reasoners can ensure that they discharge the task of making their
proposals followable by those for whom they are to count; they cannot make others see or act in accord with the reasons they provide.

   In proposing as reasonable only principles of action that are
followable by the relevant others – whether those in a more

inclusive or only those in a more restricted sphere – practical reasoners need therefore judge only that *the principle itself is followable by all in that sphere*, in the sense that its universal adoption in the relevant domain would not be incoherent. The requirement that reasoned principles be such that all others (in a restricted or an inclusive domain) *could* adopt them demands not that all of them could here or now, or on some anticipated occasions, or simultaneously, or with some defined level of success, act on those principles, but that they be judged *principles which could coherently be adopted by all*. Often action on principles that can be coherently *adopted* by all cannot at a given time be acted on by all, or even by many. Sometimes action on principles that can be coherently adopted by all cannot at a given moment be acted on by any, or at least not overtly.[31]

This account of the demands of practical reason may seem feeble and pointless. Yet it has clear practical implications: there are many banal examples of principles of action that cannot meet its demands, hence clear examples of principles of action which there is good reason to reject. These practical implications will be discussed in later chapters; but the point can readily be illustrated by considering a principle of injuring severely. Nobody can coherently think of a principle of injuring severely as adoptable by all (in any domain): if it were so adopted, some would succeed in acting on it, hence others would become their victims, so unable to act on it.[32] There is no possible world in which adoption of a principle of severe injury by all could be achieved; there is nothing agents could do that would count as or contribute to bringing about such a world.[33]

2.4 CONSTRUCTING REASON AND CONSTRUCTING ETHICS

The metaphor of *construction* may seem appropriate enough for an account of the way in which ethical principles might be built on the

---

[31] If this seems implausible, consider the following mildly fictional case: after September 1939 all Poles were committed to ending the German occupation, yet for most of them no overt expression of this principle turned out to be possible for years to come.

[32] For discussion of applications of a critical conception of practical reasoning to identify specific ethical principles see chapters 6 and 7.

[33] The starkness of the contrast between rule utilitarianism and universalizability is evident here. To the standard question 'What if everyone did that?' asked, say, of promise breaking, the rule utilitarian replies 'The effects would be bad, and so they should not' and the Kantian notes 'Not everybody can'. Cf. chapter 6, note 23.

basis of a certain conception of practical reason. It is harder to see whether or why it is appropriate to speak of *the construction of practical reason*. Yet the metaphor has a long history: in developing the first critical account of practical (and theoretical) reason, Kant used an extended set of building metaphors.[34]

The most significant texts can be found in the *Doctrine of Method* of *The Critique of Pure Reason*, where Kant likens his unfinished task of establishing a critical account of reason to the problem of needing a building, having materials and builders to hand, yet lacking any sort of plan for putting the materials together to form a building. The solution evidently was to find a 'plan'. However, the 'plan of reason' cannot be derived from any more fundamental plan: 'reason' is just the name we give to whatever may be most authoritative for orienting thought and action. If no metaphysical system or empirical discovery provides foundations for reasoning, reason will be no more than the term we use for the necessary conditions for any coordination, however minimal, by those among whom the reasoning is to count. A 'plan of reason' articulates the necessary conditions of action on which all relevant parties can converge. Faced with this coordination problem, the most fundamental principle of practical reasoning will be to reject principles and strategies that are not followable by all. If a proposal or principle is not thought followable by all others in the relevant domain, it will not be thought a possible way of coordinating with them. On this minimal, constructive account of reason, all that there is to reason is this 'negative authority' or 'negative discipline': we fail to reason as soon as we make moves which we hold that others for whom we expect reasons to be cogent cannot follow; we must expect such moves to seem bafflingly arbitrary to those others.

Kant used numerous metaphors of construction to articulate both the problem and his solution to it. The predicament is depicted as follows:

---

[34] For more detailed discussions of some sources and the significance of a constructive view of practical reason in the Kantian texts see Onora O'Neill, 'Reason and Politics in the Kantian Enterprise' and 'The Public Use of Reason' in *Constructions of Reason*, part I; 'Enlightenment as Autonomy: Kant's Vindication of Reason' in Peter Hulme and Ludmilla Jordanova, eds., *The Enlightenment and its Shadows* (London, Routledge, 1990), pp. 184–99; 'Vindicating Reason' in Paul Guyer, ed., *The Cambridge Companion to Kant* (Cambridge University Press, 1992), pp. 280–308; as well as 'Four Models of Practical Reason' in *Bounds of Justice*.

If we look upon the sum of all knowledge of pure speculative reason as a building for which we have the idea within ourselves, it can be said that in the *Transcendental Doctrine of Elements* we have made an estimate of the materials, and have determined for what sort, height and strength of building they will suffice. Indeed, it turned out that although we had in mind a tower that would reach the heavens, yet the stock of materials was only enough for a dwelling house – just roomy enough for our tasks on the plain of experience and just high enough for us to look across the plain. The bold undertaking had come to nothing for lack of materials, quite apart from the babel of tongues that unavoidably set workers against one another about the plan.[35]

Kant's answer to this predicament is that with the failure of traditional metaphysical ambitions – no 'towers that can reach the heavens' – the demands of practical reasoning can be no more than a matter of *coordination* in using *available* materials. A convincing conception of practical reasoning although highly abstract, still must start from the gritty realities of human life: it cannot provide reasons for anyone to adopt principles which they cannot adopt.

Here the importance of abstraction is evident. If reasoning must be followable by agents whose categories, beliefs and norms are rather narrow and specific, and yet is to reach beyond the restricted domains in which these terms are current, then it must be abstract. Some abstract reasoning will be followable throughout wide domains; some will only work within restricted groups. Since practical reasoning has many audiences, some more restricted and others more inclusive, it may and indeed must on different occasions rely on more abstract and on more specific views of the characteristics of those audiences.

Kant calls reasoning which aims only at restricted audiences a *private use of reason*. This is a highly unusual use of the term. His examples are of action that is premised on a certain social structure or role, such as the commands of military officers, the exhortations of preachers and the injunctions of tax collectors.[36] Other stretches of practical reasoning are inclusive, and these are what Kant terms

---

[35] *Critique of Pure Reason* (1781), A707/B735 (Prussian Academy pagination). The standard English translation is by Norman Kemp Smith (London, Macmillan, 1929). However, this passage is my own translation.

[36] Some well-known passages that are highly relevant are to be found in Kant's 1784 essay 'What is Enlightenment?'; others in the less well-known 1786 essay 'What is Orientation in Thinking?'. Translations of both essays can be found in H. Reiss, ed., *Kant: Political Writings*, 2nd edition (Cambridge University Press, 1991), and see note 34.

public uses of reason; they address not some restricted group but 'the world at large'.[37] This unusual distinction between private and public uses of reason is in fact a distinction between reasoning premised on the assumptions of a restricted group, which will have restricted currency and authority, and reasoning which is not based on restricted assumptions, and is in principle followable by all in a more inclusive domain, so can have more inclusive currency and authority.

A constructive account of practical reasoning itself is only a first step, and does not show which specific 'buildings' could or should be built once this basic 'plan' of reason is adopted. A constructive account of ethics could be built using this basic 'plan' in conjunction with a sober and accurate, indeed critical, view of the builders within the relevant domain(s) and of the materials and skills believed to be available to them. The construction of ethical principles could start from abstract but adequately accurate accounts of the 'agents of construction' or 'builders', whose capacities and capabilities determine and whose vulnerabilities correspondingly limit what they can build out of the 'materials' of which they dispose. The empirical premises that are genuinely available may legitimately include many that abstract from mundane realities, but cannot legitimately include premises that idealize these realities.

The methods of 'coordination' used in constructing an account of principles we have reason to adopt must be similarly disciplined. Practical reasoning that seeks to give an account of the ethical constraints, the lives and forms of life – the 'buildings' – that can be made out of available materials must start from sober consideration of the real possibilities for those who are to build and to live with what they have built. They must meet the condition of being followable by those for whom the reasoning is to be relevant. These

---

[37] Kant's illustration of inclusive reasoning is in some ways unfortunate in that he instances the publication of a learned work – which inevitably assumes an all too restricted audience, 'What is Enlightenment', p. 57. In another way publication is an apt illustration, since authors know too little about those whom they 'address' to settle for too specific assumptions about those who are to follow what they write (if they do they may pay varied costs). I have used the terms *inclusive* and *restricted* rather than *public* and *private* to mark distinctions in intended *scope*, and derivatively in the presumed authority of stretches of reasoning, partly in order to make it plainer that the issue is in the first instance one of scope and the assumptions appropriate to principles of differing scope, but mainly to avoid the oddity of a usage that led Kant to classify action in public office as private.

starting points set a task rather than provide a solution. Even taken together, abstract starting points and a critical account of practical reason may look too slender to resolve the task. They amount to no more than the injunction to use only available materials and procedures thought to be followable by others. Yet abstraction and a constructive account of practical reasoning, taken together, may provide a lot. I shall argue that (fortunately) they do not provide enough to regiment what can be built: an amazing variety of lives and forms of life can be built within these constraints; but also that (equally fortunately) they require action to meet certain identifiable standards. Would-be builders who observe the constraints of reason will find that these *partly* shape the 'buildings' they can produce, while those who try to ignore them will find that some others think some of their proposals for action baffling, arbitrary and unfollowable. When the constraints of reason are ignored, coordination and communication fail: only the Tower of Babel can be built.

Constructivism in ethics, it should now be clear, is not a novel philosophical method or procedure. To construct is only to reason with all possible solidity from *available* beginnings, using *available* and *followable* methods to reach *attainable* and *sustainable* conclusions for relevant audiences. The reason for singling out the metaphor of construction, and for emphasizing the matter-of-fact demands that those who construct and their constructions must meet, is that many approaches to questions about justice and about virtue have been too vague or too sanguine both about the materials available and about the standards of practical reasoning. Those universalists who try to orient practical reasoning by assuming idealized conceptions of persons, reason and action, or transcendent moral ideals or real moral properties, do not test their arguments sufficiently against the limitations of the human condition and the constraints of human knowledge. Particularists, who so often claim to take more sober account of the realities of human life, frequently fail to do so. Even when they do not introduce their own idealizations, they may support a meagre, even parochial vision of the real range of possibilities and capacities for societies or lives, whose aspirations they fix and blinker by current norms, commitments and sensibilities and of whose capacities and need to reason with differing others they take inadequate account.

Constructivism is in the end no more, but also no less, than an attempt to work towards a result that is neither unattainable for those whose lives are both led using the categories and norms of a restricted milieu and connected to those of others with differing categories and norms, nor unsustainable for what they could become. It may be thought of rather prosaically as starting from available materials (rather than from some ideal inventory of unavailable materials), assuming only an abstract account of others' capacities, capabilities and vulnerabilities that is appropriate to the restricted or inclusive scope of the reasoning in hand, taking account of the degree of coordination possible between 'builders', and working towards 'buildings' which all in the relevant domains can help 'build' and can 'inhabit'.

Sceptics will probably not worry that any such constructive procedure will prove too constraining. They are more likely to suspect that it will turn out to be the emptiest of formalisms.[38] I believe that it will not: the case is yet to be made. In the chapters that lie ahead, the case for an integrated account of justice and of virtue which does not rest on unvindicated assumptions will be built up in consecutive stages. The stages and tasks of construction that lie immediately ahead are as follows.

Chapter 3 will consider the *locus* of ethical concern. It will argue that action, hence principles of action, rather than either the sources or the results of action, must be the primary focus of practical reasoning, including any ethical and political reasoning, and including reasoning about virtue. However, this focus on principles leads neither to the prescriptive uniformity that some friends of the virtues dread, nor to the radical indeterminacy that others of them suspect.

Chapter 4 will consider the *scope of ethical consideration*. In considering *scope*, I shall argue, we cannot fruitfully pose the classical questions 'Who or what counts as moral agent or subject?' or 'What are the criteria of personhood?', which lead only to

---

[38] The charge of empty formalism has been repeatedly made against positions which purport to justify universal principles. It has been repeatedly levelled against Kant, notwithstanding the equally frequent claims that he is guilty, on the contrary, of rigid prescriptivism. Both charges have also been repeatedly made against contemporary 'Kantian' ethics. The accusation of formalism can be found in the work of Hegel and of Heine, of Nietzsche and of Mill, and now flourishes in utilitarian and communitarian writing. For some chapters and verses see *Constructions of Reason*, part II. For contrasts between Kant and contemporary 'Kantian' work, see 'Kant's Ethics and Kantian Ethics' in O'Neill, *Bounds of Justice*.

inconclusive debates that demand and do not get satisfactory answers. In their place I shall pose the practical question 'Whom or what do particular agents have grounds to include within the scope of their practical reasoning and of their ethical consideration?', and propose in answer that they cannot reasonably exclude from the domain of reason or of ethical consideration others with whom or on whom they take themselves to interact or act. For this reason the scope of ethical consideration, as of reasoning itself, may vary.

The last three chapters will turn from these preliminaries to the construction of justice and virtue. Chapter 5 will elaborate the *structure* of ethical claims to which practical reasoning may lead. It will draw on the constructivist conception of practical reason outlined in this chapter to argue that the first concern of practical reasoning must be to identify ethical *requirements*, which are best analysed as requirements for action rather than for recipience. It follows that *obligations* or *duties* are ethically more basic than *rights*. Moreover, taking obligation as the basic ethical category provides the framework *both* for a full account of rights *and* for a closely linked understanding of certain important *virtues*.

Chapters 6 and 7 will offer some account of the *content* of obligations which human beings, however diverse, who fall within one's another's domain of ethical consideration, would have to acknowledge as legitimate constraints on their action. Some of these obligations constitute the demands of justice, others the demands of certain important social virtues. Although the obligations of justice and of virtue constrain both action and policies, they neither regiment lives nor preempt either the vast range of unrequired or optional excellences of which human beings are capable or the countless activities and projects of no particular ethical significance which they may pursue.

CHAPTER 3

Focus: action,
intelligibility and principles

The four ranges of conceptions of practical reason discussed in chapter 2 grasp action in very different ways. Teleological conceptions of practical reason grasp it by way of the *ends or states of affairs* of which acts and the sources of action are means or components; act-oriented conceptions by way of the *descriptions or principles* which it is to embody. There has been a lot of dispute about the adequacy of these ways of focusing on action. In general, universalists and historicizing particularists have thought that a focus on act descriptions is appropriate, although they have disagreed about the sorts of descriptions that are appropriate. But more radical particularists have thought that a focus on principles must lead to ethical and to more general catastrophes; some of them assert simply that there are no moral principles.[1] These issues must be settled before moving on to the construction of an account of ethics.

Action could be guided (to some extent) by fixing the *ends* it is to achieve, the *source* from which it is to emerge, or the *form* it is to take. Different accounts of ethics focus on these different ways of guiding action. Some accounts focus on ethical demands which guide action indirectly by focusing on the *ends* or *results* which action is to produce; others do so yet more indirectly by focusing on *dispositions* or *traits of character*, from which action and attitudes, and ultimately further ends and results, are to flow. However, most accounts of ethics focus more directly on the *form* action is to take, so aim to guide action more directly by fixing the *types of action, attitude and sensitivity* which are to be prescribed and proscribed, recommended or warned against.

---

[1] Cf. the first sentence in Jonathan Dancy, 'Ethical Particularism and Morally Relevant Properties', *Mind*, 92 (1983), 530–47: 'This paper is about the non-existence of moral principles'.

Universalists have taken all three paths. Contemporary consequentialists seek to guide action by reference to its contribution to certain results. Both Plato and Aristotle may be read as viewing traits of character as the source which is to guide both action and sensitivity that is to lead towards the Good. Contemporary 'deontological' writers on justice and right hope to establish which form or type of action, policy and institutional structure are required, without assuming any prior focus either on the ends or on the sources of action.

Contemporary particularists generally focus on the source or form of action as the way in which ethical concern can be made practical. Some hold that action and attitudes are to be guided by focusing on states of character, and specifically on virtues, which they see as *sources* of action. Others have focused on the very specific *types* of action whose embodiment in equally specific social practices can make ethics practical. These differences in initial focus have large implications.

Those who focus immediately on action, rather than on its sources or results, need to explain *how* action is to be grasped and guided. Almost without exception[2] they think of action as specified by *descriptions, which can form the content of principles* that enjoin or abjure action, whether by prescribing or proscribing, recommending or rejecting action that falls under those descriptions. Practical reasoning is articulated in practical principles, and practical principles are thought of as holding universally for some domain of agents (whether more restricted or more inclusive) rather than as bearing only on a particular case or situation.

However, universalists and particularists disagree about the *sorts of descriptions* that can properly be contained in action-guiding principles. Particularists object strongly to the abstract character of act descriptions which universalists identify as the proper content of universal principles. They insist that we do not and cannot grasp, guide or judge action by using abstract descriptions, or principles which incorporate them. Action must rather be grasped and

---

[2] An exception is provided by those who rely on physicalist accounts of act individuation, who individuate action by purely physical descriptions which are unlikely to form the content of any practical principles on which agents act. Some physicalists are not interested in ethics; but see section 4.1 and Hillel Steiner, 'Individual Liberty', *Proceedings of the Aristotelian Society*, New Series 75 (1974–5), 33–50 and *An Essay on Rights* (Oxford, Blackwell, 1994).

interpreted in terms of '*thick*', culturally and socially specific descriptions,[3] which render it intelligible and accessible to the particular, restricted audiences who are familiar with those descriptions, but equally may make it unintelligible and inaccessible to those familiar only with different thick descriptions. This conviction that the intelligibility of action depends on grasping it under 'thick', locally significant categories makes many particularists suspicious not only of abstract starting points and of universal principles of (more-or-less) cosmopolitan scope, but more generally of ethical writing which centres on justice and in particular on rights.[4]

These contentions are convincing in part. The friends of the virtues are right that any attempt to reason practically must be followable by those whose action it seeks to guide; and they are right that reasoning that uses unintelligible act descriptions will not be followable.[5] Moreover, they are right that intelligibility is always intelligibility for agents with a specific outlook and formation. But it does not follow that universalist writers on justice, who think that abstract act descriptions can be used in principles with more-or-less cosmopolitan scope, neglect intelligibility. Reasoning that abstracts from culturally specific, locally intelligible act descriptions can remain intelligible to those from whose daily 'thick' descriptions it abstracts. Particularists are simply wrong to think that intelligibility is inevitably threatened by abstraction. All act descriptions, whether thicker or thinner, are abstract to a degree, and the more abstract are not necessarily the less intelligible:[6] intelligibility and abstraction are in fact close and necessary

---

[3] See Charles Taylor, 'What is Human Agency?' in his *Human Agency and Language: Philosophical Papers*, vol. 1 (Cambridge University Press, 1985), pp. 15–44; Williams, *Ethics and the Limits of Philosophy*; MacIntyre, *After Virtue*.

[4] Most particularists – but not radical particularists – argue for thickly formulated principles of no more than local scope: as noted above, section 1.1, what bothers them is not that a principle might have universal *form* but that it might be 'too abstract' and might hold for an inclusive, diverse, indeed more-or-less cosmopolitan, domain.

[5] Intelligibility and followability have already been discussed in section 2.2, where their importance for any conception of theoretical or practical reason was noted.

[6] Some very abstract act descriptions are commonly thought of as particularly 'tough-minded' and hard to follow – e.g. those used by accountants. Yet they are *less* widely intelligible than the *more* abstract act descriptions of elementary algebra. On the other hand, some very *thick* act descriptions are intelligible to very few – e.g. those of particular crafts. There are no general reasons for thinking that thick act descriptions are more comprehensible than thin ones.

allies rather than antagonists. The illusion of antagonism has perhaps been produced by confusions between abstraction and idealization of the sorts discussed in section 2.1, or by a selective focus on certain distinctive sorts of abstract act descriptions.

Once the spurious antagonism between intelligibility and abstraction is set aside, it is evident that action and principles of action *might* be a primary focus of intelligible practical reasoning. However, this thought leads many particularist critics of principle-based ethics to a second range of criticisms, which focus less on abstraction than on universality, and specifically on the claim that ethical principles might or should have not only universal form but (more-or-less) cosmopolitan scope.

Although particularist supporters of virtue and community are convinced that a focus on abstract and universal principles of action has high costs, they disagree strongly about what the costs are. Some of them think that universal principles can guide action all too firmly, but disastrously: they will mandate rigid and insensitive regimentation of life. Other particularists think that action cannot be guided by universal principles which are nothing but empty formulae. Yet a focus on universal principles in fact leads to neither of the practical disasters that particularists fear. Properly understood, an ethics of action and of principles neither prescribes with regimented uniformity nor strands us with radical indeterminacy.

The latter points cannot be fully established by the argument of this chapter, which considers *only* the appropriate focus of ethical reasoning. However, this focus must be fixed before embarking on accounts of the domain, structure and content of ethically important principles. Questions about the proper domain of ethical consideration will be discussed in chapter 4; questions about the structure and substantive content of ethical principles in the following chapters.

3.1 FOCUSING ON RESULTS: INTELLIGIBILITY AND CONSEQUENCES

Some views of ethics challenge the need to focus on intelligibly described action. The best examples of such challenges can be found in certain forms of consequentialism. Consequentialists take *results* or *states of affairs*, rather than action, as the primary locus of value and focus of ethical concern, and derive the rightness and justice of acts and states of character from the goodness of the states of affairs that they (are expected to) produce. States of affairs may be identified in ways that are unintelligible to agents whom they affect or who bring them about, and claims about principles of action, or about the intelligibility of those principles, may be dispensable in some forms of consequentialist reasoning.

However, although action is not the basic category for consequentialist ethics, consequentialists who seek a plausible account of practical reasoning must nevertheless specify and discuss action in intelligible terms.[7] There are two reasons for this. First, capacities, capabilities and activities, described in intelligible ways, are themselves likely to be important components of some states of affairs that are to be judged good or bad. Secondly, and more decisively, consequentialist reasoning will be unable to guide action if it treats acts as mere instruments for achieving and avoiding states of affairs that need not be intelligible to those whose action, attitudes and sensitivities are to be guided. The 'options' for action that consequentialist procedures are supposed to rank can be picked out and identified by agents as pointing towards some rather than other consequences only insofar as they are intelligibly described. Only if agents can understand options as falling into certain patterns, as matching certain norms, as fitting familiar categories, can they confidently link them to specific results. Hence any practical, action-guiding use of consequentialist reasoning must be usable in a world of agents who employ and act under intelligible descriptions.[8] Whether consequentialist practical reasoning starts from desired results and searches for optimal means to achieve them, or starts from 'available' options and seeks to calculate and evaluate their results, it assumes a backdrop of intelligibly described action. Consequentialism *in practice* offers no method for evading the need for intelligible and followable act descriptions. It can be used to guide action only if options specified

---

[7] The classical difficulties of consequentialist reasoning alluded to in chapter 1 are bracketed to make the point; they should not be minimized. Many forms of consequentialist reasoning rely on breathtakingly idealized views of knowledge of causal regularities, of capacities to evaluate states of affairs and of the metric structure of those evaluations.

[8] For comments on the use of intelligible act descriptions, and often of norms, to make consequentialist reasoning *practical* see Onora O'Neill, *Faces of Hunger: An Essay on Poverty, Justice and Development* (London, George Allen and Unwin, 1986) and Jon Elster, *The Cement of Society* (London, Routledge, 1989).

in this or that way can be judged likely to lead to results of this or that sort, and this can be determined only when options are described in terms that are intelligible to agents (as purely physicalist or physiological descriptions might not be) and reliably linked to consequences under intelligible descriptions. Not every causal regularity is usefully action guiding. Practical reasoning that locates all value in results will be useless unless it ranks practices and acts as described in ways that are intelligible to those who are to follow and use the reasoning.

3.2 FOCUSING ON THE SOURCES OF ACTION: VIRTUE AND ACTION

If consequentialist reasoning must assume that acts are intelligible to agents, it seems unlikely that any other view of practical reasoning could avoid this demand. In any case, other contemporary writing on ethics, whether universalist or particularist, does not seek to avoid it. It views action as falling under and grasped by multiple and complexly interlinked descriptions, that are intelligible to those who act on them and to others, and that can be incorporated into practical principles that enjoin or prescribe or proscribe, recommend or reject intelligibly specified action.

Nevertheless some particularists insist that universalist writing on justice does not take the demands of intelligibility seriously enough, not only because it is unbothered by abstraction, but because it focuses too little on the sources and embodiments of action. Many particularists concentrate variously on the particular dispositions, states of character, sensitivities and commitments from which action flows, and the particular practices, communities and traditions in which it is embodied, preserved, articulated and developed, and from which further action flows. They favour 'agent-centred' or 'practice-centred' over 'act-centred' ethics; they insist that abstract principles may lack intelligibility and in any case will fail to capture the subtlety and complexity of a virtuous state of character or of good practices.

There are, of course, good reasons for looking behind action to its sources and embodiments. We need to fit acts into patterns that make sense of their interconnections; we need to understand the complex relations between what agents do and what they might have done; we have to take a view of phenomena such as weakness of will, remorse and regret, moral psychology and moral learning, and of the relation of right feeling to right action. We need to talk about the character of agents, the ethos of institutions and the traditions of communities. In thinking about these, and about many other complex matters of moral phenomenology, moral psychology, community and tradition, the categories of virtue and vice will be indispensable. However, the need to consider all these aspects of ethical life does not show that ethical concern must focus *primarily* on the characters and practices which are the sources and embodiments of action, rather than on action itself.

On the contrary, granted that any satisfactory ethical outlook must deal not only with action, but with virtue and vice, with practice and community; granted even that virtue and vice are the most significant ethical categories; still virtue and vice could not be discussed without presupposing that practical reasoning focuses *primarily* on action, and hence on descriptions of action, which may form the content of principles of action. (Perhaps if virtues and vices were simply 'original existences', it might be possible to treat them as unanalysable primary bearers of value. However, this conception of states of character is controversial and hard to defend.)

Virtues and vices are in fact usually construed by their proponents either as dispositions or as traits of character of individuals, or as the practices and traditions of communities.[9] On such accounts the category of action is neither dispensable, nor dependent. Dispositions are simply tendencies to do acts of this or that sort. If virtues and vices were merely dispositions, action, intelligibly described, must be the basic focus for thinking about virtue or vice. If virtues and vices are not dispositions, but traits of character, which are not invariably, but only more or less reliably, expressed in action, once again the category of action must be the basic focus for an account of virtue or vice. The advantage of viewing virtues and vices as character traits rather than as dispositions is only that this allows for the 'looseness of fit' between

---

[9] I shall not explore the distinctions that might be drawn between *disposition* and *character*. See, however, John Waide, 'Virtues and Principles', *Philosophy and Phenomenological Research*, 48 (1988), 455–72; Michael Slote 'Utilitarian Virtue' and Peter Railton, 'How Thinking about Character and Utilitarianism might Lead to Rethinking the Character of Utilitarianism' both in Peter A. French, Theodore E. Uehling and Howard K. Wettstein, eds., *Ethical Theory: Character and Virtue*, Midwest Studies in Philosophy, vol. xiii (University of Notre Dame Press, 1988), respectively pp. 384–97 and pp. 398–416.

action and the sources of action. It allows for the expression of virtue to be variable and even unreliable, and for an account of weakness of will. It allows for states of character to remain unexpressed despite appropriate circumstances, or to be expressed not in appropriate action but only in congruent feelings or sentiments, or perhaps only in regret or remorse. These variations would tell against ascription of a disposition, or rather in favour of ascribing a different disposition. However, whether virtues are thought of as dispositions or as traits of character, they are still individuated by reference to characteristic, intelligible patterns of action and sensitivity. The fact that virtue ethics takes the sources of action as the fundamental locus of ethical concern in no way exempts it from taking intelligibly described action as the basic focus of ethical reasoning: traits of character are intelligible and distinguishable only if their characteristic expression in action and attitudes is intelligible.

Despite skirmishes in which particularists suggest that practical reasoning must be basically concerned with the sources of action, their deepest worry is not about act-centred ethics, but about act-centred ethics which advances abstract, universal principles. They worry that reliance on the sorts of act-descriptions that are abstract enough to form the content of universal principles with inclusive, more-or-less-cosmopolitan scope will lead to ethical catastrophe. Like certain utilitarians, current proponents of virtue ethics and of communitarian political thought are moved mainly by the thought that appeals to abstract rules and principles, the mainstay of act-centred ethics, amount to superstitious 'rule worship' and point to ethical bankruptcy.[10]

3.3 UNIVERSALITY, UNIFORMITY AND DIFFERENCES

The most serious ethical charge which contemporary particularists make against universalists is not, in the end, that abstract and universal principles are unintelligible, but that living by them is ethically disastrous. Either universal principles will prescribe or

---

[10] For the utilitarian version of the complaint see J. J. C. Smart in J. J. C. Smart and B. Williams, *Utilitarianism: For and Against* (Cambridge University Press, 1973). For other versions see Winch, *Ethics and Action*; MacIntyre, *After Virtue*; McDowell, 'Virtue and Reason'.

recommend with rigid insensitivity to difference and diversity, so demanding inflexible and uniform treatment, or they will prescribe or recommend nothing at all. Many particularists, including communitarians, virtue ethicists and some 'radical' feminist writers, concur with these charges.[11]

The allegation that action guided by universal principles must overlook or regiment human differences is traditionally labelled *ethical rigourism*. It is surely to be taken seriously: if it is true, those who live by universal principles cannot take account of others' specific characteristics or circumstances, in short of their particularity, so will not respect others' distinctive needs or senses of identity. Yet those who criticize universalist thinking for these supposed flaws seldom explain *how* or *why* universal principles must lead to these objectionable results.

The most elementary sense in which a principle may be said to be universal is (cf. section 1.1) if it applies to or holds for all rather than merely for some cases in its domain. In this sense a universal principle of action prescribes or proscribes, recommends or rejects some type of act or policy for all, rather than for some but not all, of a certain range of beings. The second sense in which a principle may be said to be universal is that the range of beings is seen as extensive: the scope of the principles is inclusive, perhaps (more-or-less) cosmopolitan (again cf section 1.1 as well as section 4).

These rather meagre features are not, however, the ones to which particularist critics of universal principles most object. Their polemic against universal principles is targeted on an assumption, and a fear, that universal principles are *ipso facto* principles that prescribe or proscribe, recommend or reject *uniform* treatment for all the cases for which they hold. In this they target a third and quite separate conception of universalism in ethics: they suggest that universal form and cosmopolitan scope must lead to uniform prescription. There are at least three strong reasons for rejecting this presumed equivalence.

---

[11] For communitarian views see some of the references in chapter 1, notes 5 and 7. Feminist views often draw on the work of Carol Gilligan, who contrasts the 'male' ethics of justice, which appeals to universal principles and is blind to significant differences between people, with the 'female' ethics of care, which is expressed not in universal principles but in virtues such as care, love, patience and responsibility for and sensitivity to self and others. See Gilligan *In a Different Voice*. See also Sara Ruddick, *Maternal Thinking: Towards a Politics of Peace* (Boston, Mass., Beacon Press, 1987); Kittay and Meyers, *Women and Moral Theory*.

In the first place, uniformity is a matter of the content of a principle and not of its form or scope. Some principles of universal form, whatever their scope, prescribe or recommend differentiated, i.e. non-uniform treatment. For example, principles such as 'Each should be taxed in proportion to ability to pay', or 'Good teachers should set work that is adjusted to each child's level of ability' respectively prescribe and recommend universally, but both will *require* varied rather than uniform implementation in a world of varying cases. Universality evidently does not entail uniformity.

Second, even when universal principles specifically prescribe some degree or aspect of uniformity of action or treatment, they underdetermine action, so must *permit* varied implementation. A principle such as 'Everyone should be punctual' prescribes a policy for time-keeping, but leaves everything else undetermined. This is true even for quite narrow and specific principles: practical principles, unlike some rules of some formal systems, are necessarily indeterminate, so are never true algorithms. Even those that might be thought of as quasi-algorithms, such as practical principles that prescribe 'shadowing' certain true algorithms, will leave much open. There is a familiar algorithm by which the player who opens a game of noughts-and-crosses can win; yet one who follows the algorithm may play the game fast or slowly, in good or ill spirit, on paper or in the sand.

Third, universal principles of action hold universally only relative to some domain of agents (which domains are relevant will be discussed in chapter 4). Principles such as 'Cast your vote on election day', recommendations such as 'An apple a day keeps the doctor away' are indeed universal in form, but they prescribe or recommend universally only for a certain domain. In the first example the domain is presumably the adults living within a restricted politically defined territory; in the second it is less clearly defined, yet evidently limited in scope (nobody imagines that it is useful where there are no apples). Universal principles require nothing of agents beyond their domain.

These three considerations show that uniformity of requirement cannot be inferred from the universality of principles: universal principles can *at most* prescribe or proscribe, recommend or reject that some *aspect* (perhaps a trivial aspect) of action be uniform for beings falling within a given scope.

These conclusions could have been reached by other less formal routes. For example, recent debates among advocates of differing conceptions of justice show that those who *agree* in proposing universal principles of justice *disagree* over the extent to which these prescribe significant uniformities. This is particularly evident in debates about equality, for equalities are uniformities of particular sorts. It is a substantive, difficult and controversial question whether and in which respects universal principles of justice would demand equalities of various sorts for various domains. There are, after all, countless possible equalities which vary in value and achievability. Achieving some is a matter of deep significance (e.g. equal respect), achieving others is a matter of sheer indifference (e.g. equal ignorance about long-past events), while others are at all costs to be avoided (e.g. equal amounts of surgical intervention), not achievable (e.g. equal weight) or even in principle incoherent (e.g. equal enjoyment of positional goods). 'Equality' is always an incomplete predicate, and arguments about it are pointless and fruitless without clarity about the completion of the predicate under discussion.[12] Fantasizing that universal principles automatically require, prohibit, recommend or reject uniform treatment is no way to establish which, if any, uniformities or equalities are ethically required, permissible, or forbidden, important or unimportant.

Once the requirements of universality and uniformity are distinguished, it becomes clear how absurd it would be to object against an account of practical reasoning that proposes universal principles that it prescribes rigid uniformity or demands neglect of differences. On the contrary, virtually any account of practical reasoning will have to endorse universal principles, and such endorsement need not entail a commitment to uniform treatment and need not deny differences. Hierarchical conceptions of justice, for example, may differentiate social roles, but their fundamental principles (e.g. 'Each to his or her station in life') will still apply to all whom they assign to those differentiated positions. In the *Republic* Plato never rescinds the initial account of justice as living by the universal principle of giving each his due, but rather argues

---

[12] See Amartya Sen 'Equality of What?' in S. McMurrin, ed., *Tanner Lectures on Human Values*, vol. I (Cambridge University Press, 1980); G. A. Cohen, 'Equality of What? On Welfare, Goods and Capabilities' in Nussbaum and Sen, eds., *Quality of Life*, pp. 9–29, followed by a reply by Amartya Sen, 'Capability and Well-Being', pp. 30–53.

that the proper interpretation of that principle shows that what is due to different sorts of human beings differs. The real disagreements between universalists and particularists are over the *extent of the domains* across which certain principles should hold, over the *content of ethical principles* and over the *degree to which* they prescribe uniform or differentiated action within their domains. These disagreements will be addressed in later chapters.

Once formal universality is seen as the meagre matter that it is, it seems unlikely that *any* account of justice, or many of virtue, could wholly avoid invoking *formally* universal principles. Even if appeals to the singular commands of some authority (the judgements of Solomon, the *fatwah* of an Ayatollah, the Nazi *Führerprinzip*) can be read as lacking implications for anything other than the particular cases for which they were issued, the *context* within which these authorities command is structured by a background of discourse, custom and law, in which universal principles play their part. While there may be many sound and important objections to be made against specific universal principles, or specific interpretations of universal principles, it seems highly unlikely that it is a serious weakness in theories of justice, or more generally of universalist ethics, or even of the more restricted principles of particularist ethics, that they prescribe uniformity.

If these are plausible thoughts, universal principles do not point to the nightmare vision of ethical principles (of justice or of other sorts) that are inevitably and relentlessly blind to human differences and mandate rigid uniformity, as so many friends of the virtues claim to fear. Principles indeed abstract from differences: but it does not follow that they must assume idealized accounts of human agents that not merely bracket but deny human particularities and differences. Universal principles indeed apply across a plurality of differing cases, but need not prescribe or proscribe, recommend or reject rigid uniformity of action or entitlement.

3.4 EMPTY FORMALISM, RULE-FOLLOWING AND RADICAL PARTICULARISM

However, one further group of formal objections to any ethic of universal rules or principles is sometimes thought to cut far deeper, although in the converse direction. These objections claim that uni-

versal principles, far from demanding uniform action for differing
cases, are empty formulae which cannot guide action.

One way of reaching this worry is to view it simply as a corollary
of abstraction: if universal principles must be abstract, they must
underdetermine action so cannot guide it. This worry misconceives
what principles must be like to guide action. The fact that
principles underdetermine action means only that they do not
provide those who adopt them with an auto-pilot for life, and
not that they do not structure and constrain it. Judgement is always
needed in using or following – and in flouting – rules or principles;
but principles are none the less important. (Cf. section 6.7 on
judgement.)

Some radical particularists offer further reasons for thinking
that principles are empty formulae that cannot guide action. One
of their principal inspirations lies in Wittgenstein's considerations
on rule-following. They take it that the view of rules of action
required by *any* act-centred practical reasoning has been undercut
by Wittgenstein's claims that rules cannot supply objective
standards that determine us to go on in one way rather than
another. The notion of 'doing the same thing' is not fixed by rules
or principles: hence universal principles, rather than demanding
uniformity, determine nothing at all.

Wittgenstein's considerations are multiple and deep.[13] His
ostensible target is not rule-governed action itself, but certain
'Platonist' conceptions of rule-governed action. According to those
conceptions, which Wittgenstein suspects are deeply tempting,
rules are binding, external algorithms, which bear on us 'mech-
anically'. To follow a rule is really to be ruled by a rule. On the face
of it, this critique of rule-following will undercut ethical thinking
that appeals to rules or principles only if the suspect ('Platonist')
conception of rules or principles is unavoidable or avoidable only at
unacceptable cost. Of course, some writers *may* have advocated the
'Platonist' view; but examples are remarkably elusive outside
the writings of critics of rule-following.

To many people the thought that Wittgenstein's considerations

---

[13] The discussion is pervasive in many of Wittgenstein's works, but see particularly
Philosophical Investigations, ed. G. E. M. Anscombe and R. Rhees (Oxford, Blackwell, 1953),
sections 185–241 and *Remarks on the Foundations of Mathematics*, trans. G. E. M. Anscombe, ed.
G. H. von Wright, R. Rhees and G. E. M. Anscombe (Oxford, Blackwell, 1965); *Lectures on
the Foundations of Mathematics*, ed. Cora Diamond (Sussex, Harvester, 1967).

on rule-following are important for ethics have seemed simply implausible. Even if, like Simon Blackburn, they were 'aware of the colonial ambitions of the rule-following considerations', they 'thought that the territory of ethics was safe from annexation'.[14] John McDowell, however, has argued that would-be ethics of rules or principles *must* fail, because they must draw on the contested conception of rule-following, so are led into incoherence.[15] Ethics is rather, he argues, centred on virtue. He portrays virtues as 'reliable sensitivities'[16] or 'perceptual capacities', which preempt all possible appeal to ethical principles:

If one attempted to reduce one's conception of what virtue requires to a set of rules, then, however subtle and thoughtful one was in drawing up the code, cases would inevitably turn up in which a mechanical application of the rules would strike one as wrong – and not necessarily because one had changed one's mind; rather one's mind on the matter was not susceptible of capture in any universal formula.[17]

His claim is not just that ethical principles, including principles of justice, as it happens, do not prescribe uniformity or are not algorithms. It is that ethical sensitivity *cannot* in principle be captured by rules: it is uncodifiable. It is a prejudice that 'acting in the light of a specific conception of rationality must be explicable in terms of being guided by a formulable universal principle'.[18] Rule-following, even following algorithms of arithmetic, provides no criterion of 'right' continuation: all rules are incomplete, and to 'follow' them is to interpret them in a certain way. No rule can have written into it a determination of what it would be to follow it. Rules do not lay down complete answers.

Kant – that great proponent of universal principles – made a remarkably similar point in the schematism section of the *Critique of Pure Reason*, where he wrote:

---

[14] Simon Blackburn, 'Rule Following and Moral Realism' in Steven Holtzmann and Christopher Leach, eds., *Wittgenstein: To Follow a Rule* (London, Routledge and Kegan Paul, 1981), pp. 163–87; p. 170.

[15] John McDowell, 'Virtue and Reason'.

[16] Ibid., pp. 332–3. What makes them *reliable* is a bit obscure: it cannot be that they perform in the *same* way from case to case, or with the *same* effects.

[17] Ibid., p 336; cf. 'Non-Cognitivism and Rule Following', pp. 145–6.

[18] John McDowell 'Virtue and Reason', p. 337; cf. 'Non-Cognitivism and Rule Following': 'The idea that the rules of a practice mark out rails traceable independently of the reaction of the participants is suspect', p. 146.

If understanding in general is to be viewed as the faculty of rules, judgement will be the faculty of subsuming under rules; that is, of distinguishing whether something does or does not stand under a given rule. General logic contains, and can contain, no rules for judgement . . . if it sought to give general instructions how we are to subsume under these rules, that is, distinguish whether something does or does not come under them, that could only be by means of another rule. This in turn, for the very reason that it is a rule, again demands guidance from judgement. And thus it appears that, though understanding is capable of being instructed, and of being equipped with rules, judgement is a peculiar talent which can be practiced only, and cannot be taught.[19]

As specific examples of the way in which the interpretation of rules is open, Kant instances certain uses of practical rules: 'a physician, a judge or a ruler may have at his command many excellent pathological, legal or political rules . . . and yet may easily stumble in their application'.[20] Like Wittgenstein, he holds that practical rules or principles are never enough to determine action. The puzzle is to see why the Kantian and Wittgensteinian views are so close in their insistence on the incapacity of rules or principles to provide complete guidance and so far apart in their estimate of their practical and ethical significance. How can Kant speak of 'many excellent rules', if he has just pointed out a great deficiency in all rules? Why did he not conclude that rule-following is impossible? Where do McDowell and those who share his view part company with Kant, when he insists that rule-following considerations undermine much that Kant, and contemporary universalist writers (who often think of themselves as Kantians), think central to ethics?

The first assumption that seems to differentiate McDowell's formulations of Wittgensteinian considerations on rule-following from Kant's view of rule-following is that he takes it that advocates of rules think that they are to bear on action as external causal mechanisms. Clearly, if one thinks of rules in this way, using the images Wittgenstein deploys to delineate the suspect conception of rules, and sees them as 'rails' or 'machinery', then it will be a nasty flaw if they are not algorithmic. If the rules are to rule us, then they had better not be indeterminate. However, it is hard to see *any* temptation in the thought that practical rules have to rule us in this

[19] Kant, *Critique of Pure Reason*, A132–3/B171–2.   [20] Ibid., A134/B173.

way. Rules, after all, are abstract entities; they do not act or cause; they are at most guide-lines for those who act or cause. Writers who hold that practical rules and universal principles are ethically indispensable do not mean that these abstract principles control agents, but that agents may follow or flout, revise or reject them.

Why do some Wittgensteinians sense real temptation in the suspect conception of rules as 'rails' or 'mechanisms' that determine action 'from outside'? Who actually thinks of rules of action as working through a 'psychological mechanism' that 'churns out the appropriate behaviour with the sort of reliability which a physical mechanism might have'?[21] Evidence is scant. Perhaps a certain way of viewing some psychological and pathological studies of cases in which human creations are projected onto supposed external realities (others, the world, God) provides a morsel of evidence. Such mistaken projections are sometimes found in the early stages of childhood: Piaget found that very young children sometimes (mis)interpret ethical rules as having independent force.[22] Literature on guilt and responsibility also sometimes depicts agents who impute responsibility to and displace feelings onto what they conceive of as outside forces: and, if no flesh and blood scapegoat is to hand, then onto mere abstractions such as rules and principles. When we cannot blame the serpent, we can still blame the system. People may seek illusory shelter from responsibility behind 'the regulations' or 'my duty'. This psychological trait may be either naive or corrupt: naive in Piaget's young informants, corrupt in cases such as Ibsen's character Mrs Solness or in Adolf Eichmann.[23] However, evidence that rules or principles can be hypostatized and then miscited as exculpating causes of action undercuts their proper use as elements in the practical reasoning agents undertake, in the communication they achieve, and in the action and policies they live by or reject. The practical view of rules and principles as something which we adopt and follow, or argue about and reject, is part and parcel of our lives and practices. What is indeed aberrant

---

21 McDowell, 'Virtue and Reason', p. 337; cf. 'Non-Cognitivism and Rule Following', p. 147.
22 Jean Piaget, *The Moral Judgement of the Child* (London, Routledge and Kegan Paul, 1932; Glencoe, Ill., Free Press, 1950).
23 See Peter Winch's discussion of Ibsen's misguidedly 'dutiful' character, Mrs Solness, in 'The Universalizability of Moral Judgements' in *Ethics and Action*, pp. 151–70; Hannah Arendt, *Eichmann in Jerusalem: A Study in the Banality of Evil* (London, Faber and Faber, 1963).

is the fantasy that rules and principles take on independent life and then use or control us.

This illusory conception of rules is one, central target of Wittgensteinian criticisms of rule-following. Wittgenstein insists, for example, that rules do not act at a distance, indeed do not act at all,[24] and that there is no logical machinery.[25] He destroys the fantasy of rules that not merely determine, i.e. specify (in some respects, under some interpretation) what is to be done, but determine, i.e. bring about, what is done. One aspect of rule-following considerations is insistence that rules are not efficient causes that preempt agency and responsibility. This prophylactic thought is convincing and clarifying, but irrelevant as criticism of act-centred ethics, which has never (so far as I can see) relied on this aberrant view of rules.

Kant, for example, takes it that the rules that are relevant to ethics or to justice are practical principles which may be referred to, adopted, modified or rejected by free agents. Kant's particular views about the ethically important rules or principles are often challenged or rejected in contemporary universalist writing, as well as by those who oppose 'Kantian' positions. But there too rules and principles are viewed as guidelines and not as efficient causes. To follow rules is to use them, not to be overcome by them.

Hence much (but not all) of McDowell's case can and would be accepted by any universalist. Universalists generally agree that any use of rules must be linked with other considerations. They think that even when we rely on quasi-algorithmic rules and principles much is left open (adding can be fast or slow, done when I am sitting still or climbing the stairs, directed at my sheep or my bank-balance). They insist that observing intricate and demanding formal rules can leave much scope for skill and strategy (chess), indeed for style and spontaneity (speech). They take it that the principles we find most plausible in ethics and politics leave even more open. In all these cases universalists think that much, *but not everything*, depends on how the rules are interpreted and enacted. Hence much also needs to be said about the moves that go into

---

[24] Wittgenstein, *Remarks on the Foundations of Mathematics*; cf. 'The rule does not do work, for whatever happens according to the rule is an interpretation of the rule', p. 249.

[25] Wittgenstein, *Lectures on the Foundations of Mathematics*; cf. 'I am speaking against the idea of "logical machinery". I want to say that there is no such thing', p. 194.

following and interpreting rules.[26] If rules are always indeterminate and incomplete, much will depend on the strategies of judgement by which agents move from principles to action.

However, the most radical aspect of McDowell's Wittgensteinian critique of rule-following in ethics is neither the well-known and uncontested point that rules underdetermine action, let alone the irrelevant polemic against the conception that rules are mechanisms. Rather it is a third, more radical thought, that underdetermination is nondetermination: what seems like rule-following is no such thing; rules yield not incomplete guidance but no guidance. Wittgenstein's famous counting examples – why should the counter, who has gone as far as 1,000 counting conventionally by 2s, not now proceed 1,004, 1,008?[27] – suggests that the notion of the 'right way to go on' is empty. Nothing objective lays down right interpretations of concepts, right projections of predicates, right implementations of rules. Even if we do not suffer from projective fantasies, so do not imagine that the rules are using us, the image of rule-following obscures the truth that our (measure of) agreement about how to go on in any process or activity is not derived from rules but based on quite other sources. It is a myth that there is something 'objectively there which transcends the "mere" sharing of forms of life'.[28] All that is there as background is the fact that we agree to some extent on the projection of predicates and the interpretation of rules. McDowell, and other writers on 'rule-following considerations', quote Cavell's stirring formulation of this 'vertiginous' formulation of radical particularism:

We learn and teach words in certain contexts, and then we are expected, and expect others, to be able to project them into further contexts. Nothing insures that this projection will take place (in particular, not the grasping of universals nor the grasping of books of rules), just as nothing insures that we will make, and understand, the same projections. That on the whole we do is a matter of our sharing routes of interest and feeling, modes of response, senses of humour and of significance and of fulfilment, of what is outrageous, of what is similar to what else, what a rebuke, what forgiveness, of when an utterance is an assertion, when an appeal, when

---

[26] Of which a small amount will be said in section 6.7. See also Barbara Herman, *The Practice of Moral Judgement* (Cambridge, Mass., Harvard University Press, 1993).

[27] Wittgenstein, *Philosophical Investigations*, para. 185.

[28] McDowell, 'Virtue and Reason', p. 339.

an explanation – all the whirl of organism Wittgenstein calls 'forms of life'. Human speech and activity, sanity and community, rest upon nothing more, but nothing less, than this. It is a vision as simple as it is difficult . . . [29]

McDowell's deeper claims go beyond the claim that rules are not complete codifications, that they are inevitably indeterminate. He also insists that there must be in each case some context or material which the supposed rule-follower takes in a certain way. There must be, so to speak, a matrix or manifold: some version or analogue of Cavell's 'whirl of organism'. When we take ourselves to follow rules and principles we assume a background of life and experience, of response and of reaction, which forms a precondition for theory and practice, for judgement and communication. A spontaneous and initially inarticulable ability to orient some responses, to project some predicates, to see some likenesses forms the shared background of life.

This spontaneous responsiveness may be indispensable; but it is not the whole story. The evident truths that rules cannot tell us what to do and that they are indeterminate do not show that we do not use rules. On the contrary, rule-following is a commonplace activity, and (far from being a myth) is integral to most forms of social life and activity. No doubt, if the presuppositions of rule-following did not obtain, no rules would be followed. But these presuppositions are widely met, and rule-following flourishes. Of course, when we follow rules there is not something there in the world which we follow (it is not like following a road); rather we shape our responses and actions in certain ways.

These rather humdrum points perhaps vanish in McDowell's analysis because he is arguing specifically against the 'Platonist' conception of rules. His target is the view that rules, if there were any, would have to be objectively 'there in the world', a matter for *discovery*, rather than something that we bring to our organization of the world, a register, as it were, of our agreements and disagreements about what to do. *Rules and principles enter our lives not because they dominate us, but because we dominate them.* They are the way in which we organize the many sorts of coordination and agreement on which Cavell comments, the record of significant agreements

---

[29] Stanley Cavell, *Must We Mean What We Say?* (Cambridge University Press, 1976), p. 52.

and sharings, demarcations and differentiations. Rules are made, not given; once they are made they may be learned and discerned, followed or flouted, rejected or revised. It is because they are ubiquitous in our lives that it is important to consider whether there are any quite general reasons for retaining or rejecting certain rules.

The central part rules have in our lives does not challenge the points on which Kant and Wittgenstein agree. Rules can be indispensable and yet indeterminate; they can be indeterminate and yet action-guiding. Agents can use rules to shape action, because rules do not function as mechanisms and in spite of the fact that they provide no algorithms for action. In using rules we shape our lives, we make judgements – often nuanced judgements – both about the situations we face and about the lines of action we will pursue.[30] In short, the rule-following considerations provide no grounds for thinking that rules or principles, provided they are not conceived of in the misleading Platonic way, are impossible, or dispensable, or corrupting, or even dispensable in articulating the nuanced agreement, discussion and complex articulation of action to which those who are sceptical about rules point. Rules are not the enemy but the matrix of judgement.

Despite the significance of Wittgenstein's rule-following considerations, many Wittgensteinian writers on ethics[31] have (rather oddly) not worried that rules were wholly non-determining, hence empty and useless, indeed mythical. Rather they have worried that rules might demand relentless uniformity, that they might determine everything. Like McDowell, Wittgensteinian writers often insist that rules cannot adequately codify moral knowledge; unlike McDowell they fear that this makes rules dictators rather than a myth. Although many Wittgensteinian writers are particularists, few are radical particularists: most of them criticize universal principles, for example of justice, for mandating uniformity rather

---

30 For a discussion of differences between Kantian and Wittgensteinian articulations of the relation between rules and judgement see David Bell 'The Art of Judging', *Mind*, 96 (1987), 221–44. For very different comments on Kant on judgement see Otfried Höffe, 'Universalist Ethics and the Faculty of Judgement: An Aristotelian Look at Kant', *Philosophical Forum*, 25 (1993), 55–71. See also section 6.7 below.
31 Consider Winch, *Ethics and Action*; D. Z. Phillips and H. O. Mounce, *Moral Practices* (London, Routledge and Kegan Paul, 1970); Diamond, *The Realistic Spirit*; R. Beardsmore, *Moral Reasoning* (London, Routledge and Kegan Paul, 1969); Rodger Behler, *Moral Life* (London, Methuen, 1983).

than for lacking all power to determine action.[32] Their particularism is displayed in the seriousness with which they consider cases, in their insistence that examples are the pivot of ethical judgement, in the thought that careful eliciting of 'what we do want to say' about cases is the goal of ethical discussion. But this is a less-than-radical particularism: it conceives of ethical discussion as presupposing a shared grid of categories, of thick descriptions, which are themselves 'not a matter for discussion', but rather the unchallengeable framework of ethical judgement which we share. Most contemporary particularist writers with Aristotelian leanings also take a non-radical view. They indeed see ethical judgement as a matter of perception of the particular case, but most of them think that judgement of that case rests not on mere, sheer perception but on perception that is formed by 'our' shared categories and practices, hence implicitly by certain culturally specific rules with restricted scope.[33]

Particularists, wherever they draw their inspiration, have difficulty in dealing with ethical disagreement. For McDowell and Cavell the sheer fact of agreement must be the basis of ethics. They stress the perception of particular cases rather than procedures for dealing with types of cases, and there is little they can say when disagreement appears. Yet ethical difference and disagreement are pervasive in contemporary life and the prospect of ignoring them or of dealing with them by mere convergence of perception is vanishingly slender (the analogy between sensory and ethical perception is strained). For reasons that any Wittgensteinian would recognize, we cannot just point and hope that the light will dawn for others; or even that we point to anything determinate. When we deal with disagreement we need to contrast and debate, to compare and infer; in doing so we formulate and we follow varied rules of varying scope. This pervasive rule-following is sometimes self-conscious and even institutionalized (e.g. in legal or administrative life), but often it is neither. Rules and principles may be embedded deep in individual characters or social traditions, whose practices and habits, virtues or vices they constitute. In such cases those who

---

[32] For further discussion and examples of Wittgensteinian worries about ethical principles see Onora O'Neill, 'The Power of Example' in *Constructions of Reason*, pp. 165–86.

[33] But contrast Wiggins 'Deliberation and Practical Reason', for a combination of Aristotelian leanings and radical particularism.

act may have little conscious awareness of rules, and perhaps no clear sense of the degree to which they leave matters open, or about their status or revisability. Even so their use of rules and principles to guide action will be readily apparent.

Radical particularism may fail in a further way. Even when there is no actual disagreement about the proper articulation of a case, practical disagreement about what to do may linger. Judgements about the nature of a case do not yield practical judgements about what is to be done. Even those who have come to agree on a nuanced articulation of a particular case may still be unsure what they should do. Much writing on ethics that is hostile to rules and principles elides this point. It construes judgement as if its task were to appreciate particular cases, and forgets that we often need to act and respond as well as to perceive and appreciate.[34] A focus on particular case, and nothing else, elides the importance of *productive judgement* as opposed to *appreciative judgement*. Appreciative judgement or appraisal sometimes seems enough because certain cases, once seen *under a supposedly agreed description*, appear so unambiguously desirable or deplorable that an illusion that nothing further need be said is created. Yet different examples would show that even the finest-grained agreement on the appropriate articulation and description of cases may leave us uncertain how to act. Anybody who doubts this may think of the cases of slavery or racism or sexism that seemed so obviously unproblematic in the recent past, or of cases of neglect of distant kin which seem so unproblematic to many of us, but would have troubled our pre-decessors. Contemporary examples too may be troubling for any view that rules are otiose, since here too full, nuanced, agreed descriptions may offer no ethical guidance. How do we view the case of a competent and uncomplaining, if unnecessarily burdened, mother? Even when we agree on all descriptions, we may disagree deeply about what is to be done by whom. Is this a case of rank injustice or of admirable fulfilment of role? Would it be wrong to condone what is going on or wrong to challenge it? Even the most nuanced and sensitive articulation of cases does not

---

[34] Some actually deny the primacy of the practical for ethics. Cf. Cora Diamond, 'The moral issue *what she should do* so interests us, . . . that we . . . do not see the relevance of . . . genius for *appreciation*', in 'Missing the Adventure: Reply to Martha Nussbaum', in her *The Realistic Spirit*, pp. 309–18, p. 316.

determine what it would be right or just, good or virtuous to do about them. It is only because so many practical principles are embedded in characters and institutions, so have become received views, that it can sometimes *seem* that fixing on a description is all that is required. But the moral life is a matter of action, not of connoisseurship.

This difficulty escapes particularists of various sorts partly because so many of them take a minimal view of capacities to communicate and resolve disagreement. If practical reasoning were little more than a matter of working out how 'we' would best describe certain matters, assuming a given grid of intelligible categories, it would require only that we make cases intelligible to 'ourselves'. If so it could show neither what we should do about cases which we do not find intelligible, nor how we might explicate or resolve disagreements between those whose categories differ, but whom we cannot regard as lying beyond the pale of ethical considerations, or as inaccessible to reasoning. It is striking how often Wittgensteinian writers on ethics, whether more or less radical, in an effort to cast doubt on reasoning that uses rules, are driven to interpret cases of apparent ethical disagreement as reflecting incommensurability, in the face of which reason is powerless.[35]

However, once we imagine in any concrete way what it might be to articulate disagreement, even in a fairly homogeneous social world, or to resolve it, we realize that to do so needs more than the intelligible articulation of cases in terms of some received set of categories. For to appraise is not in the end just to converge on agreed descriptions of cases: it is also to affirm that cases that fall under agreed descriptions are to be dealt with in this or that way. In reaching ethical judgements we affirm not just the perceptions or appraisal of the moment, or of an in-group, but principles that may be or could be woven into and judged worth weaving into activities, lives and institutions. Principles and rules, to be sure, do not provide everything. They neither make us act, nor pick out fully determinate acts. However, without them we would drift through the flotsam of available descriptions and perceptions, unable to orient ourselves on a course of action or life, to navigate among

---

[35] Again see O'Neill, 'The Power of Example' in *Constructions of Reason* for examples and further references to this pattern in Wittgensteinian ethical writing.

existing possibilities or institutions, to chart our way to new ones, or to reason with those with whom we are not already in agreement.

Against a background of shared responsiveness, we not only can but must use principles of inquiry and of practical reasoning, as well as varieties of ethical and political principles, to chart a course. The voyages that principles and rules enable us to take are not to be thought of as forced deportation: they are more like voyages of exploration, in which we may find reason to redraw the charts with which we embarked. A fundamental use of principles and rules is to revise the very conceptions and boundaries of intelligibility and the formulations of rules on which we initially rely. However, there is no reason to think that such revision must be wholly unreasoned, or that ethical and political differences must reduce us to an inarticulate 'Don't you see!'.

3.5 SOME CONCLUSIONS

In this chapter I have argued for a series of linked claims. First, action is the primary focus of all practical reasoning, including practical reasoning which treats either the sources or the results of action as the primary matter of ethical concern. Second, action must be grasped under descriptions that are intelligible to those who reason about it. Third, the need for intelligible description of action does not mean that practical reasoning must or can avoid abstraction, or that it cannot use principles. Fourth, universal principles, which abstract from many predicates, need not prescribe uniform action, even within their domain; they may prescribe differentiated action, and they must underdetermine action. Fifth, while the degree of underdetermination of action by principles is open, there is no reason to think that the underdetermination is radical in the sense which Wittgenstein's discussion of rule-following is sometimes thought to suggest.

Taken together, these arguments are intended mainly to defuse anxieties about principles, and specifically about principles of universal form or inclusive scope. However, they do not show which practical principles, or which sorts of practical principles, are ethically important, and they do not show for which domains universal principles of various sorts might hold. Some culturally specific practical principles, which many particularists find acceptable, are thought of as holding universally but only for quite particular and limited domains; others, which universalists maintain, such as the abstract principles of the Human Rights Movement and of contemporary work on justice, are presented as having the widest cosmopolitan scope. As we can see, universal principles are barely avoidable, and lead neither to dangerous rigourism nor to vacuous formalism. However this conclusion not merely does not fix everything: it fixes remarkably little.

Ethical thinking can move beyond the groundless rejection of abstraction and universality that has preoccupied so much writing on virtue and community not by rejecting principles, but by establishing and defending specific claims about action-guiding principles. I shall aim to do this in the following chapters by constructing an account of the *scope*, the *structure* and the *content* of ethical principles.

CHAPTER 4

Scope: agents and
subjects: who counts?

Universal practical principles neither impose wooden uniformity
nor reduce to empty formalism. They are a vehicle and focus for
much practical reasoning and for ethical and political life and
discourse of many sorts. Nevertheless universalist practical
reasoning will be of no use in thinking about justice or virtue unless
there are also acceptable ways of fixing the *scope*, the *structure* and
the *content* of ethically important principles. The first of these is
surprisingly difficult.

Establishing the proper scope of practical principles is no trivial
preliminary. On the contrary, tendentious ways of denying others'
ethical standing or *status*, whether as agents or as subjects, may
restrict the scope of ethical principles and may be used to support
ways of life that effectively marginalize and oppress others by
excluding them from the scope of others' ethical consideration. At
various times status as agent or as subject (or both) has been denied
or diminished for 'barbarians', for foreigner and foe, for heathen
and heretic, for serfs and slaves, for those of other race or culture,
for women, children and 'dependents', for animals and artificial
persons. There may now be more agreement than there once used
to be that all human beings are at least subjects of justice; but
justification even of this limited agreement is insecure. Contemporary discussions in ethics and political philosophy remain full of
smouldering and inconclusive wrangles about who should count as
agent or as subject (alternatively: as (moral) person, as bearer of
rights), hence about the proper scope of ethical consideration.

On one view, whose traces are common in universalist writing
even when its full commitments are repudiated, scope is to be fixed
by providing definitive analyses of the concepts of agent or subject,
which might perhaps be best achieved within some form of
perfectionist ethics backed by an appropriate metaphysics. Ethical

standing is to be established by showing that beings with certain essential characteristics – a self, a soul, reason, sentience, consciousness and various versions of personhood are favourite candidates – are agents and subjects, or at least subjects, and that beings who lack these characteristics are not. Universalists who reject metaphysical foundations find it difficult to sustain these lines of argument, but tempting to purloin their conclusions. Some particularists also lean discreetly on similar views, whose underpinning they too would find hard to provide. Other particularists try more forthrightly to identify who counts as agent and subject by appeal to the particularities of lives: those particular others who are part of *our* world or community, to whom *we* are related or attached, are agents and subjects *for us*; others are not. Yet another range of approaches to questions of standing seeks to resolve them by appeal to *recognition* by others. But it seems unlikely, despite the phenomenologically convincing and sociologically well-explored links between recognition by others and effective agency,[1] that these approaches will escape the pull or the difficulties of other approaches. If *appropriate recognition* by others is the issue, the problem of fixing the scope of ethics is named rather than resolved: its resolution will still hinge on showing which characteristics call for recognition, so may still call for independent backing, for example for a metaphysics of the person, or for a perfectionist account of the Good for Man. If *actual recognition* by others is to define the scope of ethics, we return to some variety of particularism, by which certain actual exclusions from and inclusions within the domain of ethical consideration are tendentiously endorsed.[2]

This cornucopia of proposals for establishing who or what has ethical standing, so fixing the proper scope of ethical consideration, is unsatisfying. None of the more popular proposals clearly avoids both the need for metaphysical backing and the limitations of particularist starting points. A constructive approach to questions

---

[1] The line of intellectual descent for this approach runs from Rousseau and Hegel, and is well represented in twentieth century philosophy and sociology, both in communitarian writing and in critical theory, as well as in kindred sociological work. See the references in chapter 1, note 21.

[2] Discussion of recognition has the apparent convenience that it addresses the scope and the content of ethical principles together: we settle scope in settling who is or should be recognized and content in settling what it would take to recognize them. However, since both questions are complex it may be prudent to address them separately, and to use the vocabulary of recognition sparingly.

of standing and scope would have distinctive advantages if it could resolve them without either relying (openly or covertly) on strenuous metaphysical claims, or blandly and groundlessly endorsing the actual views of scope and ethical standing of a particular time and place.

These two cul-de-sacs can, I shall suggest, be avoided by treating problems of standing and scope not as theoretical but as practical, that is as *questions that arise for and must be addressed by particular agents who need to determine to which other beings they must accord the standing either of agent or of subject (or both)*. A practical approach to standing and scope need not look for a wholly general, theoretical criterion by which to distinguish agents from non-agents, or subjects from mere things. It would be sufficient if it could offer usable and convincing procedures for answering the practical question 'Whom (or what) must we (or I) acknowledge as agent and as subject in taking this action (alternatively: adopting this attitude, supporting this policy or relying on this practice)?'. In doing so it would also provide a procedure by which the scope of practical reasoning for that agent in a given context can be fixed.

In answering questions of this type the first move is to establish the *scope of ethical consideration* which agents have reason to accept in a given situation. Even if this can be fixed, the *scope of various ethical principles* may remain unclear: principles of action may be differentiated to deal with differing cases, and may be formulated in more and less specific versions. Some *restricted principles* will have a scope that is quite legitimately narrower than the full scope of an agent's ethical consideration; other *inclusive principles* might cover all beings within the range of that consideration. Even when the proper scope of ethical consideration is established, it will be a further matter to show whether any principles must have inclusive scope (see section 6.1 and the introductory pages of chapter 7).

4.1 ETHICAL STANDING: UNIVERSALISTS AND PARTICULARISTS

Universalists have discussed questions of scope in varied terms: the issue is often formulated as one of establishing the criteria that will define who is a (moral) person, agent or subject, who has ethical standing or who merits ethical consideration. Although few contributors to these debates now defend explicit forms of perfectionism, or provide the backing such a position might require, remnants of undefended perfectionism are often evident in the background. Even in universalist writing which explicitly disowns perfectionism – such as much (but not all) contemporary work on justice – the traces of latent and unargued perfectionism are often particularly prominent in the treatment of standing and scope, for example, in discussions of 'criteria of personhood' or of 'moral standing' or of 'moral considerability'.

Clear examples of this can also be found far beyond theories of justice, for example in writing on bioethics, and especially in medical ethics, where there are compelling reasons for clarifying who or what counts as an *agent* or *subject*.[3] Discussions of the criteria for agency in this literature often centre on issues of patient autonomy and medical paternalism, and debate the standing of those with certain incapacities to act. Discussions of the criteria for being a subject centre around harder cases (the brain dead, the foetus, the anencephalic) and debate the standing of those with minimal or missing capacities either to act or to experience. There is good reason for this dual focus: any account of ethical reasoning that excludes either range of issues or assimilates them to one another will be impoverished and fail to address certain questions.[4] Yet it is all too plain that universalist discussions of ethical standing in bioethics and beyond during the last twenty-five years have lead mainly to interminable and inconclusive controversy. The protagonists hunt endlessly for some definitive, essential charac- teristic that will distinguish who is an agent, so might be entitled (for example) to autonomy and self-determination, and who is, whether or not an agent, still at least a 'moral patient' or 'subject' and entitled to care or at least to 'moral consideration'. The answers given range widely, even wildly. There are still many who take possession of an immortal soul as the key criterion of ethical

---

[3] In certain other ways medical ethics is cavalier about *agency*. Many works assume without much discussion that the primary agents whom they address will be medical practitioners working in specific professional contexts, e.g. within a specific national health service, or within commercially organized medical practice, yet also suggests that their conclusions will have a wider validity – for example that they can establish claims about 'rights to health care', or 'patients' rights' that are to hold quite generally. Such culturally specific assumptions about who counts will carry over from assumptions to conclusions.

[4] An exclusive focus on subjects who are not agents is often compounded with an excessive attention to rights of recipience and neglect of other ethical categories (cf. chapter 5); an exclusive focus on agents with an excessive attention to questions of autonomy and liberty rights. Focus only on those who are both agents and subjects neglects some hard cases.

standing, and there are some tough-minded secular thinkers who substitute having a sense of oneself as a continuing subject of mental states for having a soul.[5] Others start by taking the standing of 'normal' human beings as a base line and then aim to determine the standing of adjacent cases.[6] Others follow Bentham in championing sentience as the criterion of ethical standing, so expanding the bounds of ethical standing through parts of the animal kingdom; yet others try to extend it to include plants and other natural systems.[7] There seems little prospect of resolving these debates about 'ethical standing' within the terms in which they are usually conducted. Without a more explicit vindication of some background perfectionism, or more generally of the necessary metaphysics, it may quite simply be impossible to establish necessary and sufficient conditions for qualifying as an agent (or person), or as a subject (or holder of rights). Yet most contemporary universalists are uninclined to argue for this type of background position. Nor do they provide any other framework within which such issues could be resolved; often there is more agreement on 'intuitions' about supposedly hard cases than on justifications of proposed criteria of ethical standing.

The long-running public and philosophical debates on abortion illustrate these impasses vividly. Most parties to these debates have aimed to identify essential criteria, of the sort with which explicit perfectionists would hope to make good their claims about ethical standing, and in particular criteria that would fix the ethical status of the foetus (at some or all stages of gestation) once and for all; once this is fixed they have only to conclude who (or what) has or lacks a right to life.[8] This may be why theologians and religious

---

[5] Michael Tooley, 'Abortion and Infanticide', *Philosophy and Public Affairs*, 2 (1972), 37–63; Michael Tooley, *Abortion and Infanticide* (Oxford University Press, 1983); Peter Carruthers, *The Animals Issue: Moral Theory in Practice* (Cambridge University Press, 1992).

[6] See Vinit Haksar, *Equality, Liberty and Perfectionism* (Oxford, Clarendon Press, 1979).

[7] Utilitarians are generally keen to follow Bentham on sentience. Cf. works such as Peter Singer, *Animal Liberation: Towards an End to Man's Inhumanity to Animals* (London, Jonathan Cape, 1976) and *Practical Ethics* (Cambridge University Press, 1979); Peter Singer and Helga Kuhse, *Should the Baby Live?* (Oxford University Press, 1985); James Rachels, *The End of Life* (Oxford University Press, 1986).

[8] Of course, this is more controversial than appears on the surface. What a right to life comprises is fixed by others' obligations. Are these only obligations not to kill? Or perhaps only obligations not to kill those who are not a threat? Or do they also include obligations to rescue from present danger? Obligations to provide the means of life? Cf. chapters 6 and 7.

believers, who often accept a perfectionist view of man and matching metaphysical claims, seem comfortable with the terrain on which the debate is conducted, if manifestly distressed by their opponents' views. It may also be why those who do not avowedly accept, let alone establish, any perfectionist or kindred position make so little headway in convincing those who do. The result is an endless conflict of assertions about the ethical standing of the foetus. Some of the most thorough discussions of ethical standing suggest that an adequate solution may have to draw at least on a minimal perfectionism.[9] Without perfectionism, attempts to find the essential demarcating characteristic that confers ethical standing often look suspiciously like a hunt for some property or other which will more-or-less track, even if it cannot justify, antecedently accepted intuitions about who (or what) should count as (moral) subject in which contexts.

Yet particularist strategies for fixing who or what has ethical standing are no more convincing. Claims to discern who has ethical standing by inspecting the actual scope of 'our' particular community or nation or relationships are often decently clad in the vocabulary of commitment, care, and attachment,[10] but neglect the hard cases for these approaches. These arise where none of these wholesome bonds is to be found: those who fix the scope of ethical consideration by reference to the limits of 'our' community or 'our' attachments and relationships must seemingly exclude from ethical consideration those for whom 'we' care not a whit or whom 'we' see as outside 'our' community, as well as those to whom we are bound by hatred or rivalry rather than by friendlier ties. Communitarians and virtue ethicists often complain that certain other positions (for example, contemporary work on justice) give no account of personal bonds, or of the special ethical claims created by shared patriotism and community, relationships and attachments. Yet if the scope of ethical consideration were fixed by any of

---

[9] Vinit Haksar argues for a minimal perfectionism as the way to settle questions of scope in *Equality, Liberty and Perfectionism*.

[10] Here again Wittgensteinian, communitarian and 'radical' feminist writers provide examples; see chapter 1 notes 5, 12, 13. See also the *Symposium on Duties Beyond Borders, Ethics*, 98 (1988). For less political particularist views of the scope of (some sorts of) ethical consideration see Bernard Williams's discussions of ethical attachment and commitment in *Moral Luck* and in *Ethics and the Limits of Philosophy* as well as Lawrence Blum, *Friendship, Altruism and Morality*.

these, foreigners and other 'outsiders', not to mention the unloved and the unattached, must seemingly be excluded from the scope of ethical consideration, and so denied ethical standing. An emphasis on actual relationships may be an understandable corrective or supplement to positions that treat impartiality or justice as the whole of ethics, but no appeal to wholesome particularities alone can provide a convincing account of ethical standing, since it must exclude those to whom we have either unwholesome attachments or commitments, or none at all.

Yet some of the efforts, and of the disappointments, of universalist and particularist approaches to standing and scope are unnecessary. Both may fail to vindicate their views of the proper scope of ethical consideration because they try to show more than is needed. For what is needed may *in practice* be much less than a comprehensive and definitive criterion of ethical standing. Rather agents need a justifiable procedure for fixing standing, which they can use in acting, in taking up attitudes, and in supporting policies and practices. An account of ethical standing that is adequate for practical purposes can, I shall argue, be obtained without invoking either unvindicated assumptions about the basis of ethical standing or contingent particularities: a less ambitious view of what has to be established about ethical standing provides enough for practical purposes.

4.2 CONSTRUCTING THE SCOPE OF ETHICAL CONCERN

A practical way of fixing the scope of ethical consideration need not supply a complete account of who or what counts as agent, or as subject. It must, however, provide at least a procedure by which agents can work out to whom (or what) they must accord ethical standing, so view as falling within the scope of their ethical consideration. An adequate practical procedure might then leave gaps, and might lead to different answers in different practical contexts. From the point of view of some conceivable, comprehensive, 'perspectiveless' theory of ethical standing, this would seem defective, but the defects need not raise practical problems. A practical procedure is, after all, designed to answer the practical question 'To whom must we (or: I) accord ethical standing in taking this action?'. Provided the notional gaps which it leaves in an account of the scope of ethical consideration are not of practical importance for the agent, and provided it does not yield incompatible answers for a single course of action, this might be enough. For example, it would not matter *for practical purposes* whether we do or do not count our Neanderthal ancestors as agents and subjects, or that children alive today count as subjects for us, but not for the agents of the year 2500 AD.

Various discussions of ways in which agents might orient ethical deliberation have accepted that for practical purposes less-than-comprehensive answers to certain questions may be enough. A classical, but restricted, example of such an approach is the appeal to 'circumstances of justice' in constructing an account of justice that is practically adequate, although theoretically incomplete. Hume uses a celebrated and succinct formulation of the *circumstances of justice* to construct an account of the content of justice: ''tis only from the confined generosity of men, along with the scanty provision nature has made for his wants that justice derives its origins'.[11] Rawls uses a more elaborate version of the same idea in *A Theory of Justice*, where he distinguishes in more detail between objective and subjective circumstances of justice. Among the objective circumstances of justice he includes the cohabitation of many mutually vulnerable beings under conditions of moderate scarcity. Under subjective circumstances of justice he includes a 'thin' account of human beings, that allegedly does not draw on any 'metaphysics of the person', but simply notes that agents have limited altruism, limited cognitive powers and differ fundamentally in their basic political and philosophical convictions.[12] Both Hume and Rawls view the 'circumstances of justice' as materials out of which *a theory of justice for certain social conditions* may be built; more specifically they use them as premises for an account of the content rather than the scope of justice in certain conditions.[13]

---

[11] David Hume, *A Treatise of Human Nature* (1739), ed. L. A. Selby Bigge, revised edn (Oxford, Clarendon Press, 1958), p. 495.

[12] Rawls, *A Theory of Justice*, pp. 126–30.

[13] Rawls fixes the scope of justice in other ways. In *A Theory of Justice* he provisionally restricts the scope of justice to that of a society 'conceived for the time being as a closed system isolated from other societies' p. 8. This assumption has given rise to numerous criticisms and some revisions. For some criticisms see Charles Beitz, *Political Theory and International Relations* (Princeton University Press, 1979); Thomas Pogge, *Realizing Rawls* (Ithaca, NY, Cornell University Press, 1989); for some revisions see John Rawls, 'The Law of Peoples' in Stephen Shute and Susan Hurley, eds., *On Human rights: The Oxford Amnesty Lectures* (New York, Basic Books, 1993).

Inevitably, their approaches say nothing about justice in circumstances of perfect abundance or complete altruism. In their view this omission is not practically important. Limited altruism in conditions of scarcity, combined with divergent views or feelings on fundamental issues, provide significant and sufficient materials for determining a useful account of justice because these conditions are enough (under the assumption that desires or preferences determine action) to guarantee conflict, so to preclude an antecedent harmony or guaranteed coordination between agents. The circumstances of justice are in the first place, so to speak, the circumstances of injustice: they are circumstances which generate the problems for whose resolution justice is needed. It is practically unimportant if an account of justice doesn't cover situations for which it isn't needed.

Although many details of the approach Hume and Rawls take may be questionable, their line of thought is suggestive and can be put to other purposes. Their underlying idea is that for practical purposes it is not necessary to have a comprehensive theory of justice. Equally, agents do not need a comprehensive account of ethical standing that covers all possible cases; but they do need procedures that can be deployed in circumstances they actually face.

If the elusive definitive analyses of personhood, agency, subjecthood and the like remain unavailable, it won't help to demand that agents base their views of the scope of ethical consideration on an objective account of ethical standing: this is precisely what they lack. They will need to construct rather than to presuppose an account of ethical standing, and the material they will have to hand to do this includes numerous interlocking assumptions about others on which they base their *activities*. Activity, in the widest sense, may be taken to cover *individuable acts and responses, feelings and attitudes, support for policies*, and *participation in practices*. The presuppositions of activity commonly include rather specific assumptions about others who are taken to be agents and subjects, or both, and about connections to those others.

Although some of these assumptions may be false or tendentious, they have two features which make them appropriate material for constructing an account of the scope of ethical consideration. First, these assumptions are not arbitrary posits, but disciplined by the demands of acting and responding effectively in the world, and corrigible in the light of improved information or understanding. Second, the assumptions on which activities are based remain in place: they cannot be assumed for action or in taking up attitudes or in supporting policies and relying on practices, but then denied when ethical questions arise. In particular when agents *commit* themselves to the assumption that there are certain others, who are agents or subjects with these or those capacities, capabilities and vulnerabilities, they cannot coherently deny these assumptions in working out the scope of ethical consideration to which they are committed. Commitments to others' ethical standing are taken on as soon as activity is planned or begun: what is needed is a procedure for working out what these commitments are in a given context.

Still, if the presuppositions of activity, in the fullest sense of the term, are to provide the materials for a practical account of the scope of ethical consideration to which agents are committed we should ask what, if anything, guarantees that their presuppositions will be appropriate. May not some activity acknowledge as agents or subjects beings who are neither? Or – perhaps more likely – fail to acknowledge as such beings who are one or both? These questions look coherent enough. Yet if we lack a metaphysics of the person, or definitive accounts of agency or subjecthood, it is unclear by what standards they could be given definitive answers. Will not attempts to do so lead back into the sort of quagmire in which abortion debates have bogged down?

A constructive account of the proper scope of ethical consideration, which begins from the presuppositions of activity cannot entirely meet these concerns. Yet appeal to the starting points to which agents commit themselves can offer more than merely subjective conclusions. In particular, acknowledgement or denial of others on which activity is based is rarely *capricious*, although acknowledgement or denial of their standing in popular and in theoretical discussion can be *capricious* or *disingenuous* or both. The assumptions which activity *assumes* are both open to revision and subject to a range of cognitive and practical disciplines, so can aim both for reasonable coherence and for adequate accuracy.

4.3 ACKNOWLEDGING PLURALITY, CONNECTION AND FINITUDE

Three rather abstract and deeply interconnected aspects of the countless specific assumptions which structure all activity are particularly relevant for fixing the appropriate scope of ethical consideration. These are the assumptions *that there are others* (seen as *separate from* the agent); *that those others are nevertheless connected to the agent* (either or both can act on the other); and *that those others have limited but determinate powers*. For convenience I shall speak of assumptions of *plurality, connection* and *finitude*. Where assumptions under all three headings are made, there will be a basis for agents to determine which others they are committed to according ethical standing and consideration. Where activity is not predicated on any assumed conjunction of forms of plurality, connection and finitude, the scope of ethical standing and consideration will remain wholly undefined.[14]

Each element in this formulation needs comment and clarification. However, one point is relevant to all three types of presupposition. These are not presuppositions about states of consciousness. Each term refers to abstract aspects of the presuppositions of activity which *may or may not* be present to agents' consciousness. Activity may be premised on assumptions which agents deny, ignore, dispute or repress. This makes it easy for them to deny, doubt or diminish others' ethical standing, even when their activity evidently takes for granted that those others are agents and subjects. Conscious or effective recognition of others' standing, like conscious or effective recognition of the content of their legitimate claims, may demand complex personal, social and political struggles. Struggles for recognition, justice and consideration are often struggles about the scope as well as about the content of ethical consideration. An abstract account of the presuppositions of activity can be used to fix the appropriate scope of ethical consideration, but cannot

---

[14] The conception of connection, of being part of one and the same world, is quite different from Hannah Arendt's conception of the human condition as one in which agents *share a world*. On Arendt's much stronger notion, agents who share a world act in a single 'space of appearances', and vie for one another's recognition, so must be taken to share language, conventions and normative ties. Here agents are said to be connected if they assume that they can act on or be acted on by others, or both. For this they need only believe that there are others to whom they are linked by some causal pathway. There are disagreements about the extent to which Arendt relies on an expressive or on a communicative conception of speech, an agonal or a cooperative conception of activity, but there is no doubt that she begins her discussion with a rich – and controversial – view of what it takes to share a world. Hannah Arendt, *The Human Condition* (University of Chicago Press, 1958); Maurizio Passerin d'Entrèves, *Modernity, Justice and Community* (Milan, Franco Angeli Libri, 1990).

guarantee conscious recognition of that scope, or prevent its being diminished or curtailed or denied in practice.[15]

The basic type of presupposition of activity that can be used to fix the scope of ethical consideration by and for a given agent falls under the heading of *plurality*. Activity is premised on *plurality* whenever it assumes that there are others whom the activity may affect, or whose activity may affect the agent. The specific assumptions about others, about the ways in which they may be affected and about their capacities and capabilities for activity and reactivity, and correspondingly about their vulnerabilities to others, will, of course, vary greatly. Some activity assumes identifiable others who can (indeed are likely to) respond in complex, intelligent, immediate and focused ways; at the other end of the spectrum, some activity assumes only that unspecified others could be affected or react minimally to the remote results of that activity. Plurality is assumed whenever activity assumes sources of activity, however minimal, that are to some extent, however minimal, independent of an agent's own activity. Plurality is not assumed in activity that takes it that no others can be affected or respond, whether directly or indirectly. For example, action that is seen as unable to reach or affect others or elicit some response from them (radically isolated activity; trivial aspects of much activity) assumes no plurality of others and provides no context for ethical consideration. Ethical consideration would be out of place for anyone who thought no others existed, as it is out of place, for example, in considering countless trivial adjustments of posture which are assumed with adequate accuracy not to affect others.

Activity can be predicated on plurality without any assumption that others *will* act or react,[16] provided that it assumes others with

---

[15] In addition to literature on recognition, writing on the moral pathologies of extreme situations, such as death camps and prison camps, is revealing here. Evidently many who organized and ran these camps combined strong assumptions that those whom they tormented and killed were agents and subjects (otherwise the whole hideous apparatus of torture, humiliation and secrecy, let alone the mythology of the International Zionist Conspiracy, makes no sense) with surface avowals that the treatment was appropriate since inflicted on beings who lacked ethical standing – 'Untermenschen'. Elements of similar pathological incoherence may be more widespread: see Stanley Milgrim, *Obedience to Authority: An Experimental View* (London, Tavistock Publications, 1974).

[16] *A fortiori* it will not assume that others will react in hostile ways. The claim that some activity is predicated on a plurality of others is entirely neutral about the character of motivation, which might range from universal benevolence, to particularist attachments, to Hobbesian fear, to any mix of these and intermediate sorts of motivation.

capacities and capabilities so to do. A book that falls still-born from the press (as Hume's did not) will not be bought or read, but may yet have been published on the assumption that it *could* be purchased and read (perhaps *could* convince and be admired). A burglar who cases the joint assumes householders who *can* take precautions, even if in a particular case they have not done so, and doors are left invitingly open. A regime that tortures opponents assumes that they *could* suffer and *might* resist, even if in the event its victims give in as soon as threatened. An attitude of resentment assumes that others acted knowingly in ways that are hurtful and that they could have done otherwise, even if in the particular case the others in fact were unwitting or unable to do otherwise. Wherever activity is based on the assumption of others who *can* act and react, the standing of those others cannot coherently be denied, whether or not those others in the event actually act or react.

The claim that ethical consideration has a context *only* when plurality is assumed may seem too restrictive. Since Aristotle, plurality has been seen as an uncontroversial element in any account of the context or circumstances of justice, but it may seem that other sorts of ethical consideration would be in place even for solitary beings, hence even when activity assumes no plurality. Many views of ethics emphasize reflexive duties and virtues, such as self-respect, self-control or self-development. However, taking plurality as *one* element of the circumstances of activity which can be used to determine the scope of ethical consideration creates no problems even for the case of *radically solitary beings*, if such are conceivable. For radically solitary beings there are no others: their ethical consideration reaches no further than self-consideration. By contrast, *ordinarily solitary agents*, for example, hermits, castaways or recluses assume that there are others, whom (genuine) hermits and recluses shun and (typical) castaways seek to contact. Although a constructive procedure for fixing the scope of ethical consideration which starts from actual assumptions of plurality cannot cover the case of radically solitary beings, this is not a major (and perhaps not any sort of) practical deficiency, since by hypothesis their ethical consideration reduces to duties to self and virtues of the self.[17]

---

[17] Since agents have also to make working assumptions, indeed adequately accurate working assumptions, about their own capacities, capabilities and vulnerabilities, the materials for them to construct an account of reflexive duties and virtues will also be to hand.

Predicating activity on there being at least some others is, to be sure, a minimal, abstract assumption; but it is far from trivial. Among other things, it suggests that those who claim to act on the assumption that there are no (genuine) others will lack reason to accord anybody ethical standing so will not extend the scope of their ethical consideration to include any others. Like radically solitary agents, those who assume that there is no more than a plurality only of quasi-agents, who are not genuinely distinct sources of activity, will not be committed to according ethical standing or ethical consideration to others. For example, 'agents' who supposedly think of themselves and others as elements in one pseudo-plurality, whose parts are wholly coordinated, whether by preestablished harmony or by physical law, do not premise activity on plurality, and acknowledge no others who could have ethical standing or merit ethical consideration.[18] Plurality has seldom, if ever, been wholly and genuinely denied in practice, but various philosophical positions have treated harmony and the erosion of plurality not as the elimination but as the culmination of ethical perfection. Although it may be plausible to think that (some degree of) agreement and community are needed for ethical bonds, total abolition of plurality undercuts all but reflexive ethical consideration and practical reasoning by abolishing its locus; it preempts not only ethical conflict but almost all ethical consideration.[19] The limit case of community is totalitarian fusion of identities, the elimination rather than the perfection of ethical consideration of others.[20] If activity assumes no plurality, the

---

[18] Monads, the elements of physical systems, the hypothetical denizens of 'perfected' totalitarian societies do not then stand in ethical relations with one another. What passes for their activity is not premised on connection to any assumed plurality of agents.

[19] It follows that the context of ethics is missing wherever plurality is denied, as for example, Aristotle thought it tended to be in Plato's *Republic*: 'I am speaking of the supposition from which the argument of Socrates proceeds, that it is best for the whole state to be as unified as possible. Is it not obvious that a state may at length attain such a degree of unity as to be no longer a state? – since the nature of a state is to be a plurality, and in tending to greater unity, from being a state, it becomes a family and from being a family, an individual; for the family may be said to be more one than a state, and the individual than the family . . . we ought not to attain this greatest unity even if we could, for it would be the destruction of the state', Aristotle, *The Politics* 1261 a15–23, ed. Stephen Everson, trans. W. D. Ross, revised by J. L. Ackrill, J. O. Urmson and J. Barnes (Cambridge University Press, 1988).

[20] Cf. Vaclav Havel, 'The Power of the Powerless', trans. P. Wilson, in Jan Vladislav, ed., *Living in the Truth* (London, Faber and Faber, 1986) for a penetrating account of this tendency, and of its fortunate limitations.

domain not only of justice but of *all* ethical reasoning would be preempted.

Assumptions of plurality do not stand alone. Agents whose activity is based on assumptions of plurality will also assume that they are in various ways connected to others, in the sense that at least one party could act on, i.e. affect, the other, however indirectly.[21] *Assumptions of connection* are framed and form part of vast layered sets of assumptions about causal connections and patterns. All activity assumes a world that will change in certain ways but not others, that can be changed by certain interventions but not others. Assumptions about connections to others form part of these sets of interconnected assumptions. Where no *possible* causal connection to others is assumed, ethical consideration has no defined scope. For example, the inhabitants of Anglo-Saxon England and their T'ang Chinese contemporaries both no doubt saw themselves as connected to many others in this weak sense. Yet the two groups lived in unconnected worlds, ignorant of one another's very existence: their activity assumed no connection to those in the other group, whom they accorded no ethical standing, and did not include within the scope of their ethical consideration.

It would be absurd to wonder whether T'ang Chinese and their Anglo-Saxon contemporaries acted either well or justly toward one another. Members of each group could legitimately limit their ethical consideration to exclude their contemporaries of whom we now know, but who lived beyond their horizons. Their accounts of ethical consideration would not be practically defective because silent about relations with others, about whose existence, connectedness, capacities, capabilities and vulnerabilities they quite reasonably made no assumptions at all.[22] This notional gap

---

[21] Agents might *know* or *believe* that there were others to whom they took themselves to have no connection, such as the aliens of an inaccessible planet. But their *activity* will not be premised on this belief.

[22] This conception of connection is much weaker than the conception of shared attachments or traditions by which certain anti-cosmopolitan writers try to legitimate actual state or community boundaries as boundaries of ethical consideration. For example, Michael Walzer suggests that 'the idea of distributive justice presupposes a bounded community, within which distributions take place, a group of people committed to dividing, exchanging and sharing first of all among themselves', in 'The Distribution of Membership' in Peter Brown and Henry Shue, eds., *Boundaries* (Totowa, NJ, Rowman and Littlefield, 1981), p. 1 and cf. his *Spheres of Justice: A Defence of Pluralism and Equality*, pp. 30–1. See also *Symposium on Duties Beyond Borders*, *Ethics*, 98 (1988); C. Brown, ed., *Politicial Restructuring in Europe: Ethical Perspectives* (London, Routledge, 1994).

in their views on ethical standing was wholly without practical costs.

In assuming plurality and connection, agents also assume that the others to whom they are connected have specific, finite powers. Plurality itself perhaps entails *some* sorts of finitude: unlimited size or powers cannot coherently be ascribed to distinct embodied others.[23] However, in assuming connection agents will generally take far more specific views of the ways in which others can affect them and they others. Their actual assumptions about others' finitude – about their capacities, capabilities and vulnerabilities – cannot coherently, or honestly, be dropped or replaced with imputations of different characteristics, such as 'idealized' capacities and capabilities, or forms of invulnerability, when considering others' ethical standing: *What is assumed for purposes of activity must also be assumed in fixing the scope of ethical consideration.*

Of course, assumptions about others to whom agents are connected, and about those others' specific capacities, capabilities and vulnerabilities, on which their activities rely may be mistaken. Nothing guarantees that there will not be blindness and error, but in every case assumptions that inform activity are not likely to be capricious, and they are corrigible. In daily life agents seek to base activity on adequately accurate views about the world and its causal patterns, about their connections to others and about those others' capacities, capabilities and vulnerabilities, for the solid reason that inaccurate assumptions about any of these may lead to failure, to retaliation or to other harm or injury. For the same good, realistic reasons, agents will generally try to revise any presuppositions of their activity if inaccuracies under these headings come to light. By contrast, the positions agents proclaim in speech and in theory face far weaker reality tests. This is evident from the frequency with which the very assumptions of plurality, connection and finitude on which activity is based are surreptitiously, cynically or solemnly denied.[24]

---

[23] Not to mention disembodied others; the traditional paradoxes of rational theology raise questions which need not be addressed here.

[24] For a glaring example consider Nazi claims that those they persecuted were subhuman – although their apparatus of torture and humiliation assumed victims vulnerable as only human beings are vulnerable. See this chapter, note 15. Or consider the ease with which some writers argue that justice has boundaries although their activity makes it plain that they know and assume that actual borders (state borders, cultural borders, community

4.4 DENYING PLURALITY, CONNECTION AND FINITUDE

Those whose activity is quite evidently premised on specific assumptions about plurality, connection and finitude, often claim to make quite different assumptions under one or more heading, so in effect disowning what their activity takes for granted. In denying what their activities assume and acknowledge, they unjustifiably, but often advantageously, suggest that certain others do not have ethical standing and so fall outside the scope of their ethical consideration. They may deny that those others exist or are connected to them, or may misrepresent their capacities, capabilities and vulnerabilities, and hence the likely effects of their own activity on those others. Each sort of denial is an intellectually and ethically disreputable way of seeking to modify and manipulate the scope of ethical consideration; each can play a powerful part in strategies of selfishness, self-centredness, self-defence and even of self-deception. Each may mask what activity acknowledges, and substitute a distorted account of its presuppositions.

When acknowledged plurality is denied, others whose separateness is taken for granted in activity are depicted as so closely integrated (with the agent or with some other) that they lack distinct identities or interests, so cannot be objects of ethical consideration in their own right. This can be a powerful but spurious way of 'fixing' the scope of ethical consideration. Assertions that certain relationships are so intimate that they achieve a fusion of identities have often been used to justify claims that those at the 'dependent' end of such relationships lie beyond the scope (at least) of justice, in an 'exclusively private' sphere, or even that they lack all ethical standing.

Historically such strategies of exclusion have been used to assert the rights of fathers and husbands to act, speak and stand for children and wives and at times the rights of masters to speak for servants. Yet claims that plurality is overcome and that justice or other ethical concerns are superseded where dependence, or

borders) are porous and that those on the other side are distinct but connected others whom their activity will affect in determinate ways. See the contributions by David Miller and Robert Goodin to the *Symposium on Duties Beyond Borders*, *Ethics*, 98 (1988) and Thomas Pogge, 'Cosmopolitanism and Sovereignty' in Brown, ed., *Political Restructuring in Europe*, pp. 89–122. Or consider the ease with which large categories of persons have been excluded from certain sorts of ethical consideration, e.g. Pateman, *The Sexual Contract*.

privacy, or kinship or intimacy begin are manifestly implausible. Nobody in our world – or presumably in other human worlds – acts or responds to others on the assumption that sharing and integration are so complete that (as Aristotle suspected of Plato's *Republic*) plurality is wholly overcome. Allegations that 'dependents' are not distinct beings spuriously invoke fictions of ideal integration which do not in fact inform action or attitudes, feelings or involvements. In practice, most activity directed at children, wives or other supposed or actual 'dependents' acknowledges and assumes that, on the contrary, they are distinct agents and subjects, with multiple, rather useful capacities and capabilities to act and to feel, to respond and even to take initiative. It does not assume any complete unity of interests and concern between spouses, or within family or household. If separateness and plurality are assumed in activity it is inconsistent to deny them and to substitute ideal conceptions of integration and unity in considering the appropriate scope of consideration.[25]

Fictions of total integration that 'overcome' plurality are often buttressed by fictions of the incompetence of 'dependents', who are said to lack ordinary capacities and capabilities. Children, the ill and the handicapped may be genuinely dependent and incompetent in some respects in which most adults are not; servants and wives are seldom dependent in such ways. Even when there is genuine one-way dependence, it is usually neither so general nor so debilitating that dependents are not seen as distinct agents and subjects.[26] More often 'idealized' and highly contentious conceptions of dependence and independence are invoked as convenient tools for the dirty work of spuriously excluding others from (certain domains of) ethical consideration. The assumptions on which activity is actually based are usually more accurate: those not in the maturity of their faculties and the pride of their health are rarely seen by those who act on them as other than agents and subjects, if with certain determinate limitations. Dependence, which may arise from many sources – and frequently from oppression and injustice

---

[25] See O'Neill, 'Justice, Gender, and International Boundaries'.
[26] This forms one of the main themes of discussions of paternalism and, under the misleading heading of 'patients' rights', of a range of further issues in bioethics. These debates do not aim to show that patients have rights that others lack, but that suggestions that they lack rights others have cannot be vindicated by illegitimate exclusion from some domain of consideration.

– is not generally seen either as fusing or as destroying identities, so overcoming plurality, or even as reducing those of limited capacity to mere subjects.[27] In itself dependence is a commonplace feature of all but solitary human circumstances, and activity that assumes that others are dependent in certain ways does just that: it provides *no* reasons for their exclusion from ethical consideration.[28] The limitations of agents' capacities may indeed provide reason to restrict and differentiate activity, perhaps by creating structures that compensate for incapacity; in itself it provides no good reasons for excluding from ethical consideration.

Just as certain denials of finitude can be used to augment the dirty work performed by denials of plurality, so can exaggerations of others' capacities and capabilities, and the corresponding denials of their vulnerabilities. When others' capacities or capabilities are exaggerated, unreasonable claims about their self-sufficiency and their cognitive and other forms of independence may be put forward, and their vulnerabilities, suffering and pain may be played down or denied. Yet the adequately accurate views of those capacities and capabilities, which are commonly and prudently assumed in acting, often show up the spurious standing of such distortions. Well-organized exploitation of others' vulnerabilities is often coupled with bare-faced assertion of their invulnerability: the powerful assume, accurately enough, that the weak must go along with their proposals, yet then interpret their compliance, outrageously enough, as evidence of informed, legitimating consent. Once exaggerated assertions about others' capacities and capabilities are smuggled in, vulnerable people to whom they are misascribed may come to be thought of as entitled to just dealing in the market but not to the help they may need. Here too activity speaks louder than words, and displays the assumptions actually made about others more accurately and more honestly. Examples of dishonest denial can be found in some economistic and libertarian attitudes to just dealing: others are depicted as (hyper) rational choosers and consumers and as little else, and their

---

[27] Arguments against strategies of blaming victims for the limitations that have been inflicted on them are well explored. One of the clearest deployments is still J. S. Mill's in *The Subjection of Women* in *On Liberty and Other Writings*, ed. Stefan Collini (Cambridge University Press, 1989).

[28] It may, of course provide reason for differentiating the ways in which ethical concern is expressed.

vulnerabilities and ignorance, as well as the ties of sentiment and loyalty that constrain them, are ostensibly denied, although they may be used to take due (or rather undue) advantage in the cut and thrust of market and politics.[29] Evidence that idealized capacities and capabilities are not merely falsely but fraudulently ascribed is revealed by the skill and efficiency with which those who purport to hold these views of others adjust their activities to take advantage of the very limitations they deny.[30]

However, in some cases lack of capacities, and consequently of capabilities, is so great that denial both of agency and subjecthood may seem accurate enough. Certain hard cases that have occupied medical ethics – the foetus, the brain-dead patient, the irreversibly senile or demented patient – are cases where bodily separateness and connectedness are not in doubt, yet where elementary capacities for activity, perhaps for all experience, are missing. Will not an approach to questions of scope that starts from the assumptions agents make in acting have to conclude that such beings are not agents, perhaps not even subjects? If it does so, will it have to conclude that they may be denied ethical standing and excluded from the scope of ethical principles and consideration? If conclusions about the scope of ethical consideration are derived from the assumptions to which agents commit themselves in acting, will not any *genuine* lack of capacities to act or experience that is duly registered in the premisses of activity, legitimate lack of ethical consideration? Will not an adequately accurate assumption that others are asleep or unconscious, in a coma or demented, so unable to act or experience, provide reasons not to ascribe agency or subjecthood to them, so legitimate their exclusion from ethical consideration?

---

[29] Once again denial is sometimes defended as mere abstraction: however, abstraction *brackets* contentious predicates, whereas models of man that impute idealized forms of rationality and self sufficiency do not bracket but *predicate falsely*. Whatever the theoretical advantages of idealizing models of man, practical reasoning that assumes this sort of idealization relies on assumptions that are nearly always repudiated in acting.

[30] But need the ascription be dishonest? Suppose others' agency were denied in action – for example, by spraying them as we do certain insects. (An example I owe to Angus Ross.) If others were sprayed, but there was evidence of assumptions about their agency (e.g. making sure that they did not know who was doing it; intercepting their communications) then agency is still assumed. An imputation of agency is lacking only when *no* aspect of activity assumes the contrary. If some agents *genuinely* do not take certain others as agents, there will be no way to convince them that those others fall within the scope of their ethical consideration.

If agents who lack decisive analyses of agency and subjecthood, but assume that connected others have ranges of capacities and of capabilities for experiencing and acting, also assumed that these capacities and capabilities were wholly lost and wholly acquired in an instant this picture might be convincing. Agents might then reasonably assume that certain beings 'qualify' as agents and as subjects at some times and not at others, so should be accorded ethical consideration at some times and denied it at others. However, given the realities of the lives of finite agents, including all human agents, lack of current capacities and capabilities for activity and experience at a given moment is not generally grounds for assuming that they could not or will not have such capacities and capabilities, nor therefore that they should not be accorded ethical consideration. Capacities and capabilities wax and wane. Even meagre capacities and capabilities for action and activity of all sorts arise gradually through complex biological, psychological and social processes; so too do many capacities to feel, to experience and to suffer. Capacities to act and to experience do not come and go like the shadows of clouds; they are not episodic, although they can grow and fade. These points are duly reflected in the assumptions that underpin activity. When we act or respond we see others as sources of activity and as centres of experience, and accord them ethical consideration not merely because of the capacities and capabilities of the moment, but because of a certain picture of the growth, fading and interconnection of such capacities and capabilities. Even elementary capacities to experience and to feel are seen as a complex and often as a fragile achievement, and as the matrix and herald of capacities to act.

There are also hard cases, like those which have preoccupied bioethicists, in which the capacities that seem important to full agency are indeed missing, but are not simply absent, as they are uncontroversially absent in sticks and stones, but rather are *nearly* or *incipiently* there. The foetus and the nonhuman primate, the comatose and the senile share many biological, psychological and social capacities and even capabilities with those fuller and more complex capacities to act and to experience. Agents see them nearly as subjects, and perhaps incipiently as agents, because they see them as some way towards becoming subjects and agents, or as receding only a short way from having been agents or subjects. Even when they know that many or most capacities to act will remain minimal or absent for (the rest of) an entire life they may detect signs that point towards it. In such cases others whom agents do not now see either as agents or even as ordinary subjects may be not merely causally affected by activity, as things are, but affected by activity in distinctive ways which are recognized as signs of *proto-agency*, and as traces of *incipient subjectivity*.[31]

These considerations are, however, relevant *only* to the consideration of scope: they show nothing about uniform treatment or requirement. Even if certain inclusive principles hold across the entire domain of ethical consideration (cf. sections 2.3, 6.1 and the first pages of chapter 7), they will not mandate uniform treatment of all cases within their scope. Hence agents may have reason to include proto-agents and incipient subjects within the scope of their ethical consideration, and also reasons not to treat them exactly as they treat those capable of a wider range of activity. For example, we may make assumptions about young children and the profoundly retarded which require us to accord them ethical standing; yet it would be absurd, and often cruel, to treat them in the very same way as we treat those in the maturity of their faculties. The foetus and the senile may fall within the domain of ethical consideration of those whose activity bears on them; yet from this alone nothing specific follows about the activity to which they are entitled. All that follows is that those whose activity is based on a measure of acknowledgement of the distinctive features of proto-agents and incipient subjects cannot invoke their partly missing capacities as sufficient grounds to exclude them from the scope of ethical consideration.

Just as boundaries of ethical consideration can be manipulated by denying plurality and finitude that are implied by activity, so they can be manipulated by denying connection. This is sometimes done by depicting others as lacking the very connections which various activities assume. Yet where agents' action and plans, their feelings

---

[31] This argument does not claim that proper activity towards beings assumed to have property P provides the model for proper activity towards beings that are assumed potentially to have property P. Not all whom we recognize as proto-agents are seen as potential agents; not all in whom we see traces of subjectivity are seen as subjects to be: consider deep coma and anencephaly. Reasons for regarding proto-agents and incipient subjects as falling within the domain of ethical consideration are not sufficient for treating them just as we might treat those seen as having some or many capacities for acting and experiencing.

and practices, commit them to adequately accurate views of connections to themselves, they cannot consistently discount those connections as soon as ethical questions are raised.

Spatial separation of certain sorts *may* be the basis for a genuine lack of connection, as in the case of the T'ang Chinese and the Anglo-Saxons, and in such cases denial of connection is adequately accurate. But in other cases of spatial separation, denials of connection are not adequately accurate. For example, the division of the earth and of its inhabitants into mutually exclusive, bounded groups by state boundaries has provided a powerful and systematic way of discounting or at least diminishing the ethical standing of 'foreigners' who live beyond 'our' frontiers, even by those whose activity is in fact premised on the view that those whom they purport to exclude are others to whom they are connected in varied ways.[32] Those who view 'foreigners' and other 'outsiders' as people with whom they can trade, translate and negotiate, reason and remonstrate, whom they can resent and despise, and who can carry complex and intelligent roles, cannot coherently rescind such assumptions of possible connection in order to limit the scope of their ethical consideration, or confine justice within the boundaries of states or communities. Whenever their activity assumes a plurality of finite and connected others, they are also committed to including those others within the scope of their ethical consideration.[33]

4.5 COSMOPOLITAN SCOPE: DISTANT STRANGERS AND FUTURE GENERATIONS

The most difficult cases for a practical approach to fixing the scope of ethical consideration arise when activity affects others about whom agents apparently need make *no* assumptions of any sort, whom they therefore seemingly need not accord ethical standing. Where others seemingly need not be acknowledged at all for

[32] See Pogge, 'Cosmopolitanism and Sovereignty' and O'Neill, 'Justice and Boundaries' in Brown, ed., *Political Restructuring in Europe*.

[33] This is not an argument for the justice of a world state. Principles of justice do not require uniform treatment of fellow citizens, or of foreigners. It is simply an argument to show that, at least in our world, foreigners count. A system of states might be just, but this couldn't be shown by demonstrating the internal justice of each state, let alone of some states.

purposes of activity, will it not be legitimate to regard activity that might affect them as activity that affects things, that does not bear on agents and subjects, or even on proto-agents and incipient subjects?

The easiest of these hard cases are those in which spatial separation approximates but does not match the degree of separation and disconnection between the T'ang Chinese and Anglo-Saxons, in that at least some assumptions about possible connection are made. By itself *knowledge or belief that others exist* will not bring them within the scope of ethical consideration of those whose activity assumes that neither can act on the other. If the others inhabiting a distant planet are detectable from earth, but (it is believed) *cannot* be reached or affected or communicated with, and cannot reach those on earth, they are not objects of ethical consideration for those on earth. But if others belonging to a tribe in a remote valley are (as it happens) isolated, but (it is believed) *can* be contacted, then they fall within the scope of ethical consideration for those who *could* contact them. This will be revealed in the fact that activity will reflect assumptions about those others, which may be adequately accurate and will be corrigible. If the remote tribe are taken to have ancient wisdom or fabled wealth they may be sought; if they are taken to have formidable weapons or diseases they may be avoided or attacked. We view others as connected as soon as we see a *real possibility* of activity by either party as bearing on the other, even if no actual activity, let alone interactivity, now connects them or is planned. The case of very distant others is no different from that of others in the middle distance. Agents who assume that certain others *will not* act on them, nor they on those others, often nevertheless base their activity on the view that those others *could* act on them and they on those others. Cautious embezzlers, for example, plan to take their employers' money without revealing themselves: they assume that detection *is possible* but will not happen if they take evasive precautions; equally cautious companies do not make the paranoid assumption that every employee is bent on fraud, but prudently assume the *real possibility* that some may be, so set up fraud-prevention systems.

In the contemporary world, people act on quite strong assumptions even about the most distant strangers: for example, the affluent assume that poor and distant foreigners will not attack or be permitted to settle in their part of the world, and more generally that outsiders will not be permitted to undercut local wages. Put more brutally, a background assumption of most affluent lives is that state power will effectively keep most distant strangers more or less in their place and in their poverty.

A different range of hard cases arises when others are not spatially but temporally distant. Here too there may be separations where *no* possibility of connection is assumed. Most evidently, those whose lives are separated by many generations do not assume that there is any real possibility of interactivity. The hard cases arise because descendants depend on their ancestors for their very existence, yet ancestors seemingly will have lived their lives making minimal if any assumptions about those descendants. More generally, activity by predecessors seemingly need rely only on vestigial assumptions about far future generations, yet sets the basic conditions of their lives. By burning fossil fuels prodigally we accelerate the green-house effect and may dramatically harm successors, who can do nothing to us. By leading our lives in one way rather than another we create a future world whose inhabitants may be richer or poorer, healthier or more diseased than they would have been had we lived differently. The immense influence of current activity is not in doubt, yet need it be reflected in assumptions made about members of those future generations, whose members cannot be individuated, and whose numbers are unknown?[34]

However, the fact that future persons cannot be individuated or counted is a bad reason for thinking that present activity cannot or need not be based on assumptions about them. Activity is constantly taken on the basis of quite strong assumptions about others whom we cannot individuate, but can specify. People who insure possessions assume that others (they know not who or how many) might damage or steal them; gamblers assume that others (they know not who or how many) will also have staked money so that winnings can be paid; hotel-keepers assume that members of the public (they know not who or how many) will book the rooms and eat the meals they prepare. Activity that is predicated on assumptions about others who cannot be *individuated* by the agent often proceeds on the basis of adequately accurate assumptions about others who can be *specified*.

[34] Cf. Derek Parfit, *Reasons and Persons* (Oxford, Clarendon Press, 1984).

So the fact that we cannot individuate or count members of far future generations does not, by itself, mean that we act without making assumptions about them, nor that it is impossible to base an account of ethical consideration for them on those assumptions. Individuability of particular others is not a prerequisite for adequately accurate assumptions about specifiable others. It may then be possible for agents to fix the ethical standing they must accord those in remote places and far future generations, as of neighbours and contemporaries, by considering the assumptions they actually make about them in acting.

These assumptions are of various sorts. One way of looking at the matter is by considering the commonplaces of human life, including the overlap of generations, which will be taken for granted, in more and less accurate form, by each generation in turn. On this view, agents may with adequate accuracy see themselves as connected to *some* future others who in turn take themselves to be connected to *some* further future others, and so on through an indefinite future. Individual agents quite normally take themselves to be connected in this way to individuable and unindividuable others to whom they assume chains of possible (inter)activity.[35] In such a connected chain of assumed possible (inter)activity, agents at each stage act on the assumption that they act on possible (inter)actors. They thereby view themselves as part of numerous chains of possible (inter)activity, which may stretch beyond localities and lives, although they cannot individuate those to whom they are more remotely connected.

They will make few and weak assumptions about others who are temporally more distant, as they also make few and weak assumptions about others who are spatially and causally more distant. Still, assumed connection is assumed connection, and while it does not follow that consideration for future generations can or must be expressed as we express consideration for contemporaries it does follow that we cannot exclude from the scope of ethical consideration those others whose shadowy future lives and connection to our activity we acknowledge in acting.[36] This way of looking

[35] For example they may leave bequests to unborn grandchildren, or unknown achievers of new knowledge or fame.
[36] See the essays in Peter Laslett and James S. Fishkin, eds., *Justice Between Age Groups and Generations*, Philosophy Politics and Society, Sixth Series (New Haven, Yale University Press, 1992).

at ethical standing preserves the thought that consideration cannot reach to others to whom agents do not take themselves to be connected by any chains of possible activity. The T'ang Chinese and Anglo-Saxons did not see themselves as linked by any such chains, although presumably both saw themselves as connected by (very tenuous) chains of activity to distant successors (whose lives might have surprised them). On this account, activity acknowledges remote contemporaries and future generations when agents assume that its effects will persist and will affect spatially and temporally distant others. Distance in space or time will make much uncertain; however, where there are matters that can be predicted with adequate accuracy their impact on distant as on nearby others will generally be assumed in acting. Uncertainty as to *which* action and interaction between *which* individuals or groups will actually occur does not mean that agents will act without making commonplace assumptions about their likely impact on spatially and temporally distant others, and does not undermine the procedure for fixing the scope of ethical consideration.

For the aim is not, as it would be in essentialist or similar approaches to ethical standing, to define a class of (moral) agents or subjects, but to show how agents may work out both to which *individuable* others and to which *merely specifiable* others they must accord ethical standing. Connection will peter out at differing boundaries for different agents and in activity of differing sorts in differing circumstances; it will be lost whenever agents do not affect others on whom they might have acted had things gone differently, and be at an end whenever there is no other pathway by which they might have affected them. The finalities of permanent emigration, of permanent loss of contact, of death itself may be just that. These are further reasons why ethical consideration may legitimately have different scope for different agents acting in a given context, and for any given agent acting in different contexts.

These ways of looking at ethical consideration for spatially and temporally, hence causally and socially, distant others can seem at once overwhelming and fragile. They can seem overwhelming if we note that from assumptions that underlie activity on others who might interact with or act on yet others there may follow vast branching chains of possible pathways of (inter)activity, which draw countless remote lives within the domain of ethical consideration for a given agent. They can seem trivial when we note that the assumed implications of chains of possible connection will be no weightier than the assumed impact of the initial activity through the chain. After all, nearly all activity on spatially or temporally distant others has minimal or no effects, and assumptions made in acting will be adjusted to this reality. Even if we acknowledge possible connection to temporally and spatially distant others, the import of including them within the domain of ethical consideration may seem hardly to weigh on us.

However, this shifting image of the import of assumed connection to distant and future others stabilizes when we consider *how* activity is most likely to affect them. Activity on distant and future others may either be transmitted through chains of individual action like a 'Chinese whisper' passed successively between individual agents or generations of agents; or it may be coded in more permanent form in the social and natural world that is shared with remotely connected others.

The first mode of transmission is fragile: if each link in the chain may distort or redirect, fragment or buffer activity in countless ways, then activity will reasonably be based on quite strong assumptions about immediate recipients but on vestigial or on no assumptions about remote recipients. The second mode of transmission is more robust: activity that will be imprinted on the enduring natural and social world will be predicated on quite powerful assumptions about its remote as well as its immediate recipients. An activity that is given robust long-lasting physical or institutional embodiment *will reliably have effects that are independent of particular pathways of transmission*, and their durability will be assumed in activity. So then will the fact that the changed natural or social environment will be there to affect whoever is around.

There are many examples of activity that is predicated on strong assumptions of these sorts that will reliably affect the lives of remote others. Activity on the natural world that brings land under plough, irrigates deserts, plants trees or preserves wilderness will generally assume, and sometimes intend, that their results will raise production and perhaps limit pollution, so that more can survive or live well. Activity that pollutes or consumes or destroys important nonrenewable resources will often assume and sometimes intend that fewer will be able to live or live well in the future. Activity that aims to alter health or hygiene will also often assume, and sometimes aim at, effects on birth-rates or death-rates. Activity may also incorporate assumptions about the social worlds remote and unindividuable others will inhabit. Such assumptions are made by those who build or neglect cities and villages that could shelter and form future lives; who create, reform or destroy institutions and laws; who foster traditions of solidarity or of estrangement that can uplift or poison lives and cultures; who accumulate or dissipate capital and cultures; who improve or erode means of communication and interaction; who sustain, disperse or abandon ways of life. In such activity and policies agents make potent assumptions about the lives that will be available to distant contemporaries and remote successors.[37] These are robust, acknowledged ways by which activity extends beyond the literal boundaries of individual contact and local context.

In considering activity that takes cognizance of the natural, social and cultural structures through which activity at a distance and activity through time are reliably mediated we also gain some hold on ethical problems that arise from the 'unintended' consequences of activity. The evidently incomplete and often partly inaccurate view of the results of their own activity on which agents rely is particularly patchy for the case of remote effects on distant others. Agents are often ignorant of, and certainly do not intend, their contribution to the results of patterns of activity to which they contribute. Europeans who colonized the Americas no doubt assumed and often intended much harm to its native inhabitants, but they did not assume let alone intend the ravages European diseases would inflict on populations without immunities. Those who rush to buy in a boom market may not foresee and certainly do not intend the price rises they jointly produce. Evidently a practical and constructive approach to fixing the scope of ethical consideration can work only from the assumptions that activity relies on, so is blind when agents are blind. The limitations of the approach are reduced only because blindness can be reduced: ignorance, including ignorance of 'unintended' consequences of one's own and others' activity, is in principle corrigible.

Agents inevitably lack reasons to include within the scope of their ethical consideration at a given juncture any others, whether

---

[37] See chapters 6 and 7 for discussion of the content as opposed to the scope of justice to distant and future others, of environmental justice and of 'green' virtues.

individuable or merely specifiable, whom they genuinely (even if inaccurately) do not view as connected to themselves. Failure to see connections will be registered in the presuppositions of activity and hence will lead to 'gaps' in the according of ethical consideration. Such 'gaps' are not, however, permanent fixtures: agents who come to a better understanding of their connections to others, of others' capacities and capabilities, of the ways in which their own activity is likely to bear on others, may also come to see and foresee their contribution to the (previously) unintended consequences of patterns of activity. They will then have reasons to amend and refine the assumptions on which they base their activity and so their views of the scope of ethical consideration to which it commits them.

A constructive account of the scope of ethical consideration does not suppose that agents ever come to hold wholly accurate views about others to whom their activity connects them, or of their capacities, capabilities and vulnerabilities, or of the likely effects of their own activity. Agents may base much activity on inaccurate beliefs about others, about their connections to others, about others' capacities, capabilities and vulnerabilities, and about the effects both intended and unintended of their activity on those others. Only if these inaccuracies and omissions were complete and incorrigible would reasons not to include others within the scope of ethical consideration be in place. In practice these inaccuracies and omissions are often incomplete. Moreover, inaccuracies and omissions are always under some pressure for correction because of the disruptive effects they can have on activity. Although the assumptions agents make in acting will never be more and may often be less than adequately accurate, they may, if taken seriously and corrected when shown inadequate, provide the basis for an adequately accurate account of the scope of ethical consideration agents have reason to accord.

This constructive approach to ethical standing, and hence to the scope of ethical consideration, will not deliver what a perfectionist or other metaphysical account of ethical standing would have offered, were it available. Nor will it endorse the claims of one or another particularist account of ethical standing. It offers no way of *discovering* the 'real' basis of ethical standing, no criterion for demarcating the class of agents or of subjects. Its practical merit is that it offers enough for agents to construct an account of the scope of ethical consideration to which they are committed at a given juncture. The reason for thinking that such a construction provides answers which are not merely subjective is that it requires agents to accord ethical standing differently if they find reason to change their assumptions about their connection to others, about others' capacities, capabilities and vulnerabilities, or about the consequences, including the unintended consequences, of their activity.

In the contemporary world, in which most if not all agents take themselves to be linked to some distant and future others, this constructive approach points to a more-or-less cosmopolitan view of the proper scope of ethical consideration for contemporaries and an open-ended view of the proper scope of ethical consideration for successors. In earlier worlds – that of the T'ang Chinese and the Anglo-Saxons – agents might reasonably have come to a narrower account of the appropriate scope of ethical consideration. However, this contingent and approximate cosmopolitanism is *only* a matter of scope: real possibilities of acting on others, or of being acted on by them, are constantly lapsing unused, and as they do so agents will continue to have reason to accord those others ethical consideration only if they take it that other possible pathways connecting them to those others are maintained or open up. On a constructive account, the proper scope of ethical consideration is not and cannot be fixed by settling which beings have the characteristics which are necessary and sufficient for ethical standing. Even if no comprehensive or theoretical account of the grounds of ethical standing can be discovered, a reasoned way of resolving practical questions about others' ethical standing can be constructed on the basis of the corrigible assumptions agents make about connected others whom they take to be agents or subjects.

CHAPTER 5

Structure: obligations and rights

Justice and virtue may both be principled; their significant domains of ethical consideration may both be identifiable for practical purposes: yet they may offer incompatible orientations to life. So far nothing has been shown about the structure, the content or the compatibility of principles of justice or of virtue. All that has been shown is that some popular arguments for their incompatibility and against principle-based accounts of ethics are unconvincing, and that the domain of ethical consideration relevant for activity of all sorts – for individual action, for taking up attitudes, for supporting policies – can be fixed by constructive procedures which do not assume unavailable starting points.

An account of the content of justice and virtue can be helped by preliminary consideration of some *structural* differences between types of universal principle. Accounts both of the structure and of the content of justice and of virtue will be built upon those of practical reason, of principles and of the scope of ethical consideration. So it is as well to take stock of the materials that are available.

The assembly of materials and methods began by discussing and challenging the common, but unclear, view that justice is abstract and universal, while virtue responds to particularities. Abstraction, taken strictly, emerged as a feature of all reasoning, hence of all practical reasoning, and indeed of all thought and language, so not something that discussions of virtue can or do avoid. While many friends of the virtues legitimately attack reliance on idealized conceptions of agency or rationality, which they detect in the assumptions underlying certain theories of justice, they are mistaken in arguing that this defect provides either reason for or the possibility of rejecting abstraction. On the other hand, proponents of abstract, universalist accounts of justice have often been too sanguine about the prospects for building an account of justice on nothing but abstract accounts of the human condition and a thin, instrumental conception of practical reason. Additional materials are needed.

The inventory has been augmented in several ways. Chapter 2 provided a further, critical conception of practical reason, which was constructed out of the requirement that reasons be exchangeable among, hence followable by, all those for whom they are to count as reasons. Chapter 3 identified principles of action as a main focus for practical reasoning, and hence for an approach to justice or to virtue, but also showed that many of the fears which proponents of virtue ethics voice about principles and rules are groundless. These fears could be justified only by adopting a straw-man conception of rules and principles, which depicts them as complete instructions – even algorithms – for idealized agents that prescribe uniformly, preempt judgement or even function as quasi-mechanical generators of action. However, practical principles, ethical principles included, neither need nor can have any of these regrettable features. Acting on universal principles does not demand (strictly speaking it precludes) uniform treatment or insensitivity to differences. Principles do not dominate or determine those who act on them or live by them: rather agents refer to or rely on principles in selecting and steering their activities.

Once these misplaced fears about principles were set aside, a focus on universal principles could be seen for what it is. Since principles of action are fundamental to practical reasoning, hence to ethics, so too are universal principles. To say that a principle is universal is only to say that its scope extends across the whole of some domain, and not to fix the extent of that domain. However, this clarification of the demands of universal principles left questions of scope unsettled. Chapter 4 presented a practical procedure by which to fix the scope of ethical principles, and argued that whenever agents base their action on the assumption of connection to other agents and subjects, they must include those others within the scope of their ethical consideration.

This procedure for establishing the scope of ethical consideration suggested that many significant demarcations, such as state and community boundaries, or the boundaries of private life, may not generally be legitimate limits to ethical consideration. Action that assumes and relies on capacities and capabilities for intelligent action or responsive interaction in others who live on the far side of such demarcations cannot consistently exclude those others from ethical consideration. In acting we cannot avoid committing ourselves on questions of scope, whether or not we actually raise ethical questions. For example, those who sell or buy coffee grown by foreigners in distant regions take for granted that coffee growers are intelligent and competent agents and subjects who can deliver an acceptable product and negotiate market relations, and would feel aggrieved and complain if the supermarket offered sub-standard coffee. Those who plan to torture and oppress enemies take for granted that those others are agents and subjects, whom suffering and threats might persuade, or destroy. Those who assume that others in a distant future will have to put up with environments they despoil take for granted that those others will have correspondingly restricted life chances. In our world, we therefore cannot coherently deny that the scope of ethical consideration must often be more-or-less cosmopolitan. However, unless the content of ethical requirements can be fixed, knowing the scope of ethical consideration will have few implications for the many activities in which agents find themselves involved.

Fixing the scope of ethical consideration in this way does not settle whether abstract and constructive methods can establish ethical principles. It remains an open question which sorts of principles, let alone which specific principles, these methods can establish. Universal practical principles could, after all, be of many different types. Most will be designed to regulate restricted aspects of life in limited ways, and may make no claim to be ethical principles. They may be premised on and their scope restricted to specific institutions and roles, or to the pursuit of specific objectives. Established laws, institutional regulations, norms of roles as well as maxims of prudence, rules of games and of skill all embody universal practical principles that are tailored to specific aspects of life. Whether these laws, norms and other rules can be judged by more fundamental, inclusive ethical standards remains an open question. I shall begin with an account of the *structure* of principles that might play a more fundamental role in chapter 5, and then consider the *content* of principles that play this role in chapters 6 and 7.

5.1 PRINCIPLES AND REQUIREMENTS

If there are practical principles that can reasonably be thought of as ethical principles, they cannot derive their authority from an arbitrary starting point. A vindication of ethical claims cannot be based on the 'demands' of some supposed idealized or transcendent reality, or on the characteristics of particular agents, or on the features of certain social practices or institutions. Equally, the fact that a certain principle has been enacted as a law, adopted as an institutional rule or is a norm for a given role, or even has become part of the sacred creed of a tradition, does not show that it is a matter either of justice or of virtue. If it is, this will be due to other considerations.

However, the authority of ethical principles (if there are any), cannot derive from the supposed authority of reason, unless that authority too can be vindicated. The constructive conception of practical reason vindicated in chapter 2, which was not premised on unavailable starting points, has a correspondingly limited authority. It rejects as unreasoned principles of action which are not adoptable by all within the domain. Practical reasoning demands that principles be *universalizable* because non-universalizable principles of action will not be adoptable by all in the relevant domain, so cannot coherently be recommended to or required of all.[1]

The authority of various alternative conceptions of practical reason – 'Platonist', instrumental and normative – all, I have argued, either need unavailable starting points or have too limited an authority. By contrast, the starting points for a conception of practical reason as universalizability are available – and, used in conjunction with plausible, non-idealizing conceptions of instrumental reason, it may turn out to have adequate authority. Moreover, once it is accepted as a basic requirement for practical reasoning that non-universalizable principles are to be rejected, this demand can lend authority to some stretches of instrumental

---

[1] Hence *universalizability* is distinct both from *formal universality* and from *cosmopolitan scope*, from *universal prescriptivism* and from conceptions of *ethical universalism*, such as those stated in Golden Rules, which advocate action on principles that *would be accepted* or *would be desired by all*. Universalizability is a spare, modal notion and incorporates no claims about the content or ethical significance of motivation or preference. It merely demands that principles adopted be ones that *could be principles for all in the relevant domains*.

and normative practical reasoning, and reveal the lack of authority of other stretches. Despite these solid advantages, many will suspect that if practical reason is only the double modal standard, that *requires* agents to live by principles which they take it others too *can* adopt, it will provide too little to establish serious ethical claims. The suspicion must be taken seriously.

A modal conception of practical reason has one rather obvious advantage that may help allay this suspicion. The principles which it will endorse or reject will make or state *requirements*, and practical principles which state requirements are linked to one another by well-defined *deontic* relationships. Even limited ethical requirements, if they can be established, may guide action in significant ways. By contrast, principles which are merely hortatory or advisory, which simply recommend or warn, will be relatively free-standing, so less tightly linked to one another, and so may prove less able to guide action. An initial search for ethical principles may therefore gain by starting with ethical requirements. Of course, some may fear that principles of requirement can lead no further than an account of justice. This fear too must be taken seriously.

A constructivist conception of practical reason will identify some ethical requirements if it can show that there are principles of action which *cannot be viewed as adoptable by all*. The criterion is not merely that a given principle be such that, as it happens, some or many individuals lack the capacities or capabilities to act success-fully on that principle at some times (a situation which constantly arises), but rather that the principle be such that it *could not* be adopted by all within the domain of ethical consideration. If any such non-universalizable inclusive principles can be identified, there will be reason to reject them. If their rejection is required, a gamut of more specific principles that require, prohibit and permit certain types of activity, practice or institution for more restricted domains may also be identifiable. For example, if we cannot view a principle of inflicting violence as adoptable by all (see sections 6.4 and 6.5 below for further discussion), its rejection will be required and this may have a large range of further implications.[2]

---

[2] Lives or institutions that are based on the rejection of violence may yet condone or permit, even require, elements of violence. For example, the use of state power or self-defence might be required if a basic principle of violence was to be rejected. Nevertheless the rejection of violence requires a lot because it is not compatible with inflicting, supporting or condoning either systematic or gratuitous violence.

Requirements are therefore worth looking at first simply because they can guide action more powerfully than other types of ethical consideration, such as those expressed in recommendations or warnings, which are less closely interlocked.

Requirements have these advantages for guiding action because they link act-types to act-types and agents to agents in definite ways. The *deontic links between act-types* arise because the deontic status of each act-type determines the deontic status of omitting acts of that type: act-types that are required will also be permitted and their omission will be forbidden; act-types that are forbidden will not be permitted and their omission will be required; act-types that are neither required nor forbidden will be merely permissible. The *deontic links between agents* arise because the deontic status of an act can be characterized both from the perspective of the agent and from the perspective of others with whom the agent stands in various sorts of relationship. For example, if A owes B an act of a certain type, or its omission, B will be entitled to such performance or omission by A; if B is entitled to have A perform or omit an act of a certain type, A will have an obligation so to do. These and other deontic relationships link act-types and agents; they allow systematic arguments that link various practical requirements. If there are any ethical requirements, these links will provide a scaffolding by which their several claims can be extended and connected.

Much contemporary writing on ethics, and especially on justice, builds on systematic deontic structures. A lot of this work is broadly liberal in orientation, and the majority of it treats the perspective of the subject or recipient as prior to that of perspective of the agent, and accordingly treats *rights* rather than *obligations* or *duties* as the fundamental ethical notion. It is guided by the recipient's question: 'What are we (or: what am I) entitled to?'. The preoccupation with recipience may be politely masked by a third-person formulation, that asks 'What are human beings, or right-holders, entitled to?' (or: 'What human rights are there?'), but nevertheless focuses on *recipience* rather than on *action*, on *rights* rather than on *obligations*.

Of course, rights do not banish obligations. On the contrary, once rights have been vindicated, obligations will be entailed: but they will not be the primary focus of ethical consideration. When the perspective of recipience is taken as the starting point of practical reasoning, the more traditional and more obviously *practical* questions about ethical requirements, such as 'What ought we (or: I) do?', 'How should we (or: I) live?' and 'What is to be done?' will be answered only as a secondary and derivative matter.[3]

Older ethical traditions, which emphasized the importance of obligation rather than of rights, of action rather than of recipience, even in discussions of justice, may have insisted on a distinction that marks no difference, or no ethically important difference. Perhaps there is nothing or little to choose between beginning with right-holders and their entitlements and beginning with obligation-bearers and their duties, since the two approaches afford equivalent views of one set of ethical requirements. If so, any decision to prefer one perspective to the other would reflect no more than expository convenience. On the other hand, the two perspectives may not be equivalent. If they are not, it may matter which is taken to be more significant. Hence a basic move in arguing for principles which state ethical requirements must be to establish whether and why they should be formulated as principles either of action or of entitlement, or whether perspective is a matter of indifference.

5.2 JUSTICE: OBLIGATIONS WITH RIGHTS

Although traditional and contemporary discussions of justice both treat ethical requirements as fundamental, contemporary work is distinctive in taking *rights*, and so the entitlement(s) of subjects, so seriously that obligation is often treated as the subordinate notion. Of course, *obligations* are neither banished nor undercut when rights are treated as basic, since any principle that defines a right always by implication defines some obligation. This is the basis of the widely presumed equivalence between the perspectives of rights and of obligations, and also of the firm conceptual links between different deontic claims. These conceptual links between obligations and prohibitions, entitlements and rights, permissions and

---

[3] Agents' questions are the older ones. These three versions are favoured by Kant, by ancient and contemporary writings on virtue (see Crisp, ed., *How Should One Live?*) and by (!) Lenin. Recipients' questions rose to prominence with the Rights of Man. For some explicit discussion about which is basic to ethics see Simone Weil, *The Need for Roots: Prelude to a Declaration of Duties towards Mankind*, trans. A. F. Wills (London, Routledge and Kegan Paul, 1952); Williams *Ethics and the Limits of Philosophy*; Onora O'Neill, 'Practical Thinking and Socratic Questions', *Ratio*, 28 (1986), 89–95.

exceptions, as well as those between less formal deontic notions such as 'ought', 'must', 'may' and 'had to', underpin routine practical reasoning, whether legal or institutional, political or ethical. However, the converse claim that every obligation defines some right is both contentious and, I shall argue, unsustainable. If so, it surely matters whether reasoning about ethical requirements starts with rights or with obligations.

The picture we can draw of ethical requirements if we begin with rights takes account of complex relations between agents and those for whom they must acknowledge ethical consideration. Any right must be matched by some corresponding obligation, which is so assigned to others that right-holders can in principle claim or waive the right (or where not competent to do so, that others be able at least to claim it on their behalf). Unless obligation-bearers are identifiable by right-holders, claims to have rights amount only to rhetoric: nothing can be claimed, waived or enforced if it is indeterminate where the claim should be lodged, for whom it may be waived or on whom it could be enforced. This condition can be met for *universal rights* when they are matched by corresponding universal obligations that are allocated to all others, and for *special rights* when they are matched by corresponding special obligations that are allocated to specified others.

Liberty rights provide a paradigm of universal rights. For example, a right of access to public spaces entails corollary obligations that all others in the same domain not obstruct access to public spaces. Many liberal advocates of rights (above all libertarians) insist that universal rights not only *may* but *must* be liberty rights to non-interference, and that the corresponding obligations not only *may* but *must* be universal obligations to respect others' liberties. Certainly, if a universal right is a liberty right, the corresponding obligation must be held by all others. If anyone were exempt from the corollary obligation to allow others access to public spaces, nobody would have an unrestricted right of access to those spaces. The *institutionalized* rights we see as embodying the principles of universal liberty rights in practice are, of course, often rather more restricted. For example, in many jurisdictions police officers or lawful demonstrators may legitimately limit others' access to public spaces under certain conditions. However, those who take liberty rights seriously quite reasonably view such restrictions as minor accommodations that are needed if they are to be institutionally embodied and one liberty adjusted to others, as in this example a right of public assembly is accommodated to a right of access to public spaces.

Advocates of universal liberty rights are therefore convincing when they insist that these rights must be matched by universal obligations. The libertarians among them also assert that *only* liberty rights can be matched by universal obligations. They point out that whereas liberty rights can be matched by duties that all can discharge, any universal rights to 'positive' action, for example, rights to goods, services or specifically to welfare,[4] would demand corresponding obligations that cannot be discharged by all, if only because agents are embodied, hence spatially and temporally dispersed, so not all of them can have the access to one another that universal 'positive' intervention would demand.

This point is sometimes countered by pointing out that a universal right to some 'positive' performance, although it could not be met by the action of all agents, could nevertheless be met for each by the action of some specified agent. For example, a universal right to some 'positive' good or service – say, a right to food – although it could not be met by the action of all agents, could nevertheless be met for each by the action of some specified agent. Or again, a universal right to subsistence or security might be matched by a 'distributed' obligation that assigned to each a right to claim subsistence or protection from specified others or from specified institutions. In this case a universal right would be met 'distributively' by setting up institutions that define numerous special relationships that specify for each right-holder those from whom the right could be claimed and those for whom its performance could be waived. Such universal rights to goods or services can be matched not by a universal obligation, but by any of many possible sets of distributed special obligations, that 'cover' the claims of each, hence of all, right-holders.

This line of thought does not establish that universal obligations to provide goods or services are the counterparts of universal rights to goods or services in quite the way in which universal negative

---

[4] Much discussion revolves around a simple dichotomy between *liberty rights* and *welfare rights*, where welfare rights are thought of as guaranteeing those goods and services without which human welfare is gravely threatened. In fact the basic contrast is between rights that demand non-interference and those that demand a specific performance. Welfare rights would be a special and important case of the latter.

obligations are the counterparts of universal liberty rights, but rather that certain sets of special obligations can effectively institutionalize *positive* rights to goods and services for each, and so for all. Since distributively universal rights *presuppose* institutional arrangements, it is hardly surprising that they are typically established in restricted forms, for example, for the citizens of certain states, or within a certain community.[5]

Defenders of welfare rights are often eager to claim a closer analogy between liberty and welfare rights. Liberty rights too, they point out, need effective institutionalization, whereby ostensibly universal obligations are in fact assigned to specific agents and agencies. The most impeccable liberty rights, such as a right not to be tortured, cannot be implemented without a legal system and institutional structures for supervising police, courts and penal institutions. They conclude that the obligations that correspond to all universal rights require allocation if the rights are to be effective. Henry Shue has argued that for these reasons any supposed distinction between liberty rights, with corresponding unproblematic purely negative universal obligations not to interfere, and supposedly questionable 'welfare' rights (more generally, universal rights to goods or services), which are judged problematic because the allocation of the corresponding obligations to perform specific 'positive' actions is unspecified, is illusory.[6]

However, universal rights to goods and services, such as welfare rights, are in fact unlike liberty rights. It is true that rights of both sorts need institutional structures for their *enforcement*, but liberty rights do not need institutional structures to be claimable and waivable. By contrast rights to goods and services can be claimed or waived *only* if a system of assigning agents to recipients has already been established, by which the counterpart obligations are 'distributed'.

Unfortunately much writing and rhetoric on rights heedlessly proclaims universal rights to goods or services, and in particular 'welfare rights', as well as to other social, economic and cultural rights that are prominent in international Charters and

[5] Partha Dasgupta, *An Inquiry into Well-Being and Destitution* (Oxford, Clarendon Press, 1993).
[6] Henry Shue, *Basic Rights: Subsistence, Affluence and US Foreign Policy* (Princeton University Press, 1980).

Declarations, without showing what connects each presumed right-holder to some specified obligation-bearer(s), which leaves the content of these supposed rights wholly obscure. This obscurity has been a scene and source of vast political and theoretical wrangling. Some advocates of universal economic, social and cultural rights go no further than to emphasize that they *can* be institutionalized, which is true.[7] But the point of difference is that they *must* be institutionalized: if they are not there is no right. And the political rub is that there are huge practical problems in establishing any rights to goods and services for all, even in limited domains or jurisdictions, because scarce resources and political conflict make it hard to gain effective support for any of the many distributions of counterpart obligations that would make a reality of the rights.

The supposed disanalogy between universal liberty and welfare rights is not then bogus: the two are genuinely asymmetric. For example, when a liberty right is violated, then, whether or not specific institutions have been established, there are determinate others to whom the violation might be imputed (no doubt, perpetrators are often unknown and can't be brought to book when institutions are inadequate). But when supposed universal rights to goods, services or welfare are not met, and no institutions for distributing or allocating special obligations have (yet) been established, there is systematic unclarity about whether one can speak of violators, and not just contingent uncertainty about who they might be. If it is not in principle clear where claims should be lodged, appeals to supposed universal rights to goods or services, including welfare, are mainly rhetoric, which proclaim 'manifesto' rights against unspecified others.[8] This is not, of course, an argument to

---

[7] For example, there are many conceivable ways in which systems of taxation, insurance and welfare provision could set up specific forms of rights to income, employment, housing, health care or education for all, by allocating the relevant obligations to particular agents and agencies. Systems of universal *institutionalized* rights to goods, income, or services with distributed counterpart obligations, are both conceivable and coherent. Moreover, such rights have been at least partly achieved both in the welfare states of Western Europe and in the countries of formerly existing socialism. Alternative versions of these rights *may* be realizable with fewer conditionalities and reduced dependence and bureaucracy for recipients by establishing rights in other ways, for example by relying on voucher or basic income systems, and they have been established in narrower domains by relying on traditional social structures.

[8] For the phrase 'manifesto right' see Joel Feinberg, 'The Nature and Value of Rights' in his *Rights, Justice and the Bounds of Liberty* (Princeton University Press, 1980), pp. 143–58.

show that there can be no universal rights to goods or services. It is an argument to show that they would have to be a particular sort of right whose counterpart obligations were distributed according to one or another institutional scheme, hence strictly speaking a special right, and that their vindication as well as their enforcement would have to justify institutional structures as well as more abstract principles.

Proclamations of universal 'rights' to goods or services without attention to the need to justify and establish institutions that identify corresponding obligation-bearers may seem bitter mockery to the poor and needy, for whom these rights matter most. When advocates of Human Rights proclaim universal rights to food or to work or to welfare, yet fail to show who has corresponding obligations, or where claims of right or redress may be lodged, they hurl a weapon that may boomerang. *At best* a premature rhetoric of rights *may* have political point and impact. An appeal to the 'manifesto rights' of the sort promulgated in Charters and Declarations invokes and highlights ideals that *may* guide agitation, politics and legislation in a quest for institutionalized, claimable rights.[9] The resonating ideal of Human Rights, as formerly of the Rights of Man, *may* galvanize people who once conceived of themselves as mere subjects, entitled only to petition the powers that be for relief from their miseries. They *may* come to conceive of themselves as citizens, or as citizens-to-be, who can insist that justice is violated and claim what is owed to them. But *at worst* a premature rhetoric of rights can inflate expectations while masking a lack of claimable entitlements.

Even in the best case, when a proleptic rhetoric of rights helps political action and reform, universal rights to goods and services and the corresponding obligations to provide them cannot be antecedently identifiable in the same way that liberty rights and their corresponding obligations are antecedently identifiable. Unlike liberty rights, universal rights to goods and services do not simply await a better system of (legal, institutional) enforcement.

---

[9] This optimistic view of the value of manifesto rights is taken by some international lawyers, who hope to use the meagre resources of Charters and Declarations, and of treaties that cite them, as a basis for arguing towards the counterpart obligations. See, for example, Philip Alston, 'International Law and the Human Right to Food' in P. Alston and K. Tomasevski, eds., *The Right to Food* (Dordrecht, Nijhoff, 1984), pp. 9–68: 'The right to food is already an integral part of the existing structure of international law', p. 13.

Without institutions, supposed universal rights to goods or services are radically incomplete. To institutionalize them is not just to secure the 'backing' of the law and the courts, but to define and allocate obligations to contribute and provide the relevant goods and services, and so to fix the very shape of these rights and obligations.

The contrast between universal liberty rights and universal rights to goods and services, including above all universal rights to needed goods and services ('welfare' rights), is reflected in, indeed structures, many contemporary political struggles. The sharp legitimation crises that afflict state welfare arrangements in so many developed countries today contrast vividly with the relatively uncontentious status (if frequent violation) of universal liberty rights. Whereas liberty rights and their corresponding universal obligations fall on all if on any, universal rights to goods and services can only be realized by establishing one of many differing possible sets of burdensome special relationships. An account of the content as well as the allocation of obligations to provide those goods and services will take on a definite shape only as the structure of a specific scheme is fixed. All that could be known in advance is that, should a (just) scheme be devised, somebody or other will need to bear yet-to-be specified obligations. Nobody would know what their obligations were; or for whom they ought to provide what or when they should act, or at how much cost to themselves.

The two perspectives of agency and of recipience do not then provide equivalent views even of matters widely thought of as questions of justice. The perspective of rights provides a perilous way of formulating ethical requirements since it leaves many possible obligations dangling in the air. In a way, it is an advantage of the perspective of rights that it allows claims to be formulated even when the bearers and the content of corresponding obligations are unspecified; in another way it is a weakness. It is a strength insofar as it provides a ready rhetoric for political change and agitation, and may allow leverage for persuading governments who have (perhaps heedlessly or cynically) ratified treaties, proclamations and conventions that promulgate various rights that this must constrain their action. It is a weakness insofar as it offers a way of avoiding careful articulation of the structure of the claimed rights and of their justification, and tempts many to settle for rhetoric not matched or readily matchable by performance.

The perspective of obligations has the counterpart disadvantages and advantages. Its evident disadvantage is that appeals to the Duties of Mankind have less political resonance than appeals to Human Rights. Entitlements have more immediate charm than duties. It is hard to articulate and sobering to realize who will have to contribute what for whom at what cost if significant rights to certain goods and services – say, those that would guarantee basic standards of welfare even within a rich state – are to be established. The advantage of beginning with obligations is that taking this perspective requires one to be more realistic, clear and honest about burdens, their justification and their allocation. If the content of obligations of justice can be identified, they will have implications for action, whether or not a particular society has gone far towards building them into institutions; and an understanding of obligations which have counterpart rights can help in outlining a blueprint for institution building. Claimants who do not know who bears the counterpart obligations to rights they claim may grasp thin air; by contrast, obligation-bearers who are not bound to specific claimants can nevertheless make the construction of institutions that allocate tasks and identify claimants the first step towards meeting their obligations.

There are more general reasons for thinking that differences between the perspectives of agency and of recipience are important even within what is usually thought of as the domain of justice. They arise because institutionalization disrupts any simple match between obligations and rights, even for liberty rights. A seemingly unitary obligation may be matched by sets of rights held by various parties; a seemingly unitary right by sets of obligations held by various parties. The symmetry of rights and obligations is evident only in the case of *universal liberty rights, considered in the abstract*: if A has the liberty right to do x, then everyone will have the obligation to allow A to do x. However, even in this case, the symmetry fades when institutions of enforcement are brought into the picture: A's right to do x may then be matched not only by others' obligations to allow A to do x, but by the obligations of enforcers to ensure that A is not prevented from doing x. Institutionalization disrupts any simple symmetry of rights and obligations by dispersing obligations, and sometimes rights, across a plurality of agents, officials and institutions.

Symmetry is also incomplete in the case of *special rights*, where

A's right to x is structured by special relationships or specific institutions, and will usually be matched by connected obligations that fall on various persons. For example, a seemingly simple right to have goods which have been purchased handed over may be matched by connected obligations held not only by the vendor but, for example, by the vendor's employees and by law-enforcement agencies.

As already noted, symmetry is still less evident in the case of *distributively universal special rights*,[10] which can come into existence only where comprehensive institutions are established which assign special obligations to many officials and individuals in ways that make their cumulative effect universal within some domain: for example, universal rights to subsistence or security even within a state might have to be matched by connected obligations held by various welfare and tax officials, as well as by citizens' obligations to submit to taxation and to law enforcement.

5.3 REQUIRED VIRTUES: OBLIGATIONS WITHOUT RIGHTS

There may be other ethical requirements that lie beyond the domain of justice, for which the discrepancy between the perspectives of agency and of recipience are even more important. For example, many of the social virtues have been taken seriously in part because they were thought of as *required*, although they were not thought of as reflected in counterpart rights against those on whom the requirement falls. If there are ethical requirements that lack counterpart rights, the choice between the perspectives of recipience and of agency will be of great importance. Whether there are such required obligations will be discussed in Chapter 7; their structure can be outlined without establishing whether it is exemplified.

Some obligations without corresponding rights could be embedded in special relationships: *special obligations without rights* (if there are any) would constitute elements of certain roles, relation-

---

[10] There is no contradiction here. The right is *special* in virtue of performance being claimable from an obligation-bearing agent or agency with whom the right-holder has some specified relationship – e.g. the obligation-bearer is an official in the appropriate institution. It is *universal* in virtue of the fact that each, hence all, can have such a relationship with some obligation-bearing agent or agency.

ships and ways of life. Examples might be the characteristic requirements of certain roles: the attentiveness of a parent, the patience of someone working with handicapped adults, the trustworthiness of an accountant. However, other role-related traits of character might be ethically questionable: the honour of a thief, the strictness of a teacher, the zeal of an investigative reporter. These special obligations have been particularly emphasized by many particularists.

Other obligations without corresponding rights might not be embedded in any specific role, relationship or way of life: they would be *universal obligations without rights*. Many important virtues have traditionally been construed in this way. For example, honesty and fairness, beneficence and courage have been thought of as required of all, and as holding across many roles and activities, although lacking counterpart rights. The possibility and the importance of universal obligations without counterpart rights are often overlooked both by those particularists who emphasize (perhaps over-emphasize) the thought that virtues may be linked to roles and traditions, and by those universalists who insist that everything required is also owed, hence a matter of justice.

Yet the plausible thought that certain traditions and ways of life provide hospitable *contexts* for certain sorts of virtues, and not for others, does not show that traditions or cultures are *constitutive* of virtue. Far from being constitutive of virtue, roles and traditions may celebrate and demand idiosyncratic conceptions of certain virtues; they may champion spurious virtues and even vices; and they may be blind or hostile to important virtues. Traditions may be cruel or cold, fanatical and intolerant, oppressive or manipulative; they may narrow and distort the expression of some virtues, and exaggerate the importance of others; they may link specific virtues too rigidly to social status – witness Meno's confident alignment of the two.

Historicist writers often remind us that traditions grow and change, and have internal resources for self-criticism and self-renewal. This charitable and cheerful reminder provides limited comfort. Internal criticism and renewal may indeed improve a tradition by its internal standards, or by some of its internal standards; equally it may worsen and narrow a tradition, both in terms of external standards and in terms of other of its internal standards.[11] On the other hand, if we take a more generous view of the interpretive potential latent in each tradition, so think that renewal of traditions is also responsive to wider standards, we move away from a conception of the identity and integrity of traditions which would make each constitutive of virtue and vice, and the arbiter for those who live within it.[12] This move rejects the thought that actual historical traditions are constitutive of virtue, and allows that they too can be judged, praised or criticized in the light of less restricted ethical principles, provided that those less restricted ethical principles can be vindicated.

A particularist understanding of virtue has not been the only, or even the dominant, one even among those who have made virtue their basic, or one of their basic, ethical concerns. Plato, Aristotle, Aquinas, and many later overt and covert perfectionists, all offered non-historicist accounts of the virtues.[13] So did early modern writers, including Kant. None of them tied virtue solely to role and status or to particular societies or traditions. They often pointed to *examples* of virtues that were paradigmatically expressed in specific sorts of roles, relationships or 'lives', but did not *define* virtues by reference to any of these. On these classical (and latently still influential) views, virtue (like justice), can be identified independently of its historically specific embodiments.

However, if virtues are to be independent of their embodiments, they must be specified by describing the *types of activity* by which those with a given virtue will express it. They must then be thought of in terms of the *act descriptions* and *principles* that virtuous people embody in their lives and display in their action, as *dispositions* or *capacities* to act, respond and feel in determinate ways.

The difference between virtue and justice may then be not that justice is principled and virtue unprincipled, nor that justice is

---

[11] See Robert Stern, 'MacIntyre and Historicism' in John Horton and Susan Mendus, eds., *After MacIntyre: Critical Perspectives on the Work of Alasdair MacIntyre* (Cambridge, Polity Press, 1994), pp. 146–60 for a defence of internal criticism as defining progress without reference to any external vantage point, in terms of its power to resolve problems. However, changes and accumulations of changes may also generate new problems and destroy the power to solve some that were previously resolvable.

[12] A further reason why it is uncertain how far internal critique can go is that the individuation of traditions and cultures, hence of their internal critical resources, is uncertain and controversial. Is traditional Mafia culture internal to traditional Christian culture? Or distinct?

[13] This is not to deny that there have been many particularist appropriations of classical writers, and especially of Aristotle. See section 1.1.

always and virtue never a matter of requirement. Rather it may be that justice is not only required but owed, hence claimable and waivable, while virtuous action, even if required, is not owed, hence neither claimable nor waivable, and in many cases not even tied to any particular role, or status or office. If certain virtues are required, they will be a matter of obligation or duty, but will simply lack counterpart rights.[14] For example, if helpfulness to others is required, but is not owed, and there are no rights to be helped, the virtue of helpfulness would be manifest in a life informed by a principle of helping where one can and where it is needed, although, by hypothesis, in this case nobody would have a right to specific sorts of help from specified others.[15] A principle of helpfulness would define an obligation whose expression not only may but must vary hugely: yet helpfulness might be a profoundly important virtue. So too might other required virtues: they might be or provide the basis for required activity of many sorts, even if they were owed neither to all nor to specified others, and were not restricted to any special relationship. Early modern writers who spoke of *virtues* as *duties*, or of *duties of virtue* did not mistakenly assimilate virtue to right or to justice; they also did not lose sight of the possibility that there may be significant universal obligations that lack counterpart rights.

If there are obligations that lack corresponding rights, they will not be what the advocates of 'welfare rights' are looking for, precisely *because they offer no basis for claiming others' action or assistance as a matter of right*. If there are universal welfare rights, they will, as suggested in section 5.2 above, be vindicable only by arguments for certain sorts of institutionalized, distributed obligations. Nevertheless, obligations without rights, if there are any, will hardly be trivial: they may form and inform lives, institutions and societies with profound effects. Yet obligations without rights, like

[14] Virtues which are required are often classified as 'imperfect' obligations, thus distinguishing them both from perfect obligations which are claimable and owed, and from optional virtues which are in no way required. See T. D. Campbell, 'Perfect and Imperfect Duties', *The Modern Schoolman*, 102 (1975), 185–94; Onora O'Neill, 'Duties and Virtues' in A. Phillips Griffiths, ed., *Ethics*, RIP supplementary volume 35 (Cambridge University Press, 1994), pp. 107–20; see also below sections 5.4 and 7.3.

[15] Like other examples in this chapter, this one is hypothetical. The content of principles of justice and of virtue will be discussed in the next two chapters. Illustrations are useful in presenting the diversity of structure of obligation, but this diversity is independent of the particular illustrations.

obligations whose corresponding rights take shape only when institutions are built, are readily overlooked in writing that begins from the perspective of recipience.

Practical reasoning that assigns priority to rights and to recipience rather than to obligation and to action is an unnecessary and damaging, if distinctive, feature of contemporary writing on ethics. Its predominance in universalist writing is a major reason why justice and virtue have come to be seen as competing rather than as complementary orientations to life. For once rights rather than obligations are treated as the basic deontic category, both obligations which lack corresponding rights unless institutions are built, and those which lack corresponding rights altogether are quite simply hidden from view. The marginalization not only of rights to goods and services but of virtue by many who take justice seriously and base justice on rights is indeed no accident. It is built into the very starting point of those who assign priority to rights. However, the source of the trouble lies not in their focus on justice, or on action and principles of action, or even on universal principles or rules, but in a habit of looking at action and indeed more broadly at activity primarily from the perspective of the recipient rather than of the agent, so losing contact with the full range of deontic structures and with certain possibilities for practical reasoning.

This diagnosis is supported by the fact that those earlier writers on justice who did not insist on the priority of the perspective of rights integrated accounts of justice and of the virtues. Locke, Rousseau and Kant, for example, whom contemporary advocates of rights-based accounts of justice regard as their intellectual ancestors, begin not with rights but with Natural Law or duty, and discuss justice and virtue in tandem. So do naturalists such as Hume and Mill, who also do not give the perspective of rights and recipience priority.[16] The simple and seemingly innocent intellectual strategy of looking at action and indeed at all activity from the perspective of recipients rather than of agents has proved sufficient to cripple the capacity of action and principle-based ethics to give any account of the virtues.

[16] The particular accounts of the virtues these writers offer vary greatly. What is significant for this general conclusion is simply the ubiquitous assumption that justice and virtue are complementary orientations to life.

The disabling results of this intellectual strategy, with the consequent narrow focus on rights-based views of justice, explains some of the appeal of virtue ethics, which ostensibly celebrates the full range of ethical activity to be found in particular communities. It is hardly surprising that many who doubt the adequacy of consequentialist ethics, and who are worried by the narrowness of rights-based reasoning about justice, have come to feel that only an ethics that concentrates on virtue provides an alternative that does not need unattainable metaphysical foundations.

Yet, in taking this direction, some contemporary friends of virtue and community have gained ground only in order to lose it. They adopted a vantage point from which the importance of certain virtues in certain contexts could be displayed, but to do so they often accepted particularist approaches which disabled their accounts of justice and severely limited their accounts of virtue. These disabilities are stridently displayed by writers who manifest simple hostility to human rights, who offer no serious discussion of justice or its borders, who dismiss justice as an ethically inadequate, 'male' concern, or who ignore the import and import- ance of the institutions of the public domain (state, economy, society) in favour of celebrating the caring virtues of domesticity and intimacy. These are disastrous limitations in any ethical vision that aspires to relevance to the contemporary world. So too is the diminished vision of virtue which confines it to specific roles and traditions.

5.4 TAKING OBLIGATIONS SERIOUSLY

If this distancing between concern for justice and for the virtues is to be reversed, it is important not to begin from a point that obscures either. It may be a dangerous strategy to begin with rights, on the assumption that the perspective can simply be broadened once important issues of justice have been settled. Indeed, some positions that take rights as basic are formulated in ways that strictly, if perhaps inadvertently, preclude any account of virtue. For example, certain libertarian accounts of rights actually rule out obligations without corresponding rights. They interpret justice as a matter of securing the greatest possible liberty compatible with like liberty for all, and take it that the maximal set of liberty rights must incorporate a 'right to liberty' that entitles each to do anything that violates no rights.[17] Obligations without counterpart rights are thereby rendered impossible. Acts are exhaustively partitioned into those forbidden (because rights-violating) and those permitted (as elements of each agent's rights). The supposed 'right to liberty' pre-emptively occupies the only possible 'space' in which obligations without rights could make their demands.

Other libertarian writers do not argue for a pre-emptive 'right to liberty'. Although they insist on a strong account of liberty rights, and take it that this shows that any state-enforced welfare system must be unjust (since it would demand 'confiscation' of property or 'enslavement' of tax-payers, so would violate basic liberty rights), they ostensibly leave room for an account of other ethical concerns, including an account of the virtues, as do other non-libertarian writers on justice.

Yet in the end merely 'leaving room' for an account of the virtues does not take seriously the possibility that some virtues may be a matter of obligation. Liberal writers on justice can 'leave room', yet display attitudes ranging from neglect to deep hostility to the very virtues for which they ostensibly leave it.[18] Some libertarians might dispute this charge on the grounds that they prize what they characterize as 'voluntary action', and in particular what they oddly call 'voluntary giving', and see maximal liberty rights as securing space and opportunity for deeply ethical action of this sort. Some libertarian writers speak glowingly of charity, in the sense of philanthropy, whose very context would be destroyed by any enforced redistribution or enforced dependence (such as that supposedly created by welfare rights), although they worry sporadically that philanthropy too may create a culture of dependency.[19] Yet the characterizations they give of the ethical

---

[17] Otherwise the liberties would be less than maximal. See Hillel Steiner, 'Individual Liberty'; but see also his *An Essay on Rights*. For criticisms of this strategy of argument see Onora O'Neill, 'The Most Extensive Liberty', *Proceedings of the Aristotelian Society*, New Series 80 (1979–80), 45–59, and Charles Taylor, 'What's Wrong with Negative Liberty?' in his *Philosophy and the Human Sciences: Philosophical Papers*, vol. II (Cambridge University Press, 1985), pp. 211–29.

[18] The obvious example is the failure of libertarian writing to give a serious account of the social virtues. By way of examples, consider Robert Nozick, *Anarchy, State, and Utopia* (New York, Columbia University Press, 1974); Steiner, *An Essay on Rights* and Judith Jarvis Thomson, *Rights, Restitution and Risk: Essays in Moral Theory* (Cambridge, Mass., Harvard University Press, 1986).

[19] See various contributions in Ellen Frankel Paul et al., *Beneficence, Philanthropy and the Public Good* (Oxford, Blackwell, 1987).

significance of action not required by respect for others' rights is extraordinarily flimsy. Some, for example, speak of charitable giving as 'supererogatory' – as going beyond all duty. Yet they offer no account of what might make such action not merely unrequired but good. Far from showing that charity, or other action that used to be taken to exemplify obligations that lacked corresponding rights, is supererogatory, it has been shown only that it is permissible. The argument appears to lead no further than the conclusion that philanthropy, and perhaps some other elements of traditional social virtues, are among the many permissible uses of the area of discretion which liberty rights afford.[20] All that is actually established of such action is that it does not violate rights and that it is chosen;[21] the basis for thinking that it is good is never revealed.

Within frameworks that give priority to the perspective of recipience, so make rights the fundamental ethical category, it is hard to show how act-types that cannot be claimed as a matter of right can be either good or obligatory. This conclusion is deeply unsettling. The remarkable series of historical transformations that have reduced charity, once the greatest of Christian virtues, to merely permitted philanthropy, are endorsed, but not in the least illuminated by current discussions of charity by liberal theorists of all sorts. A strange alliance between libertarians who see nothing but liberty rights and social justice liberals, who mistakenly fear that acknowledging the importance of imperfect obligations would show that protection against poverty and other forms of vulnerability is *only* a matter of virtue, has steered those current thinkers most concerned with justice away from all concern with charity and with most other social virtues. The demotion of charity and other social virtues in work on justice is a consequence of relying on the framework of rights-based thought, which allows in the end only for obligations with corresponding rights and for discretionary action. Although it sounds reassuring to say that some discretionary action

---

[20] This impression is reinforced by some of the strangely coy characterizations that libertarians offer of the unrequired activities they ostensibly admire. For example, action that goes beyond duties to respect rights is sometimes characterized as 'decent' or 'nice' or as a matter of 'not being naughty'. See Thomson, *Rights Restitution and Risk*, pp. 13–18, 58, 64.

[21] Onora O'Neill, 'The Great Maxims of Justice and of Charity' in *Constructions of Reason*. For further discussion of these points see section 5.6 below.

is virtuous or supererogatory, no explanation of these terms is generally offered by those whose framework makes rights the basic category of ethics. No reasons are given to explain what it is that makes giving to others better than not giving to them, provided no rights are violated. Nothing shows why indifference or self-centredness should not be life-projects for liberals, providing, of course, that others' rights are respected; and no doubt they often are. The poverty of these ways of thinking about ethical relations cannot readily be remedied by tacking an unexplicated notion of the supererogatory onto an account of rights.

Some clue to the difficulties we find here can be seen in the very terms of debate. When helpfulness or charity or other 'virtuous' action are dubbed 'supererogatory' – going beyond obligation – by those who take rights as ethically basic, it appears that they have simply taken for granted that any obligation has matching rights. They blandly exclude the possibility of obligations without corresponding rights from consideration: they see nothing between obligations with corresponding rights and what they construe as optional supererogation.[22] Yet older discussions of obligations often took obligations without rights as seriously as they took those that have corresponding rights, and rather more seriously than some of them took supererogation. As we have seen, it is no mystery why such obligations have vanished from the ken of rights theorists. Those who begin their thinking with rights must take account of obligations which are the counterpart of rights, but in order to take account of obligations without counterpart rights they would have, so to speak, to reverse perspective and explain that the obligations that are the corollaries of the rights from which their theory began are somehow supplemented by obligations which have no such foundation. Just as Nelson avoided seeing his Admiral's order not to engage battle by raising his telescope to his blind eye, so discussions in ethics and politics can readily avoid seeing obligations without counterpart rights if they begin with rights. They can bring these obligations into focus only by an awkward swerve of thought, which they would not need to make if they had started out from the

---

[22] For example, Rawls often speaks of virtues as supererogatory, cf. *A Theory of Justice*, e.g. p. 192. For further discussion of supererogation see section 7.5 below and Marcia Baron, 'Kantian Obligations and Supererogation', *Journal of Philosophy*, 84 (1987), 237–62. It may be possible, and I shall argue necessary, to provide a proper account of imperfect obligations if a plausible account of supererogation is to be given; but they are not the same thing.

perspective of agency and obligations, and then distinguished obligations which do and do not have corresponding rights.

Since the distinction between obligations with and without counterpart rights is a fundamental and structural one within any account of obligations, it helps to have terms to mark it. The traditional terms *perfect obligation* and *imperfect obligation* can usefully be revived for this purpose. These terms have been used to mark a number of distinctions. For example, some writers call obligations which are relatively determinate 'perfect obligations'; others reserve the term for obligations which ought or may be enforced by law. The varied usage is not surprising. The root meaning of 'imperfect obligation' is simply 'obligation that is in some way incomplete'. There are many ways in which obligations can be incompletely specified, and no reasons for thinking that all forms of incompleteness will coincide.[23]

However, there are reasons for taking the distinction between obligations with and without counterpart rights as particularly important, structural forms of incompleteness, and for holding that other interpretations of the terms 'perfect' and 'imperfect' are less significant. For example, the distinction between obligations which specify what is required in more and in less determinate ways is a matter of degree, and varies with the level of specificity and institutional context assumed in describing a particular obligation. The distinction between obligations that may (or ought to) be enforced and those which may not (or ought not to) be enforced by various forms of legal or social discipline or power is hardly likely to be ethically fundamental. If certain obligations ought or ought not to be enforced in some but not in other ways, this will presumably be because they differ in other, more basic features.

In retrospect it can seem surprising that a tight preoccupation with the priority of rights has been so strong a feature of action-centred ethics and of political philosophy during the last twenty-five years. That grip may reflect several factors: the political significance of the Human Rights Movement; misplaced fears that if rights were not taken as basic, then accounts of social and economic justice could not be given; perhaps better placed fears that no adequate account of justice could be built within

---

[23] On the differing distinction marked by the terms 'perfect' and 'imperfect' see Campbell, 'Perfect and Imperfect Duties'.

result-based ethical reasoning. It also surely reflects the prestige of specifically legal models of practical reasoning, within which the perspective of recipience and of rights indeed mirrors that of agency and obligation.

Yet, given that the two perspectives of agency and of recipience are not equivalent beyond the domains of law and of comparably well-defined institutional relationships, we must choose between them. However, the choice is easy: no advantage is lost, and some may be gained, by treating the category of obligation as funda-mental. Since the perspectives of agency and recipience are equivalent across the domain of obligations with corresponding rights, it is not necessary to assign any priority to the perspective of recipience and rights in order to have available a perspective which takes full account of them. A constructivist account of ethics, I believe, may be able to offer an account both of perfect and of imperfect obligations, and can also confirm the older traditions which identified the former with justice and the latter with required virtues.

By contrast, the narrower perspective of rights may restrict our focus beyond the domain of justice in ways that matter. If there are imperfect obligations, we handicap ourselves by insisting on a perspective in which they are hidden. We risk entertaining not only the illusion that there can be nothing between respect for rights and action that goes beyond all duty, but the more dangerous thought that action that is not required by respect for rights can be no more than a matter of individual discretion: a way of filling in the 'space' beyond ethics with optional, preferred activities and chosen 'life-projects'. In taking rights as prior we fail to take obligations seriously.

5.5 EMBODIED OBLIGATIONS

The structural differences between obligations that have and that lack corresponding rights surface in their embodiments in insti-tutions, relationships and lives. Although the examples used in this section must also be hypothetical, since no principles of obligations have yet been established, they can illustrate the structural claims advanced in previous sections of the chapter, and the classification of obligations which it permits.

The most fundamental of the structural differences between

different sorts of ethical requirement that must be taken into account if obligations are taken seriously is that between perfect and imperfect obligations. *Perfect obligations* (if there are any) can hold only between identifiable obligation-bearers and identifiable right-holders. *Imperfect obligations* (if there are any) will belong to identifiable obligation-bearers, but there will be no corresponding right-holders.

This deep structural difference means that the two sorts of principle of obligation can best be embodied or institutionalized in differing ways. Moreover, any account of the embodiment of obligations has to take cognizance of the contrast, discussed in section 5.1 above, between *universal obligations*, which all can hold, and *special obligations*, which grow out of specific roles, institutions, relationships or the like.

Perfect obligations divide into universal obligations that can be owed to and performed for all others and special obligations that are owed to and are performed for specified others. *Universal perfect obligations* can impose no positive tasks; they will be the counterparts of liberty rights. For example, if there are universal, perfect obligations not to kill or coerce, these may be owed by each to all, and if so are equivalent to counterpart universal rights against each and all not to be killed or coerced. Such obligations can be institutionalized in legal and political systems that define positive rights and provide for the adjudication of violations of rights and for the enforcement of such adjudications. When this is done the obligations corresponding to the rights not to be killed or coerced will often be spread across a number of agents, officials and institutions. Even universal perfect obligations are helped and supported by congruent virtues: their principles can, as a secondary matter, be embodied in social institutions and in individual characters which reinforce their primary embodiments. A legal order may gain support from forms of social solidarity and traditions of fair play; it may be undermined by traditions of greed or cruelty.

By contrast, *special perfect obligations* require social structures or practices that connect specific agents to specified recipients of action, to whom they owe and for whom they are bound to perform, who are the holders of the equivalent special rights. For example, specific institutions such as states, markets, firms and families define, create and enable agents to create numerous special relationships within which countless special perfect obligations with their counterpart rights will link particular obligation-bearers with particular right-holders. Some special perfect obligations may be 'distributively' universal (e.g. welfare rights within some restricted domain); others are defined by episodic or continuing special relationships between obligation-bearers and right-holders (e.g. contracts, leases, promises, family ties). Since special obligations always presuppose special relationships by which agents are allocated to recipients, they are always subject to two levels of ethical vindication or query. Both the ethical claims that arise within special relationships and those of the background practices, institutions and relationships that establish or enable special relationships can be questioned.

The embodiment of imperfect obligations must take rather different forms. *Universal imperfect obligations*, like all imperfect obligations, lack counterpart rights, so unlike universal perfect obligations will be enactable by all but not for all; *a fortiori* they cannot be claimed by each from all. An imperfect, hence unclaimable, obligation that is held by all may then require action by each, but will not specify for whom or to whom that required action is to be directed. For this reason some universal imperfect obligations will be most readily embodied not in relationships between agents and recipients but in agents' characters, and can be thought of as required virtues of those agents. The range of circumstances and relationships in which virtuous action can be elicited and expressed cannot be foreseen except in the most general terms.

Virtues have often been praised and prized precisely because they are *portable ethical characteristics*, which can be carried over from one situation or relationship or stage of life to another: they are thought of as apt for the unexpected as well as for the expected turns life takes. No doubt, certain traits of character are closely associated with certain traditions, and some traits that seemed virtues in one stage of life or history seemed less valuable, or even vicious, at other stages.[24] However, for many the merit of many virtues is that they are *not* bound too closely to specific situations. The point and merit of being kind or generous would be far less if either were so bound. Such virtues are required, but their particular instances are not. When and where and to whom kindness and

---

[24] Consider the various revaluations of values mentioned in section 1.2 above.

generosity are expressed is a matter that has to vary and cannot be required.

A recurrent worry that people have about their own, and about others', characters is that they might turn out to be bound to context, so that, for example, without its familiar support carefully nurtured generosity or kindness will fade or corrupt. These concerns show how important it is to consider not only the psychological dispositions of individuals, but also the socially effective capabilities and practices that traditions of virtue foster in individuals. In recognizing the importance of good character we do not deny, but rather affirm, the importance of institutions and traditions which inculcate, transmit and sustain virtues as well as congruent support and discipline. The individual and social embodiments of virtue are mutually supporting.

Character and tradition are not, however, the sole locus of principles of imperfect obligations. The connections that historicist writers on the virtues also draw between specific roles and relationships and certain virtues have their distinctive importance in an account not of universal but of *special imperfect obligations*. Although imperfect obligations do not, by definition, require the clearly defined relations between agents and recipients that are essential for all perfect obligations (whether universal or special), many sorts of relationship provide particularly rich, or particularly poor, opportunities for the practice of certain special imperfect obligations, hence for certain virtues. When we think of devotion as a virtue of family life, of specific sorts of care as a virtue that responds to human suffering or frailty, or of self-possession as a virtue for weathering misplaced hostility, we think of these virtues as particularly suited to embodiment in some sorts of social roles and relationships, and as more marginal or less useful in others.

This perhaps suggests why some have thought of certain virtues *solely* as features of special relationships. But while it is true that certain relationships (e.g. those between relatives or friends) provide special opportunities for trust, kindness and care, and others (e.g. those of commerce and collegiality) for honesty and fairness that go beyond strict entitlement, these virtues are important beyond their characteristic contexts. In addition, it is notorious that many special relationships also provide special opportunities for unkindness and neglect, for deceit and betrayal. If the very relationships that provide preferred contexts for various virtues also provide fertile fields for the contrasting vices, these contexts cannot be constitutive of those virtues.

The evident links between certain social contexts and relation-ships and the practice of certain virtues in no way show that those virtues are only or generally bound to those specific situations. The historicist tendency to identify virtue very closely with its specific and historically contingent embodiments is not only unconvincing but ethically risky. Formation of character matters because it may help agents to act with a measure of independence from insti-tutions, ways of life and relationships. Right formation of character provides a limited insurance policy against some of the common risks and variability of lives. As with other insurance policies, some sorts of character formation turn out with hindsight to have been unneeded. The fortunes and misfortunes of life may bring many or few opportunities to reveal all of the virtues, or vices, that have been acquired; sometimes they will swamp even deeply ingrained virtues. Those who turn out to lead secure and sheltered lives may find little opportunity for many sorts of courage; those who lead solitary lives may find so little opportunity for solidarity that they can hope to manage without much of it. Lives of intense public activity may crowd out opportunities for intimate sympathy and attentiveness to others; lives of terror or of utter deprivation may stunt many capacities to act well. However, insurance policies are not usually pointless. Ordinary lives and their most typical varieties of association offer ample opportunities for most of the ordinary virtues, and of the ordinary vices; even lives lived in dire circum-stances offer some opportunities.

These familiar points bear repeating only because they are so often obscured. Whereas the asymmetry between universal obligations that are perfect and those that are imperfect – between liberty rights and states of character – is readily apparent, the distance between perfect and imperfect special obligations is often overlooked because a single context can provide a locus for both. In many associations and relationships participants take it that they are bound *both* by claims others can make *and* by further principles on which they ought to act, although no other is entitled to such action. The fact that within any special relationship another can be identified as having a claim to some sorts of act in no way shows that everything an agent ought to do to or for that other can be claimed as entitlement. We know this well enough when we reflect on the way in which one party to some relationship may press demands on the other, which may seem nearly reasonable, and hard to resist, yet are simultaneously felt to be excessive and in particular to go beyond any entitlement. Much of the delicacy of being a good parent or spouse, friend or colleague, is a matter of ensuring that action that is not a matter of entitlement is not so regarded, and that when given it is understood by both parties as no mere entitlement.

These distinctions between the four categories of obligations discussed and the types of structure in which they can most readily be embodied can be illustrated by some quite conventional views of the varied obligations of parents to children for whom they are responsible.[25] (Once again the illustrations are offered without specific vindication: if none emerges, the structural points would need different illustrations.)

Good parents usually think they are bound in *many* ways to their children. They will take it that they owe their children (and others) certain obligations which they also owe all others, to whose observance their children (like others) have rights: for example, they will take it that they are obliged not to injure. These are the *universal perfect obligations*, which abusing parents, and other child abusers, violate. They will also take it that they owe their children care and support, which their particular children, but not all children, let alone all others, have a right to receive from them: these are the *special perfect obligations* that neglectful parents violate. They will also take it that they owe their children, as they owe others, a measure of courtesy and concern: these *universal imperfect obligations* are virtues that rigid or fanatical or cold people lack, and whose lack rigid, fanatical or cold parents inflict specifically on their children, even when they scrupulously observe all their children's rights. Finally, good parents will take it that they owe their children certain sorts of love, attention and support which they do not owe to all, which are quite specific to the relationship to the child, but to which their children have no right. Certain sorts of fun, warmth and encouragement might come under this heading: these are *special imperfect obligations* which parents see as part of what is required of good parents, and which may be neglected even by parents who both observe their children's universal and special

---

[25] Cf. Onora O'Neill, 'Children's Rights and Children's Lives', *Ethics*, 99 (1988), 445–63.

rights scrupulously and accord their children the same help and concern they habitually show all others – but no more.

These various types of obligations can be represented diagrammatically:

TYPES OF DUTY OR OBLIGATION

UNIVERSAL

PERFECT: Held by all, owed to all; counterpart liberty rights; embodied above all in legal and economic systems

IMPERFECT: Held by all, owed to none; no counterpart rights; embodied above all in character and expressed in varied situations

SPECIAL

PERFECT: Held by some; owed to specified others; counterpart special rights; fixed by structure of specific transactions and relationships; can be distributively universal given appropriate institutions

IMPERFECT: Held by some, owed to none; no counterpart rights; embodied in ethos of specific relationships and practices and in characters; often, but not exclusively, expressed in action within special relationships

This classification of duties or obligations will not include all those traits of character that have been thought of as virtues at one or another time. In particular, it will not include traits of character which it is good to have, and are often spoken of as virtues, but which are optional rather than required. There may be many aspects of good lives and styles of life whose governing principles are not a matter of requirement. An analysis of deontic structures will cover only those virtues whose basic principles are not optional. However, an account of virtues that are duties provides, I shall argue, a convincing framework for an account of certain social virtues, which are indeed duties as well as virtues, as well as a promising context for looking both at supererogation and at optional excellences (see chapter 7).

This chapter has offered an account of different *structures of obligation*, and provided hypothetical illustrations of differing types of obligation. To come any closer to justice or to virtue an account of the content and justification of some of their principles is needed. This account lies ahead. The next two chapters will aim to establish some principles both of justice and of virtue, which can provide guidelines for constructing just and virtuous institutions and practices and for leading just and virtuous lives.

CHAPTER 6

Content I: principles for
all: towards justice

Can abstract starting points and constructive reasoning show what makes institutions just, or characters virtuous? The last three chapters offered accounts only of the focus, of the scope and of some central, significant structural links between practical claims. They did so without relying on the metaphysical or particularist assumptions that lie behind many conceptions not only of justice and of virtue, but of practical reasoning itself. Three basic conclusions emerged. First, practical reasoning must focus on action and use intelligible categories, so must engage with (more and less) abstract act descriptions which can be embodied in varied universal principles. However, universality in this merely formal sense is a meagre matter, which does not define a determinate domain of ethical consideration, let alone mandate uniform action or lack of concern for differences. Second, agents have reason to extend their ethical consideration to those others whom their proposed action already takes for granted, hence, in our world on some occasions, have reason to think of the scope of that consideration as more-or-less cosmopolitan. Third, the principles that are of first importance for ethical reasoning formulate constraints or requirements, hence also provide the basis for obligations and (in some cases) rights, although other ethically significant principles might formulate recommendations or exhortations, condemnations or warnings.

However, no specific principles of any sort have been vindicated. If constructivist reasoning is to lead towards accounts of justice or of virtue, it will have to justify at least some substantive principles without relying on the tried, trusted but untrustworthy strategies that have led to antagonistic conceptions of the two.[1] Attempts to

---

[1] Untrustworthy because universalist approaches that require metaphysical backing fail if it is not available, and because particularist strategies presuppose the merits of ways of life they purport to establish. Cf. chapter 1.

154

do so without vindicating metaphysically demanding conceptions of persons, reason and action have often failed to reach convincing ethical conclusions; one more attempt may reasonably arouse suspicions. What conjuring trick could build much worth having out of so little?

These suspicions can be rebutted only by showing how principles of justice and of virtue are to be constructed. This chapter offers a brief and brisk constructive account of some principles of justice; the next of some principles of virtue.[2] The initial stage of construction will identify only very abstract principles, but these may be used as the framework for constructing more determinate principles, so ultimately for guiding action and policy-making and for building institutions and practices.

6.1 INCLUSIVE UNIVERSAL PRINCIPLES

Many of the recurrent suspicions raised about any ethics of principles were discussed in chapter 3. In particular the worries that universal principles will demand uniform enactment and that indeterminate principles will offer no guidance were addressed and set aside. Other worries remain.

One resilient suspicion is that ethical principles, and in particular principles of obligation, even if they could be established would be pointless, since commitment to a plurality of obligations engenders insoluble practical conflicts. A second unallayed suspicion is that any attempt to vindicate ethical principles from starting points that are too meagre and abstract, or by relying on a conception of practical reason as meagre as that of universalizability, leads nowhere. Mill put the second worry forthrightly in accusing Kant:

I cannot help referring, for illustration, to a systematic treatise by one of the most illustrious of them, the *Metaphysics of Ethics*, by Kant. This

---

[2] I offer no reasons for thinking that there is a *complete* set of principles of justice. It makes little sense to look for *complete* sets of practical principles of any sort since principles can always be reformulated, specified and disaggregated to form more general or more specific principles. The only plausible way of telling whether this account of inclusive principles of justice is adequate is to see whether they jointly provide enough to construct a convincing way of moving towards more specific principles, institutions, practices and patterns of justice and of virtue for given times and places, with their actual resources and populations and their attainable capacities and capabilities.

remarkable man, whose system of thought will long remain one of the
landmarks in the history of philosophical speculation, does, in the treatise
in question, lay down a universal first principle as the origin and ground of
moral obligation; it is this: – 'So act, that the rule on which thou actest
would admit of being adopted as a law by all rational beings.' But when he
begins to deduce from this precept any of the actual duties of morality, he
fails, almost grotesquely, to show that there would be any contradiction,
any logical (not to say physical) impossibility, in the adoption by all
rational beings of the most outrageously immoral rules of conduct. All he
shows is that the consequences of their universal adoption would be such
as no one would choose to incur.[3]

In addressing these two suspicions it is useful to begin by considering those *inclusive* principles of action whose scope extends as wide
as the full domain of ethical consideration an agent acknowledges.
Agents need at least some *inclusive principles* of action because each
of them leads a single life, whose aspects and stages are multiply
connected, so must be coordinated. It will not be enough to
approach the various spheres, segments or aspects of an acknowledged domain of ethical consideration relying *only* on a variety of
more specific principles of more restricted scope.[4] The segments
of a full domain of ethical consideration can only be organized if
some inclusive principles cover the entire scope of acknowledged
ethical consideration, and demarcate and link the restricted
segments and spheres of life within which more specific principles
are to serve. Hence those who lead their lives in the contemporary
world will need at least some inclusive basic principles whose scope
is more-or-less cosmopolitan (cf. chapter 4). Inclusive universal
principles will not merely be abstract – all descriptions, all
principles, even the most thickly formulated, are to some extent
abstract – but too abstract to incorporate the thick concepts that

---

[3] John Stuart Mill, *Utilitarianism* (1861) in *Utilitarianism, On Liberty and Other Essays*, ed. Mary
Warnock (London, Fontana, 1962), p. 254.
[4] Of course, this is often done. An agent may acknowledge a wide domain of ethical concern,
then segment that domain and tacitly introduce conceptions of status and subordination
which are not themselves vindicated. Those who think subordination and dependence appropriate for certain others often insist that they accord those others appropriate if different
concern; they simply go light on showing what justifies the hierarchy they assume, and why
these are the convincing separations. Wittgensteinian, communitarian and many other
writers note the plurality of 'spheres' (traditions, forms) of life, but wrongly assume that
this could be the whole story, forgetting that agents have a single life to live and must link
the differing 'spheres' in which they are connected, so must live by some principles that
cover the full domain of ethical consideration to which they are committed.

have currency only in restricted portions of that domain of ethical consideration.

This does not mean that thick concepts (which are more descriptive and less abstract) and restricted principles are dispensable. In reaching judgements about what to do in a particular situation agents have to supplement and elaborate their more inclusive and abstract principles with more specific principles that are fashioned for more restricted domains. These more specific and restricted principles may articulate legal requirements, economic constraints, family understandings, professional codes, and the like, using their appropriate thick, or at least thicker, categories. However, the ethical weight and scope of these more specific principles and tight webs of requirements, and of the special rights, obligations and relationships that they define, cannot be fixed without relying on a framework of more inclusive and indeterminate principles (cf. chapter 5).

So the first step towards a substantive account of justice must be to establish some inclusive principles of justice. The most elementary principles of justice must be inclusive and must provide basic orientations, by which more restricted and specific principles, and hence indirectly also some institutions, practices and acts conceived of in specific, 'thick' terms, and their special obligations and rights, can be shown as justifiable and others unjustifiable (cf. sections 6.5 and 6.6). However, before turning to the vindication of inclusive, indeterminate principles, the accusation that inclusive principles, and above all inclusive principles of obligation, are the very ones that most readily generate insoluble conflicts must be addressed.

6.2 CONFLICT AND CONSISTENCY

On the surface the claim that principles, and especially principles of obligation, inevitably generate irresolvable conflicts is odd. If principles do not determine their own application, so underdetermine the structures, practices and acts in which they are embodied, then a plurality of principles, and above all of inclusive, indeterminate principles, will leave much open, so need not lead to conflict. Do not governments aim simultaneously to accept principles of popular sovereignty, of respect for fundamental rights and of budgetary prudence, as well as quite specific party political commitments? Do not citizens regularly and simultaneously manage to respect prohibitions on injury, perjury and fraud? What problems arise if just action has to respect a number of different inclusive principles? Is not a commitment to a number of distinct principles a commonplace of public and of personal life? And will not this be true of principles of obligation, as of other principles?

However, some critics of principle-based ethics think that if the obligations of justice require acts, practices and institutions to conform to a number of distinct unranked principles, then those who aim to live justly will be driven into an impasse. They read Kant's curious essay on a conflict between truth-telling and beneficence as a dreadful warning, and conclude that the demands of different principles of obligation will, indeed must, be inconsistent, and so that any account of inclusive obligations of justice, indeed any ethics of principles, must collapse.[5]

A plurality of principles could conflict in two quite different ways. Some principles of action, and specifically of obligation, are intrinsically *incapable* of joint instantiation. Attempts to adopt both or all as inclusive principles will constantly produce genuine and irresolvable conflict (they could, of course, be adopted as restricted principles for distinct spheres of life – say for a public and a private sphere: but not as inclusive principles). No life can be wholly governed, for example, both by an inclusive principle of subordinating oneself to others and by an inclusive principle of retaining one's independence; no institution can impose obligations both of maximal secrecy and of complete openness in all its affairs; nobody can aspire to be a genuine yet popular hermit (society 'hermits' are another matter). Pairs or larger sets of inclusive principles of this sort generate irresolvable and *intrinsic conflicts*; they *cannot* be simultaneously instantiated; those who aspire to honour both or all run into disaster. No pairs or larger sets of principles that

---

[5] See Kant's essay, *On a Supposed Right to Lie out of Benevolent Motives*, trans. L. W. Beck in his *Kant's Critique of Practical Reason and Other Writings in Moral Philosophy* (University of Chicago Press, 1949). For discussion of the problems of conflicts between principles, in particular between principles of obligation, see David Ross, *The Right and the Good* (Oxford University Press, 1930); Bernard Williams in many discussions of obligation and of consistency throughout his writings; Martha Nussbaum in *The Fragility of Goodness: Luck and Ethics in Greek Tragedy and Philosophy* (Cambridge University Press, 1986). For views on the consistency and conflict between principles akin to those presented here see Barbara Herman, 'Obligations and Performance' in her *The Practice of Moral Judgement* (Cambridge Mass., Harvard University Press, 1993), pp. 159–83 and Ruth Barcan Marcus, 'Moral Dilemmas and Consistency', *The Journal of Philosophy*, 77 (1980), 121–36.

conflict intrinsically could be justified as inclusive principles of obligation.

However, other pairs or larger sets of inclusive principles need not lead those who live by them into conflict. When principles do not intrinsically conflict they are consistent and can be jointly instantiated at least in some circumstances. Nevertheless it will sometimes or often be demanding to lead lives or structure institutions that live up to both or all. Such principles *may*, but *need not*, give rise to contingent but difficult practical conflicts. *Contingent conflicts* between principles, and specifically between obligations, are the stuff of life and of literature: telling the truth will sometimes (but not always) injure somebody; rescuing somebody from danger can sometimes (as in Kant's example, but not always) require a lie. Indeed, commitment to a single principle can generate contingent conflicts: fostering one loyalty will sometimes (but not always) short-change another; saving a life will sometimes (but not always) cost another. Even a minimal principle of respect for life will sometimes (but not always) lead to conflict.

However, these contingent conflicts are conflicts not between principle(s) but between ways of living up to principle(s) in particular circumstances. They are conflicts not between act-types but between particular tokens of certain act-types. Agents who are committed to a plurality of inclusive principles which do not intrinsically conflict may still in particular circumstances find it hard or impossible to perform some token of each in certain situations. But it is wide of the mark to view cases of contingent conflict between principles as showing that principles, or specifically principles of obligation, *must* lead to conflicts. The necessity of obligations attaches to principles of action and not to their particular embodiments in act-tokens: they require acts of a certain type, rather than particular act-tokens of that type, which may be incompatible with some act-tokens of other types. This is merely a corollary of the indeterminacy of principles (cf. section 3.3).

The possibility of contingent conflicts between principles shows not that obligations are impossible, let alone that life is tragic or absurd, but that it can be demanding. The fact that some ways of living up to several principles, or to several obligations, are not compatible sets a task: often a feasible task. Sometimes the solution is not even difficult: many possible contingent conflicts between principles, including possible 'conflicts of obligation', are routinely averted or resolved by action that fits all the relevant principles of obligation. One criterion for judging lives well-led and institutions well-built is that they shape and adjust commitments to avert clashes, and that they successfully identify action that will meet multiple requirements.

Sometimes this proves impossible: in some cases contingent conflicts between principles or obligations cannot be averted or resolved by action that meets all relevant demands. This is particularly common when action is framed and forced by unjust institutions. In totalitarian societies, for example, the obligations of civic solidarity, or even of personal or family loyalty, were deliberately pitted against one another and against state requirements. Gentler and more just conditions make resolution of some contingent conflicts easier: many ordinary lives have been led without injury or perjury, by good-enough citizens; many husbands and wives, parents and neighbours have lived without violence and with some mutual kindness; at the end of *Emma* Mr Knightley sees just what he must do if the woman he hopes to marry is not to face a conflict between filial and wifely love and duty – and does it with grace.

Needless to say, not all contingent conflicts can be avoided, and some conflicts of obligation that could be avoided are not. When this happens the demands of principles that have been flouted or skimped may be acknowledged (although they often are not) by responses that range from apology or confession, by way of restitution or reparation, to regret or remorse.[6]

These ways of acknowledging the force of unmet, and on occasion contingently unmeetable, obligations is often seen as an objection to rather than as a component of any ethic of principles or of obligations. This may be because of the persistent but misplaced suspicion that principles must fully determine action. If that were true, commitment to a plurality of inclusive practical principles

---

[6] Bernard Williams, Thomas Nagel, Martha Nussbaum and many others have explored the importance of *remainders of feeling* (e.g. remorse, regret, guilt) as acknowledgement of unmet obligations. However, *remainders of action* are equally if not more important. Rectificatory action other than punishment (which is oriented only to perpetrators, rather than to victims or to the relationships between perpetrators and victims) is surprisingly little discussed in secular ethics. It may include forms of apology, confession, atonement, forgiveness, reconciliation, compensation, reparation, restitution, recognition, penance, and no doubt other acts and activities.

would inevitably lead to irresolvable conflicts, so undermining any ethics of principles, and especially of obligations. However, given that practical principles underdetermine action, conflicts between principles undermine only principles that are intrinsically rather than contingently incapable of joint realization. Conflicts are possible, but they do not show that principles are either pointless or dispensable.

6.3 UNIVERSALIZABILITY AND THE REJECTION OF INJURY

Inclusive practical principles may be needed to coordinate different spheres and aspects of life; they may not be inevitable sources of conflict: but they may none of them be vindicable ethical principles. In seeing how inclusive ethical principles might be established it is useful to begin with inclusive principles of justice.

Much universalist writing on justice takes an intermediate step at this point, and argues that abstract conceptions of liberty or of equality, or of both, provide the further building blocks for a theory of justice. These materials will not be available, or of any use, in constructing an account of justice unless their standing can itself be vindicated. This has proved difficult.

Those who think liberty basic to justice often depict respect for equal liberties as its central inclusive principle, or as one of its central inclusive principles. One account of justice with a long pedigree proposes that each should have the largest equal liberty compatible with like liberty for all.[7] However, lack of any plausible metric for liberty undermines the sense and the point of this proposal.[8] Without a metric for liberty we cannot know which set of

---

[7] The position is now mainly associated with Rawls, *A Theory of Justice* (1971), but has earlier ancestors and many other contemporary adherents. Rawls's initial conception of the priority of liberty is more demanding than the approach Kant and Rousseau took, in that he argued not only for *equal* but for *maximal equal* liberty, so assuming that liberty has some metric. See H. L. A. Hart, 'Rawls on Liberty and its Priority' in Norman Daniels, ed., *Reading Rawls* (Oxford, Blackwell, 1975) pp. 230–52; Charles Taylor, 'What's Wrong with Negative Liberty', in his *Philosophy and the Human Sciences*, pp. 187–210; O'Neill 'The Most Extensive Liberty'. Rawls has since dropped the maximizing element of his principle of liberty. For his reasons see references in his *Political Liberalism*, p. 5, note 3. See also section 5.2 above.

[8] One way of providing a metric for liberty would rely on physicalist conceptions of act individuation, and measure the extent of liberty by the extent of spaces and times across which it can be exercised; see references in chapter 5, note 12. This may be a promising principle for dividing the world into maximal equal territories – properties – but is not very

liberties is largest. Yet a weaker principle of liberty, for example one that merely prescribes like liberty for all, may be too indeterminate to provide the basis for a plausible account of justice. Moreover, even if like liberty for all is a plausible component of justice, it is hardly self-evident, so needs justification.

Other writers have hoped to base an account of justice partly on conceptions of equality. This strategy too is unpromising because equality (cf. section 3.3) is a radically incomplete predicate, so hospitable to countless differing completions. If equality is to provide a building block for justice, sound arguments for well-specified equalities will be needed. A minimal and formal equality is, of course, detectable in the very construction of an account of the scope of ethical concern: agents must view all others to whom they assume connection as equally subjects of their ethical concern. It is common, but not illuminating, to speak of such inclusion as evidence of a minimal 'equality of respect' or 'equality of consideration'. Since this mere equality of consideration does not require uniformity of treatment, this by itself shows little about the content of ethics, or of justice. To show that more substantive and significant equalities provide building blocks for a theory of justice is a hard and contentious task.[9]

The difficulties of using liberty and equality as building blocks for an account of justice suggest that universalist accounts of justice may have good reasons for considering the simpler requirement of universalizability. Yet many will be reluctant to look in this direction. Those who insist that principles of justice must be universal often think, like Mill, that an appeal to universalizability can do nothing to discriminate between one universal principle and another.

---

useful for showing how a plurality of beings can justly share one world. See Steiner, *An Essay on Rights.*

[9] The task is hard (perhaps impossible) because we can best measure the equality of physical and economic properties. Yet equalizing these material, measurable holdings is difficult, may damage other aspects of justice (e.g. liberty) and leave those whose sensitivities differ variously satisfied (a utilitarian worry) and those whose capabilities differ in very different situations. (Equal income does not put the frail or dependent in an equal position, cf. Drèze and Sen, *Hunger and Public Action.*) However, if justice required not that everyone have the same measurable holdings, but (say) that they have the same capabilities, i.e. be equally able to take certain sorts of effective action, then since capabilities are specified by complex act descriptions, there would be no ready metric. See chapter 3, note 12.

Some suggest that *all* universal practical principles are universalizable, since any universal principle that can be acted on by one can also coherently be adopted by all, apart from exceptions which are more eccentric than ethically significant. Universalizability fails, they suggest, only for principles that, for example, mandate unique successes or attainment of positional goods, which cannot be principles for all because they can be followed only on the assumption that others who are included in a given domain of ethical consideration do not follow them, or at least do not do so successfully. Not everybody can undercut the competition, or earn more than average. These idiosyncratic principles are perhaps not universalizable – but their rejection is unlikely to provide significant inclusive principles for orienting and coordinating many aspects of life.

However, universalizability fails for significant ranges of inclusive principles which have nothing to do with unique successes or positional goods. Consequently rejection of non-universalizable principles can set demanding constraints. Universalizable principles have to meet a weak, doubly modal constraint: they must be principles which agents take it can be principles for all in the relevant domain of ethical concern. Accordingly a principle cannot be taken to be universalizable if it cannot be viewed as a principle for all, because its universal adoption (*per impossibile*) would render some unable to act, *a fortiori* unable to adopt that principle. It follows that no principle of injuring others (whether directly, or indirectly by injuring the social fabric or the shared natural world on which lives depend) can be universalized. The ordinary and predictable results even of widespread, let alone of ostensibly universal, commitment to an inclusive principle of injuring within some domain would injure some, so disable them from acting, so show the principle itself non-universalizable. Those who adopt principles which they cannot view as principles for all must see what they do as non-universalizable, that is as available to some only on condition that at least some others not do likewise.[10]

---

[10] Cf. Kant's shrewd comment on what we actually do when we act on principles that cannot be universalized: 'we find that we do not in fact will that our maxims should become a universal law – since this is impossible for us – but rather that its opposite should remain a law universally: we only take the liberty of making an *exception* to it for ourselves (or even just for this once)'. *Groundwork of the Metaphysic of Morals*, trans. Paton, p. 426 (Prussian Academy pagination).

On the other hand those who reject injury, or other non-universalizable principles, adopt principles which they reasonably judge all *can* share, which they can view as possible principles for all. Putting the matter simply, principles of action will not be universalizable if attempted universal adoption would foreseeably injure capacities and capabilities for action of some of those within the relevant domain of ethical concern, thereby ensuring that they cannot adopt those principles.[11] It is absurd to imagine that everyone might make injury an inclusive and basic principle of their lives and yet that (miraculously!) nobody could act on their principle and so nobody would be injured. If nobody is injured that is simply excellent evidence that not everyone has made injury an inclusive and basic principle of their lives. In making injury basic to their lives or institutions agents commit themselves to destruction and damage that undermines like action by at least some others, hence to seeing their own action as exclusive rather than as universalizable. The core of injustice is action on principles which if universally acted on would foreseeably injure at least some; the core of justice is rejection of principles whose attempted universal adoption would foreseeably injure at least some.

A classic objection to taking universalizability as the criterion of permissibility, and its failure as the criterion of non-permissibility, has been that more specific principles that fall under evidently non-universalizable principles can be universalized. For example, it is often said, principles of selective injury such as *injuring certain sorts of people* or *injuring on certain rare occasions* can be universalized. Perhaps taken in isolation they could be: but the appropriate question is whether someone who had rejected the evidently non-universalizable principle of injuring could coherently back-track and adopt these less inclusive principles, or whether their adoption would count against the ascription of an unrestricted principle of rejecting injury. Since adopting a principle of action is committing oneself to act when the situation is judged appropriate, a commitment to *rejecting injury* will hardly be compatible with a commitment

---

[11] To show that a principle is not universalizable is to show that *not all can adopt it*. It is usually all too easy to show that *not all can act on it*, and without practical point to show that *all cannot act on it* (if they all can't, they all won't). Hence in demonstrating non-universalizability it is sufficient to show that universal adoption would be self-defeating, in that it would undermine possibilities for *at least some* agents to adopt the principle, assuming ordinary capacities, capabilities and vulnerabilities.

to selective injury, unless there are specific features of some type of selective injury, that make it part of or at least compatible with a general policy of rejecting injury. Such cases apart, a commitment to selective injury will simply count as evidence of lack of commitment to rejecting injury.

A slightly different and perhaps more plausible objection might be that while selective injury is not universalizable, *trivial injury* is readily universalizable. The world in which everybody inflicts trivial injury may be beastly, but it is quite coherent to suppose that everybody gets in on the act. However, once again if certain inclusive principles can be shown non-universalizable (in this case an inclusive principle of injuring), laws, institutions, practices and policies must be designed to meet the requirements of rejecting that principle. It may well be that an overall commitment to rejecting injury will turn out to allow (or even to require) certain sorts of trivially injurious action; but what it allows or requires will not be generalized trivial injury. A serious commitment to rejecting injury will only be properly expressed in social, political and other structures that put rather strong prohibitions on injury and make exceptions only for equally serious reasons. Whether trivial injury is permissible in some contexts will emerge in the course of considering just what it takes to make the rejection of injury *sans phrase* a basic principle of lives and institutions.[12] The import of rejecting universalizable principles is not well judged by considering carefully tailored principles in isolation. The central point is to see what must be done if those inclusive principles which can't be principles for all are rejected, rather than to discover whether related principles could be principles for all.[13]

The fact that injury is not universalizable also does not show that justice requires lives or institutions to be based on a principle of

---

[12] In addition, the permissibility of trivial injury must be judged not merely against the real requirements of ways of life that embody the rejection of injury but of the real requirements that embody the rejection of indifference: see chapter 7.

[13] Why then does so much of the literature on universalizability worry that there is a problem if non-universalizable principles are similar to others that are universalizable? Possibly because the perspective taken is not truly practical. Instead of asking 'What should we do or be?' it assumes that it is unclear which principles are relevant, as it might be if (for example) we were trying to work out what somebody else's principle of action is in a given situation. In a practical situation, multiple principles will be relevant, and the fact that (for example) injuring *sans phrase* is non-universalizable cannot be set side because (supposedly) injuring *very slightly* is not.

non-injury, but only that they be based on *a principle of rejecting injury*. The difference is considerable. Commitment to non-injury calls for living in ways that always favour non-injury over injury. It calls, for example, for pacifism, non-retaliation and acceptance of any injustice to self or others which persuasion cannot avert. Commitment to rejecting injury demands less: it is a matter of not making a *principle of injury* fundamental to lives, institutions or practices.[14] The rejection of principles, such as those of injuring, which cannot be principles for all, provides the material both for constructing an account of other more determinate principles of justice, of just institutions and practices, and with them of just special obligations, rights and relationships, for a particular time and place.

6.4 JUST INSTITUTIONS: REJECTING INJURY

A commitment to reject injury will always be less than perfectly expressed. Legal and constitutional order prevent injury only at the cost of inflicting some injury in the maintenance of public order and of penal systems; so do stable and protective social and economic institutions; democratic structures enable and they expose. Achieving a degree of order that will control and discipline the amount and range of injury that might otherwise be inflicted concentrates powers, and the resulting distinction between the powerful and the vulnerable will often facilitate and risk inflicting injury. A world state, a centrally planned economy, a rigidly hierarchical social order might each in various circumstances help prevent some of the injuries that disorder facilitates; yet each is likely to facilitate other sorts of injury. More limited concentrations of power also create vulnerability: a feudal order, protected markets and patriarchal family structures will not avert all the injuries that disorder brings, and will inflict some that greater concentrations of power avert. And yet anarchical political structures, unfettered markets and fragmented social relations,

[14] Might there be other equally fundamental requirements of justice? Many plausible candidates turn out to be modes of rejecting injury, in that what makes a principle non-universalizable is that its attempted adoption by all would disable some from adopting the same principle. The principle of rejecting injury is at any rate fertile enough to ground a complex web of requirements of justice. Cf. section 6.7 below. A complete inventory of ethical requirements, even for the domain of justice, may be an illusory goal, given the indeterminacy of principles.

although they might help prevent some of the injuries that globally or locally concentrated power facilitates, will facilitate injuries that concentrated power deters and prevents. On the other hand, a constitutional and legal order coupled with democratic politics, regulated markets and unhierarchical communities, although they may seem to provide the institutions and structures that will best limit systematic and gratuitous injury, encompass a wide range of different possibilities whose real merits and shortcomings may vary for different situations. Rejecting principles of injuring others will be expressed in working for and through institutions and practices which are judged relatively good at avoiding and preventing injury *in actual circumstances*, so will aim for (let alone achieve) less-than-universal non-injury.

In choosing between imperfect institutionalizations of the rejection of injury that are achievable at a given time and place, some forms of injury will generally be *unavoidable*, hence not unjust. For example, in defending the innocent against aggressors, in bringing offenders to book, and in self-defence, as well as in the disciplines of commercial and social life, *unavoidable* injuries may be inflicted as components of an underlying commitment to rejecting injury. However, this does not mean that some given measure of injury is acceptable; it means only that no institutions which would do better in the actual situation could be identified and established.

A requirement or commitment to reject injury must be expressed in action that does not avoidably injure in ways that are either *systematic* or *gratuitous*.[15] The reasons are plain enough. Avoidable systematic and gratuitous injury both provide strong evidence that principles of injuring have not in fact been (wholly) rejected, but have been at (at least partly) adopted.[16] In practice, drawing the line between avoidable and unavoidable injury is often difficult.

If just lives and societies have to avoid systematic and gratuitous injury as far as possible, they must identify and seek to meet complex institutional demands that take account of actual capacities and capabilities for action of those involved and of their

---

[15] Some *unavoidable* injury is, of course, quite regular and systematic: consider the statistically all-too-regular injuries inflicted even by scrupulous law-enforcement and medical practice. It is *avoidable* systematic injury that is impermissible, and of relevance here.

[16] Remembering that principles can be followed without being present to consciousness. See section 4.3, especially p. 101.

counterpart vulnerabilities to injury. Injury can destroy or damage bodies (including minds), bodily (including mental) functioning and so capacities and capabilities to (inter)act and to respond. It can do so *directly* by affecting agents and their capacities for action. It can also do so *indirectly* by two routes. It may damage the social connections between agents, and so the conventions, trust, traditions and relationships by which pluralities of agents maintain a social fabric and complex capabilities. It may also damage the natural and man-made environments, which provide the material basis both for life and lives and for the social fabric, so once again damaging capacities and capabilities for action and increasing vulnerabilities.

A commitment to justice must be expressed by rejecting avoidable direct and indirect injury; a commitment to injustice will be expressed by condoning or inflicting some avoidable systematic or gratuitous injury. The specific requirements of justice in a given situation cannot, however, be *deduced* from these basic demands. The basic principles provide only a framework for building an account of more specific and restricted principles appropriate in a given social world, and of the elements of action, institutions and practices which will in those situations avoid or help avoid systematic or gratuitous injury (cf. section 6.7 below).

6.5 JUST INSTITUTIONS: REJECTING DIRECT INJURY

Direct injury may seem simple. It may be inflicted by killing or destroying, by wounding or maiming, by threatening or coercing, by forced labour and starvation, by intimidation and terror, by detention and deportation. Evidently no principle of acting in these ways can be universalized. Yet the action, institutions and practices through which the rejection of principles of injuring directly might be well expressed, or best expressed, in actual circumstances may need to be very complex.

The institutions or practices which specify more closely what it is to reject injury in a given situation will generally include ways of determining or adjudicating whether avoidable injury has been either systematic or gratuitous, and of imposing and enforcing responses to at least some of these determinations. These *adjudicating* (legal, administrative, communal, etc.) and *executive* (governmental, police, military, communal, familial, educational, etc.) institutions and practices may vary in many ways, as may the degree of their coordination. Some institutions or practices may establish specific ways of institutionalizing universal obligations not to injure and universal rights not to be injured, others may fix ranges of special obligations and special rights, and ways of creating further special obligations and rights. Yet others will establish obligations and rights which, on the surface, have little to do with averting injury, but which play a more indirect role. The adequacy of these multiple institutions and practices must be judged as a whole, rather than by considering a check list of obligations or of rights. Although justice always needs ways by which to decide whether avoidable injuries are systematic or gratuitous, it does not need a single system for so deciding in all domains: it may rely on quite specific and restricted ways of deciding whether specific sorts of avoidable injury are systematic or gratuitous.

Even in the least complex human conditions of which we have any knowledge – say, hunter-gatherer societies – rejection of injury would be expressed not only by avoiding systematic or gratuitous injury directly inflicted on others (killing, assault), and in ways of dealing with those who violated such taboos, but also by some understanding of an authoritative allocation of resources, hence some definition of action that would violate these standards (e.g. taking others' food or tools) and be seen as wrongs. The practices by which directly injuring acts could be adjudicated and decisions enforced could no doubt vary greatly even in these circumstances. Any detailed view on which avoidable injuries were systematic or gratuitous, or how they might be dealt with in such societies, is largely a matter of speculation; whether these practices should be thought of as achieving a pre-political form of justice, or only as stabilizing social relations is opaque.

In modern, highly differentiated societies adjudicating and executive institutions and practices are still considerably opaque, even for those who live by and with them. Moreover, the institutions and practices that secure (a measure of) justice will be of huge complexity. The rejection even of direct injury will require institutions that limit and control the power that some have over others, and hence also the vulnerability of those others. Limiting power and vulnerability may require the construction of legal orders which guarantee certain universal liberty rights, of political orders which limit powers of government, of economic orders which secure tolerable levels of subsistence,[17] and of social orders which limit subordination and dependence, and of information orders which regulate communication and above all telecommunication. Each of these aspects of a just social order will need distinctive and complex systems for determining which injuries are either systematic or gratuitous, so unjust, and varied institutions for enforcing at least some decisions.

The need for justice in contemporary societies to achieve adequate standards under all of these headings is clarified by considering alternatives. Any modern society whose institutions entrench lack of individual liberties, great disparities between rulers and ruled, extremes of poverty, or extremes of unilateral social dependence, or allow some voices to dominate the global media while others go unheard, establishes powers that need answer to nobody, so entrenches vulnerabilities and erodes capabilities for some, if not for many, people. It secures rather than limits the likelihood of injury. Its institutions and practices will lead to avoidable injury that is *systematic* and will leave wide scope for individual action and inaction that injures *gratuitously*. It is a society that institutionalizes injustice.

However, even societies that successfully identify and establish institutions that go some way to control systematic or gratuitous injury will have nevertheless to allow, and even require, some injury. The rights not to be injured that just institutions secure cannot be complete or unconditional. The institutions and practices that secure liberties are typically maintained by coercive policing and penal systems; those that limit government power may give opportunities to unjust factions and interest groups to injure either systematically or gratuitously; those that achieve even minimal economic securities may both limit liberty (they may allocate labour, tax, regulate, exclude aliens) and institutionalize some sorts of dependence to prevent others; those that weaken social subordination may destroy some traditional sources of insecurity

---

[17] Which sort of economic order will best achieve basic economic securities is a matter of great dispute. Candidates include: unfettered market structures, social market systems i.e. welfare states, basic income schemes, and (now considerably discredited) centrally planned economies. Older systems included local poor law institutions, tribal, caste, familial and charitable systems of allocation. The most just system for given conditions will have to do better than others in reliably sustaining capacities and capabilities for action, so limiting vulnerabilities, in those conditions.

(and security) as the price of strengthening other sources; those that ensure that the media are not dominated by the voices of a few may in the process also silence a few voices.[18]

These limitations demonstrate once again why neither liberties nor equalities by themselves can be viewed as building blocks of justice: any set of institutions will compromise some liberties or some equalities, or some of both. A more fundamental criterion is needed by which to judge which available compromises are better and which worse; this criterion is the adequacy with which a whole system of institutions and practices limits systematic and gratuitous injury.

The difficulty of choosing among possible institutions and practices that stabilize and express the rejection of direct injury, and their concomitant ranges of perfect obligations and rights, can be seen at all levels of political, economic and social organization. Neither the most global nor the most local of political and economic institutions, nor their combination, can reliably prevent all injury. They may be able only to establish rights and obligations which limit unanswerable exercises of power and the more damaging sorts of vulnerability and injury, and so limit both systematic and gratuitous injury and secure some measure of the most important capabilities for action for all.[19]

---

[18] It is also hard to judge which non-economic institutions and practices reject injury most effectively. Consider, for example, traditional societies with powerful family or tribal loyalties, arranged marriages, patriarchal values. Such structures demand *loyalty* from all, and severely limit opportunities for redress (*voice*) or *exit* for some or even for all, so institutionalize dependence and subordination (even slavery) for some. On the other hand, replacing traditional families or communities with 'voluntary associations' (and some societies have come a fair way in this direction) allows each some *voice* and eases *exit* from oppression – but in reducing *loyalties* also eases abandonment of dependents. When divorce is easy, and support for children and for the old can be avoided, the weak are still vulnerable – in different ways. The rub of the matter is that family structures that demand unconditional *loyalty* silence *voices* and deny *exit* so institutionalize vulnerability; but so too do structures which require minimal *loyalty*, encourage all to *voice* their concerns and allow ready *exit* from families. For the distinctions see Albert Hirschman, *Exit, Voice and Loyalty* (Cambridge, Mass., Harvard University Press, 1970). Although the literature on women's issues is relevant here, the realities of dependence are more clearly seen in writing on children, where the realities of dependence and institutionalized vulnerability are sharper. See David Archard, *Children: Rights and Childhood* (London, Routledge, 1993), and its informative bibliography.

[19] It is tempting to think that vulnerability would best be limited by securing specific equalities – or limiting specific inequalities. Such approaches treat certain *outcomes* – the achieved equalities – as the indices of justice. The difficulty with the approach is that securing equalities is institutionally difficult and may disrupt other securities. For example, it may limit liberties, disrupt certain social relations and limit democratic

These complexities and limitations apply to 'international' as much as to 'domestic' justice. A *global* system of a plurality of more-or-less sovereign states, whose inhabitants' lives are restricted for many purposes to their own state, can injure many lives. Even if each state were more-or-less internally just, and they rarely are, states may injure those whom they exclude, and a system of states may systematically and gratuitously injure insiders and outsiders, by wars and international conflict and by economic structures that control and limit access to the means of life. On the other hand, a world-state might injure lives by concentrating, yet failing to regulate or discipline, vast and damaging powers. Merely noting these points will not pick out a particular institutional scheme, that is most appropriate for a given situation, and the simplified contrast between a system of states and a world-state probably misses many of the more promising possibilities. A system of states might, for example, look rather different if disciplined and restrained by international (more strictly: inter-statal), trans-national (more strictly: trans-statal),[20] intergovernmental, and non-governmental institutions. A world state might look rather different if constrained by forms of subsidiarity, by separations of powers and by a strong non-state economic system. The (realistic) 'moral cosmopolitanism', to which the more-or-less cosmopolitan scope of ethical consideration that is in fact assumed by agents in the contemporary world points, does not show which determinate form of institutional cosmopolitanism is feasible or optimal for now, let alone best for all time.[21] It shows only that processes of institution building and reform must be judged for the systematic ways in which they might increase or lessen, and redistribute, the vulnerabilities and capabilities of all those within the scope of

politics. The institutional approach to limiting vulnerability sketched here stresses *processes*, rather than *outcomes*. One *outcome* which would probably be achieved by any society whose *processes* were designed to limit vulnerabilities would be a range of equalities, which could then be used as performance indicators for justice: but they would not themselves be the components of justice. Moreover, trying to adjust performance indicators is often a bad way of adjusting the realities they are meant to indicate.

[20] For discussion of these and other distinctions see Philip Allott, *Eunomia: New Order for a New World* (Oxford University Press, 1990).

[21] For discussion of these issues and terms see Charles Beitz, *Political Theory and International Relations*; Pogge, 'Cosmopolitanism and Sovereignty' and Onora O'Neill, 'Justice and Boundaries' both in C. Brown, ed., (London, Routledge, 1994), respectively pp. 66–89 and pp. 89–122; Thomas Baldwin, 'The Territorial State' in Hyman Gross and Ross Harrison, eds., *Jurisprudence: Cambridge Essays* (Oxford, Clarendon Press, 1992), pp. 207–30.

ethical consideration, whether or not their lives are led within the
same borders.

Thinking along these lines might lead in many directions; the
following example is only one. If a system of states is to reject
avoidable injury it will have to construct institutions which compensate for any systematic or gratuitous injuries created by the
exclusion which states practice, and by the varied sorts of dependence they buttress. Where exclusion is a source of avoidable
systematic or gratuitous injury, justice will then demand at least
that basic human rights and some sorts of economic support be
made effective beyond borders, and that asylum and immigration
be made available when these fail. Borders inevitably exclude; and
if the exclusions are sources of systematic or gratuitous injury,
justice could be achieved either by remedying these injustices
directly or by making the borders more porous. Without effective
institutions with these aims, forced exclusion can be just only if it is
not a source of avoidable systematic or gratuitous injury to any of
those excluded.

Both *global* and *less-than-global* thinking about justice makes
quite realistic and down-to-earth demands. In each context the
objective is to establish institutions and practices which (as far as
possible) prevent and limit systematic or gratuitous injury. In each
context difficult judgements about the range of possibilities, and
about the real prospects of reform have to be made. In each context
the powers both of natural and of artificial persons must be
controlled. In each context the capabilities of natural persons must
be secured and their vulnerabilities limited. In each case success
will go some way to secure some (if limited) liberties, and is likely
to be reflected in a measure of political and legal equalities (including a measure of political participation), and in social structures
that avoid or discipline extremes of dependence and of power.

The limitations of merely theoretical thought about justice are
evident. Since the institutions and practices by which power can be
limited and with it vulnerability minimized, vary with context,
there is no general answer to questions such as 'Which sort of
constitution is most just?' or 'Which type of economic system is
most just?'. However, the diversity of situation and pluralism of
belief found in different times and places do not undermine
principles of justice. Principles of justice can be justified quite
generally, and can be used to judge the specific constructions of

justice which, quite rightly, take different forms at different times and places.

6.6 JUST INSTITUTIONS: REJECTING INDIRECT INJURY

Injustice can also arise from injury that is inflicted *indirectly* through damage to the social fabric or the natural world. Much action that damages the social fabric does so by direct injury to individuals: the effects of violence and hostility, of terror and intimidation spread from individuals to the institutions and practices amid which those individuals live. However, other sorts of injury work indirectly by way of destroying or damaging the social fabric, and in particular the trust which connects and sustains lives, relationships and communities,[22] or by way of destroying or damaging the natural and man-made environments which are the material basis of lives and action.

The injustice of deception can be thought of both as an indirect way of injuring, and more immediately as action on principles that cannot be universalized. In the first place deception is unjust because it injures indirectly: systematic or gratuitous deception destroys trust and creates vulnerabilities, which facilitate direct injuries. By destroying the social fabric deception injures those whose lives are linked by that fabric. Secondly, principles of deception – of lying, breaking promises, defrauding or manipulating – are not universalizable. Nobody can coherently view deception, by whichever means, as an inclusive principle that could be available for all: rather they exploit the fact that at least *some* others maintain *some* trust and social connection to achieve their own deception.[23] Liars, cheats, fraudsters and promise breakers *require* a social background in which lying and cheating are not

---

22 Weil, *The Need for Roots*: 'we owe our respect to a collectivity, of whatever kind – country, family or any other – not for itself but because it is food for a certain number of human souls', p. 7. Her analysis of collectivities which sustain and those which fail to do so in the following paragraphs is resonant and suggestive.

23 Kant on false promises is the *locus classicus*, *Groundwork of the Metaphysic of Morals*, p. 422 (Prussian Academy pagination). The problem is not one of thresholds: the universalizability criterion is 'Can I view this principle as available for all?' and not (for example) 'How much can deceivers weaken trust before doing so backfires?'. Evidently it is often easy to get away with being a free-rider and there is not much of an argument to be made from an expectation of slight damage to trust to the inviolability of promise keeping or truth telling. These are awkward issues for consequentialists, who have to slink up to trust and deception very circumspectly.

universal, so cannot think that their principles are available to all. Like practices and policies of direct injury to persons, those of deceiving can be thought of as available for some, but not as universally available.

Those who reject principles of deception need not make a principle of sustaining trust (or honesty, or truthfulness or fair dealing) an inclusive principle of their lives. Since principles cannot be perfectly institutionalized, even scrupulous commitment to rejecting a principle of deception may fall well short of a general commitment to non-deception. At times a commitment to reject deception may demand *unavoidable* elements of deception: even if there are no noble lies, there may be necessary lies, and certainly necessary deceptive silences and reticences. For example, some lies and even some betrayals may prove unavoidable if serious injury or deeper deception are not to be inflicted. Nevertheless rejecting deception demands a lot. Deception that is either *systematic* or *gratuitous* shows that a principle of deceiving has not been rejected. The *systematic* deception of Orwell's Ministry of Truth or of actual totalitarian states,[24] as well as the *gratuitous* deceptions which are often convenient for the powerful, and for those who have something to sell, are both evidence that deception has not been rejected. However, wholly trusting, transparent societies and lives may not be sustainable by vulnerable and limited beings. The very institutions of enforcement, which undoubtedly coerce, also commonly deceive and manipulate.

Commitment to reject deception will therefore demand the construction and support of institutions or practices of which some elements might, in other contexts, constitute deceit. The special obligations not to destroy trust, and the special rights not to be deceived in specific ways, which these institutions and practices define and sustain will not be complete or unconditional obligations or rights. The social institutions and practices needed to reject deception will be complex, but cannot be complete. A just political and legal order can at best go some way – perhaps a long way – towards avoiding and preventing systematic and gratuitous deception, for example by establishing criminal and civil law, by securing forms of free speech and freedom of information, and

---

[24] See in particular Vaclav Havel, 'The Power of the Powerless'. More generally, consider literature on life under totalitarian regimes from Alexander Solzhenitsin to Jung Chang.

by demanding and enforcing some degree of probity in public, commercial and professional life. But more may be needed. As many anarchist, socialist and communitarian thinkers have stressed, legal and contractual relations may themselves undermine and weaken certain sorts of trust and certain social bonds. In a just society with a strong legal order their 'alienating' character may have to be compensated for by establishing and supporting institutions of civil society, an information order and other social practices and traditions which build and stabilize trust, toleration and practices of non-deceptive communication.

The injustice of destroying natural and man-made environments can also be thought of in two ways. In the first place, their destruction is unjust because it is a further way by which others can be injured: systematic or gratuitous destruction of the means of life creates vulnerabilities, which facilitate direct injuries to individuals. Destroying (parts of) natural and man-made environments injures those whose lives depend on them. Secondly, the principle of destroying natural and man-made environments, in the sense of destroying their reproductive and regenerative powers, is not universalizable. Nobody can coherently view the irreversible destruction of the means of life as an inclusive principle that is available for all: rather they rely on the fact that at least some others preserve rather than destroy (parts of) the natural world, and its productive capacities, so preserve some means of life, on which they and their destructive activities depend.

This is particularly significant in technologically advanced societies, whose abilities to damage and destroy natural and man-made systems are gigantic. In a populous world that is not infinitely abundant, where highly destructive technologies are widely available, examples of unjust ways of affecting natural and man-made environments multiply.[25] Those who exhaust or contaminate the earth, or poison waters, or pollute the air, rely on their own policies not being universally pursued. They cannot and do not take it that their own depredations are open to all. Like practices and policies of direct injury to persons, any destruction of nature which creates vulnerabilities and injures indirectly can be thought of as

---

[25] Traditional societies also inflicted a lot of irreversible damage: massive erosion, salination, deforestation are not new. Technologically advanced societies differ because they can inflict more sorts of damage at higher speed with global impact.

available for some, but not as universally available. Justice makes environmental as well as political, economic and social demands.

A just environmental policy cannot, however, reject as unjust all changes to or action on natural and man-made environments, each of which transforms and (in a lesser sense) destroys some of its parts or aspects. Conserving *every* aspect of natural and man-made environments would end all productive hence all economic activity and, taken strictly, life itself: total conservation points to total injury. Some transformations, hence some destruction, of parts and aspects of nature are an unavoidable component of an over-all commitment not to injure. Agriculture and herding, manufacture and construction, all transform natural and man-made systems, so destroy some of their parts and aspects, in order to produce. However, they need not do so in ways that inflict irreversible damage on the underlying reproductive and regenerative powers of natural systems; they can be done in ways which natural and man-made systems can sustain. Environmental justice is a matter of sustaining life and lives without avoidable damage to the reproductive and regenerative powers of the natural world, but not at the expense of destroying all man-made systems that use the natural world. Only when those man-made systems themselves threaten or destroy the underlying regenerative power of natural systems would justice require their destruction.[26] Environmental justice is therefore a matter of transforming natural and man-made systems only in ways that do not *systematically* or *gratuitously* destroy the reproductive and regenerative powers of the natural world, so do not inflict indirect injury.[27]

By these standards, many commonplace activities and policies are environmentally unjust. For example, avoidable erosion or pollution of fertile countrysides, pollution of waters, destruction of

---

[26] The term 'sustainable development' is often used in a quite different sense, meaning that a certain industrial or other economic process can be sustained. But much that is sustainable in this sense inflicts avoidable damage on natural processes of reproduction and regeneration. Low level polluting is an all too sustainable process, yet it may destroy the sustainability of the natural systems it damages.

[27] This is evidently a largely anthropocentric conception of environmental justice: without perfectionist starting points, more may not be vindicable. Even with generous perfectionist assumptions more may not be liveable. In particular, total non-destruction of nature cannot plausibly be vindicated. Every human way of life, even those of Jains and of vegans, is based on destroying in the sense of transforming and remaking parts of the natural world. So is every non-human life. Total conservation leads to avoidable, systematic injury.

the atmosphere and the ozone layer, as well as the destruction of biodiversity are all ways of using the natural world which it may not be able to sustain, and which may ultimately injure many lives. Done on a sufficient scale they will injure others *systematically*; done on a lesser scale they can still injure *gratuitously*. Localized destruction of parts of the natural world, such as the heedless and needless extinction of species or degradation of habitats, or failure to regulate damaging technologies, may not often injure *systematically*, but frequently does so *gratuitously*. However, these pointers do not make it easy to distinguish just from unjust environmental policies and practices. Only when there is some clarity about which technological and economic policies and activities inflict which sorts of damage on the natural world, and which of them do so avoidably, hence which injure life and lives indirectly, can the justice of specific policies and technologies for areas ranging from public health and human reproduction, to patterns of farming and food technology, to energy use and industrial policy, be judged even with any certainty. Since there are great uncertainties in these matters, and much is at stake, a precautionary approach is required: only those sorts of transformation of the natural world which are known not to threaten its underlying recuperative and regenerative powers may justly be undertaken.

6.7 TOWARDS JUSTICE: PRINCIPLES, DESIGN AND JUDGEMENT

The ranges of political, economic, social and environmental institutions, policies and practices which could express a commitment to reject injury, both direct and indirect, and with it a commitment to some measure of justice, are of huge variety and complexity. (So too are the ranges of arrangements which could thwart justice.) Within each institution or practice that might be thought just under certain circumstances, special obligations and rights and ways of constructing further special rights and obligations may be established, together with specific modes of adjudication and enforcement. Our present understanding of the best ways in which justice can be stably instituted in political, economic and social structures and environmental policies remains patchy even for the most familiar conditions. We know of some better and some less good attempts to institutionalize principles of rejecting injury, but we stumble towards more comprehensive views of an adequate institutionalization for familiar, let alone for unfamiliar, conditions. We are even uncertain how far different institutions and practices can be combined. Some argue that just social structures should foster both 'Victorian values' and unfettered market relations, others doubt the two are even compatible.[28] Some believe that market economies can be spliced with authoritarian politics, others that this is not even possible in an era of advanced information technologies. Some believe that justice within a single state remains a possible aspiration; others insist that justice now has to be thought of globally. The task of identifying compatible institutions and practices is itself exacting; the task of identifying what forms and degree of justice can be achieved in a given time or place is even harder.

Yet the suggestions about the requirements of justice offered in the last sections are neither arbitrary nor too general to be of use. In the first place they address the *range* of concerns which justice must address. Secondly, they do so drawing only on the abstract and constructive *methods* which are available for ethical reasoning. They do not invoke either starting points or conceptions of practical reason that need unavailable metaphysical support or unavailable proof that the particularities of a given society or life are not open to ethical question. Thirdly, they see institutional change in a down-to-earth and practical way: what may be achievable is piecemeal reform of institutions and practices rather than a utopian project of imposing an ideal constitution or of transforming 'manifesto rights' into realities.

The range of issues discussed reflects the considerations which determine the scope of justice (cf. chapter 4). In general terms, justice is in the first instance a matter of living lives and of seeking and supporting institutions and policies that reject injury: to do so justly is a matter of shunning both gratuitous and systematic injury, but may be compatible with and even require some unavoidable injury. The three ranges of injury discussed are closely connected to the three bases of ethical concern discussed in chapter 3. It is because ethical concern is directed to a *plurality of others* that those who reject injury must reject activities, institutions and practices which gratuitously or systematically inflict direct injury on others'

---

[28] See Jürgen Habermas, *The New Conservatism: Cultural Criticism and the Historians' Debate*, trans. Shierry Weber Nicholsen (Cambridge, Polity Press, 1989).

lives. It is because ethical concern is directed to *connected others* that those who reject injury must reject activities, institutions and practices that gratuitously or systematically deceive, thereby destroying or fragmenting trust and social bonds and so indirectly injuring the connections between lives. It is because ethical concern is directed to *finite and vulnerable others*, whose social connection and capabilities are formed and fed by the natural and man-made world, that those who reject injury must reject activities, institutions and practices that gratuitously or systematically destroy the world in ways that it cannot sustain, so indirectly injuring lives.

Critics of principles may nevertheless think that this account of justice provides too little to help anyone discern what justice requires. They will argue that the rejection of direct and indirect injury provides too little material for constructing a useful account of justice. They will object not to the paucity but to the presence of principles of justice. They will note that principles are never enough, and that to choose among possible lines of action *judgement* will be needed. Only judgement, they will point out, can distinguish ways of life that injure systematically or gratuitously from those that do not. They will suggest that the very indeterminacy of principles, on which a constructive approach to ethics builds, robs principles of all power and usefulness. Practical principles which do not entail their applications (and none do) are, they may claim, no more than vague exhortations. The very view of principles which was advanced in order to defeat charges of ethical rigorism, the rule-following considerations and the problem of conflicting obligations robs principles of power. There are no deductive arguments to show *which* more specific and restricted principles, or *which* particular activities, institutions and practices are most important for rejecting injury in a given situation. Moves from abstract to less abstract principles, from principles to institutions and above all from principles to judgements of particular situations are not deductive, so are obscure. The claim that in the end decision lies with perception remains unanswered.

However, genuflection to the notion of judgement which does not show how it works is even more obscure. Those who emphasize judgement as the alternative to principles often get no further than the claim that judgement is needed to *appraise and appreciate situations*, of which they give no adequate account, overlooking the fact that it is also needed to find a way forward among a variety of possible lines of action that are open once a situation has been appraised. Here the advantage of approaching questions of judgement by way of an account of principles shows. The advantage is that principles provide the framework both for *judgements of appraisal* and for *productive judgement*, and make them at any rate less obscure. Principles provide the guidelines for the moves that are appropriate in judging cases.

This can be illustrated for the case of productive judgements; an analogous account of appraising judgements could be given. The way in which productive judgement works can be understood by analogy with the moves designers make when they start with a set of specifications and constraints and move towards the construction of an artefact. For example, the specifications for a stove may demand that it heat well, that it be safe and reliable, and that it be made of cheap materials. *Each constraint helps to specify ways in which the others might be appropriately met.* A very cheap stove that does not heat adequately won't do; nor will a very dangerous stove that heats superbly. The designer's task is helped rather than confounded by starting with many specifications. Of course, usually many design solutions will be possible: it is typical for the specifications to be meetable by more than one blueprint, and blueprints can be realized in varying ways. The fact that a blueprint is not yet a working model does not mean that working models cannot be made, and the fact that a working model is not the real thing does not mean that the real thing cannot be constructed, nor that it cannot be tested and adjusted in use.

The move from abstract and inclusive principles of justice towards just institutions, policies and practices is analogous to moves from design specifications towards finished products. In this case too, starting with a plurality of principles defines the task and provides the scaffolding for its solution, rather than making it insoluble. The basic 'specifications' for justice are the *rejection of a plurality of abstract and inclusive principles of injuring, all of which are to be simultaneously satisfied under actual conditions.* Rather than generating impossible conflicts, starting with a plurality of principles of rejecting injury, which are mutually constraining, helps to fix the specific ways in which each can be satisfied. Since each requirement to reject injury limits the ways in which each other requirement is to be satisfied, each provides some scaffolding for judging whether possible moves from more abstract to less abstract principles is adequate.

The task of judging what is just begins with fixing principles of justice. Judging what it would be just to do is not a matter of discerning that particular acts meet (or would meet) those inclusive and very abstract principles. It is a matter of identifying more restricted principles and ways of living that fall within the constraints of justice, in that they do not either directly or indirectly inflict avoidable injury. The scaffolding provided by principles of rejecting injury limits the range of less abstract principles that can be judged just. These less abstract, and often more restricted principles in turn provide a framework for the construction of institutions and practices that can be judged just in a given time or place. Just institutions and practices provide the specifications for judging the justice of particular acts or decisions.

These stages of deliberation, of movement from the more indeterminate towards the more determinate, are like the stages of design. The various ways in which each of the most abstract and inclusive principles of justice might be satisfied by more restricted principles may be thought of as specifications for justice. The sets of institutions that might conform to these specifications can be thought of as blueprints for justice: they might include sketches of constitutions, drafts of legislation, programmes of reform, proposals for economic institutions or environmental policies and regulation. Like other blueprints, these are not working models, but their partial and imperfect realizations are just that. Those drafts and plans can be used to help construct working institutions and practices, which can then be tested and adjusted in use.

Although, like other specifications, the principles of justice will underdetermine choices between institutions, policies or action, this indeterminacy need worry nobody. Any reliable scheme of institutions, that meets all the specifications of justice reasonably well, will be a just scheme: there is no need to find a unique and optimal scheme. The constraints of justice need not provide an algorithm, yet can guide judgement in powerful ways.

One of the main differences between the construction of material and of institutional and social artefacts is that justice, and injustice, are seldom if ever built *de novo*. Complex institutions and practices are already to hand, and themselves shape deliberation about justice and hence all moves towards successor institutions or practices. What is to hand may be judged defective in varied ways, and possibly unjust; but it nevertheless constrains what new institutions, practices and policies can be forged. Hence a movement towards less unjust institutions and practices will be in part a matter of remodelling what is to hand, of repairing or redesigning parts rather than the whole, of connecting or reconnecting aspects of life that have come apart, of separating aspects of life that are linked in ways that injure, of testing and adjusting what is to hand: in short of constructing and of reconstructing parts of institutions, practices and policies so that they come to embody the specifications of justice more adequately and more reliably. In this way, abstract starting points and a constructive conception of practical reason can be of practical use in building towards just institutions, practices and policies.

CHAPTER 7

Content II: principles for
all: towards virtue

Might justice be enough? Or, if not enough, might no other
inclusive ethical principles for lives and action and attitudes, for
institutions and policies prove vindicable? This is the view of many
contemporary writers on justice (cf. chapter 1). Contemporary
friends of the virtues find the view unconvincing and repugnant.
They aim to make a complete break with 'abstract' theories of
justice and with inclusive principles of all sorts. Yet the gulf both
parties see between justice and the virtues may be an artefact
produced by approaching the two from quite different directions, a
difference of approach too often 'justified' only by inattentive and
unconvincing denunciations of the rejected approach (cf. chapters
1 and 3). Yet if virtue need no more be unprincipled than justice
need be implacably uniform, a choice between them may be neither
necessary nor plausible.

Even if justice and virtue are consistent, an integrated account of
their principles may remain elusive. Any integrated account is
likely to focus at least in part on *required virtues* (if there are any;
cf. chapter 5), since these may prove vindicable by arguments
analogous to those which can vindicate the requirements of justice,
even if they differ from justice in other ways. Principles of justice
specify ethical requirements *and* their recipients; their observance
can in principle be claimed, waived and enforced by publicly
recognized actions that can be invoked even between strangers, for
example by conventional legal means or in routine economic
activity. Justice is a matter of perfect obligation, matched by rights;
its demands fall on all, and are owed to all. Required virtues, if
there are any, will also make demands that fall on all, but will not
specify recipients and occasions for virtuous action (cf. chapter 5).
Even when required of all, virtuous action can, indeed must, be
no more and no less than a matter of imperfect obligation, hence

selective and without counterpart rights: it will be directed at some and not at others, performed on some occasions and not on others, expressed in some ways and not in others. Even when required in special contexts, the pattern and occasions of virtuous action may leave much open for judgement. Consequently virtuous action, even if required, will be unclaimable, unwaivable and not readily enforceable by the conventional methods through which claimable obligations are often enforced.

If principles of required virtue are less tightly interlocked than those of justice, need any of them be inclusive principles, whose requirements govern all domains of life? May not virtue, unlike justice, be no more than a mosaic of traits and excellences, each of them required or important only for some specific context or relationship? Could not relativism about the virtues be combined with objective claims about justice? And do not ordinary experiences (as well as notable theorists) suggest that virtue can be compartmentalized and fractured? Do we not meet people who combine strict impartiality in their public or working life with amiable warmth in personal affairs? More ominously, are not some vicious war criminals said to have been good (at least not cruel) fathers and husbands? In short, why should any virtues be more than the virtues of particular spheres or situations? Perhaps virtue also differs from justice in lacking inclusive principles.

Inclusive principles are part of any account of justice because there must be some principles that link the different spheres and domains of life (section 6.1): it will not be enough to have *only* principles whose scope is restricted to specific domains or aspects of life. Parallel considerations suggest that at least some principles of required virtue (if there are any) must be *inclusive* principles. Not merely do agents have to lead a single life, in which they act in many different spheres and relationships, but they have to approach these varying spheres of action and relationships with certain orienting habits or traits, with a certain stance or attitude to others and to the life around them. The degree to which anyone can vary character with situation and relationships is limited by their need to relate and connect those different spheres. The spheres of action must be linked not only by public institutions that coordinate or subordinate them, but by continuities of character which support continuities of activity, including feeling, relationship and community.

Without some underlying orienting stance, without certain
attitudes and responses to others and to differing aspects of life, in
short without a *character*, action would be unstable and erratic;
the basis for sustaining relationships and ways of life would be
weakened; even ways of interpreting situations and of distinguishing which ways of feeling and acting were appropriate to
given contexts ('public' or 'private'; family or business; friend or
foe) would fluctuate. People who exhibit quite different traits in
different spheres of life are often seen not as typical, let alone
successful, in their inner fragmentation, but as having pervasive
failings of character and feeling and as susceptible to swings of
judgement and action. A rigid distinction or dissociation between
spheres of life is often maintained at great psychic cost, and
frequently fails: the impartial severities of the 'public' person carry
over into intimate relationships; the indulgences or bullying of
'private' life become the corruptions of 'public' life. Habits of
dishonesty or of callousness, of friendliness or of courtesy, are not
easily kept within distinct departments of life; nor are sensitivity
and lack of sensitivity to others. Without some very general
inclusive traits of character, patterns of action, attitude, and
feeling *within* spheres of life, even psychological stability, can fail.
Inclusive principles of virtue are no more dispensable than inclusive
principles of justice.

This conclusion does not imply that the virtuous life is rigidly
uniform. Inclusive principles of virtue, like those of justice, will
underdetermine action and attitudes and will be variably expressed
in different roles and relationships: an underlying, inclusive
orientation to others or to life need not and usually will not be
displayed in a regular (let alone a uniform) pattern of action or
attitude across different spheres of life and relationships.

Even if some virtues are required, and if some principles of virtue
are inclusive, others may be optional. Traits of character may be
excellent, much prized and much recommended, without any
thought or need that they should be sought and cultivated by all, or
that they are required. Some optional excellences of character may
be tied to particular roles or relationships; others to specific
projects or pursuits. There is no reason to suppose that all
excellences of human character and life conform to a single
pattern. It is only the vindication of required virtues (if there are
any) that may be closely linked with that of justice: that of optional

excellences may be wholly different. In considering how far an integrated account of justice and virtue is possible, it is therefore useful to separate the two ranges of virtues, and to consider the justification of required virtues separately.

7.1 REQUIRED AND OPTIONAL VIRTUES

For present and preliminary purposes five ranges of virtues can usefully be distinguished. The classification is neither exhaustive nor exclusive: for example, the theological virtue of *faith* fits happily in none of the categories I shall distinguish; the virtue of *toleration* might fit in several of them.

One range of required virtues consists of *virtues of justice*. Virtues of justice embody principles of justice in characters and lives, as just laws or institutions embody them in political, social and economic structures. The two types of embodiments of justice share a common underlying pattern of justification. In modern societies principles of justice must above all be embodied in public institutions (e.g. in Rawls's 'basic structure'), but they can also be embedded in individual characters, in social traditions and in the ethos of cultural groups. The virtues of justice include justice itself, as well as varied forms of fairness, of toleration and respect for others, of fidelity and probity, and of truthfulness and honesty. Since institutions are never perfect, the virtues of justice are never redundant: if institutions are not knave-proof, it helps not to have too many knaves around. Just political and economic institutions and social traditions can easily be perverted by cultures of corruption. Since the justification of principles of justice has already been discussed, no more need be said about that of virtues of justice; this does not mean that they are unimportant.

A second range of required virtues may be thought of as *executive virtues*. These virtues are manifested in deciding on, controlling and guiding action, policies and practices of all sorts. Executive virtues might include self-respect, self-control and decisiveness; courage and endurance, as well as numerous contemporary conceptions of autonomy; insight and self-knowledge, and various traits that are both cognitive and practical, such as efficiency, carefulness and accuracy. The reason why executive virtues are required is evidently that they are *means to action*, and especially to effective action, of all sorts. They are, so to speak, instrumentally necessary or instrumentally required traits of character.

Although executive virtues are also of great importance, I shall not discuss them here either, for two reasons. First, since they are ancillary or instrumental to action, their vindication offers little problem even to those who are largely unconcerned with ethics, or whose interest in ethics is mainly with justice: these virtues are important for all domains of life, for doing ill and for doing well, for thought as well as for cognition. Executive virtues will be acknowledged even by those who are most non-committal about the possibility of showing what it is to live well.[1] Second, any extensive, let alone interesting, discussion of executive virtues would need an ample account of agency, motivation and moral psychology.

It is a matter of controversy whether the substantive *social virtues* form a third range of required virtues. Instrumental justifications have frequently been proposed for these virtues. Many forms of altruism, from sympathy and beneficence to care and concern, have been depicted as traits that are required (if covert) means to self-interest, or as required (and generally overt) means to the common good. Such claims have the standard weaknesses of instrumental justifications. Some critics query whether any social virtues really are required *means* to self-interest or to the common good, others whether *ends* such as self-interest or subjective conceptions of the common good (e.g. maximal happiness) can really vindicate the means they require,[2] or more generally whether *ends* can justify *means*. These recurrent doubts and criticisms could be set aside if there were other, non-instrumental reasons for thinking that the principles that underlie certain social virtues were universal requirements.

Since principles of imperfect obligation (see section 5.4) do not specify *who* is entitled to receive required action, they are in part unlike principles of justice. But their vindication may be like that of inclusive principles of justice, in that it too works by showing that

---

[1] See Macedo, *Liberal Virtues*, esp. ch. 7; Ronald Dworkin, *Law's Empire* (London, Fontana, 1986), esp. ch. 6, on integrity. Macedo's liberal virtues include not only what are here classed as virtues of justice but aspects of certain social virtues; Dworkin emphasizes not only justice and fairness but integrity, see pp 164–6.

[2] If an objective conception of the Good, or of the common good, can be vindicated it will be generally allowed that it can be used to ground instrumental, and perhaps other (e.g. component/composite), justifications of traits of character.

certain inclusive principles cannot be universalized, and so that their rejection is required of those who seek to act reasonably. If inclusive principles of virtue are required, more specific social virtues such as solidarity and sympathy, help and beneficence, care and concern, generosity and magnanimity, as well as bonds of love and friendship may also be vindicable. The vindication of the underlying principles of some required social virtues will be discussed in the next section; even when a virtue is required its specific expression in one or another act or attitude will be a matter for judgement.

Other ranges of virtues or excellences may be optional rather than required. Most evidently, a fourth type of virtue, which is spoken of as *supererogatory*, is epitomized in the action of saints and heroes. In going 'beyond duty' supererogatory action must unavoidably be optional rather than required. Any reasons for thinking of it as excellent, and of characters that achieve it as saintly or heroic, must seemingly differ from those which underlie required virtues. Supererogatory action will be a principal concern of section 7.4.

Supererogatory action is not the only sort of optional yet excellent action, and the virtues of saints and heroes are not the only optional virtues. There are also numerous other-than-saintly and other-than-heroic ways of acting and living which have been seen as virtuous at one time or another, but not as required, or only as conditionally required elements of some optional way of life. These optional excellences are often linked to a specific stage or status in life, to certain roles and relationships, or to certain patterns and ideals of living. Although these optional excellences are not supererogatory, they too must escape any obligation-based conception of virtue; they will be briefly discussed in section 7.4.

7.2 VINDICATING SOCIAL VIRTUES: WHY JUSTICE IS NOT ENOUGH

Until recently a claim that certain social virtues are ethical requirements would have seemed commonplace; it might now meet scepticism of several sorts (chapter 1). One sort of scepticism is voiced by those who are suspicious of the very category of obligation, for reasons linked to their suspicions of rules and abstraction. Another sort of suspicion is voiced by those who are keen on obligations, but insist that they must always have counterpart rights, so be a matter of justice, and consequently will not allow for the possibility of imperfect obligations.

The latter suspicion reflects in part an appropriate concern not to conflate social justice with certain social virtues. For example, one reason why debates about 'welfare rights' have been so fierce within liberal political writing is that many liberal theorists note that what is not a matter of right cannot be claimed, so resist attempts to identify social justice with unclaimable helpfulness or charity. They fear that unless rights to certain goods or services can be established, the vulnerable will be left at the mercy of others' sporadic and often absent good will. This fear is wholly plausible: effective limitation of the vulnerabilities that facilitate injury (especially of the vulnerabilities that arise from destitution and disease) needs more than sporadic and unclaimable individual exertion and good will. It needs institutions which allocate responsibilities and create positive rights that will prevent or limit systematic injury of the vulnerable (cf. sections 5.2, 5.4, 5.5, 6.4 and 6.5). However, the fact that certain social virtues alone cannot effectively protect the vulnerable from injury, so cannot take over the tasks of social justice, does not show that they are unrequired: it shows only that they cannot be claimed as a matter of right (cf. section 5.3). There may also be required action that is not a matter of justice.

The construction of principles of justice sketched in the last chapter used a critical conception of practical reasoning to identify three *inclusive* principles of justice which those who found themselves connected to a plurality of others have reason to accept. Since injuring cannot be an inclusive principle for all, anyone will have reason to reject inclusive principles of injuring, for which they could give no adequate reasons to others. They will therefore have reason to reject systematic and gratuitous injury, whether inflicted directly on others, or inflicted indirectly on them by damaging the social and material structures on which lives depend; they will have reason to condone only injury that is needed to avoid more extensive injury. If systematic and gratuitous injury are rejected, numerous more specific requirements of justice for an actual situation can be identified. These more specific requirements range over acts and omissions as well as over support for policies, institutions and practices, that will express and implement rejection of injury in specific circumstances.

Considered in the abstract, principles of justice are a matter of rejecting principled injury, but considered more concretely justice is a matter of constructing, maintaining and living with and through specific institutions which limit injury, in part by defining special rights and obligations and procedures for constructing further special rights and obligations (for example, by promises, by contract, through market relations, by administrative procedures) and so can help achieve a degree of political, economic, social and environmental security for all. Put more generally, commitment to universal principles of justice is most effectively expressed through specific institutions that limit risks of injury, so helping to secure and maintain basic capacities and capabilities for action for all.

Hence in asking whether justice might be enough, we are asking what it would be to live by inclusive principles of rejecting injury, and by the institutions, practices and roles which can implement them in an actual situation. We can surely make sense of the thought that justice is all that is required, and that if lives and institutions are not based on principles of injuring others, the social fabric or the material world, then all that is required will have been achieved, or at any rate attempted. Although no human society has ever lived in this way, we recognize this thought in liberal writings that say nothing about good lives or about virtue, and in particular in libertarian thinking which views just institutions as the framework for 'voluntary' activity by individuals, within which preferences rather than virtue are to be pursued.

Yet it seems quite arbitrary to insist that living by principles of justice must be *all* that is ethically required in action towards others to whom we are connected. When we take account not only of the standard and repeated patterns of vulnerability which insitutions that are designed to avoid and limit injury can (partially) mitigate, but of the varied and specific ways in which particular agents and subjects are and become vulnerable to others, it seems unlikely that justice can be enough. Even when no injury is inflicted, capacities and capabilities for action can still be under-mined and eroded in many different ways. Human vulnerabilities[3]

---

[3] In considering virtue it is important to take account of the full range of vulnerabilities that are *actually* likely to be met – hence in human life of the vulnerabilities of other, connected human beings. If angels, aliens or artificial intelligences were vulnerable in quite different ways, those whose lives were connected to theirs would have to adjust their accounts of vulnerability, hence of virtues.

are not only *characteristic* and *persistent* (so to speak, *species vulner-abilities*), but *variable* and *selective*. Just institutions can aim to avert and mitigate many of the injuries to which characteristic and persistent vulnerabilities lay people open, but cannot generally avert or mitigate activity that exploits individuals' more variable and selective vulnerability.

Human beings begin by being *persistently* vulnerable in ways typical of the whole species: they have a long and helpless infancy and childhood; they acquire even their most essential physical and social capacities and capabilities with others' support; they depend on long-term social and emotional interaction with others; their lives depend on making stable and productive use of the natural and man-made world (these are some of the reasons why radically solitary yet competent human beings are mythical). Protection from injury in the face of these ubiquitous and foreseeable vulnerabilities of the human condition is in large measure the task of justice.

However, the very social links and dependencies which all social relations, including just social relations, create, not merely shield but restructure and often focus and intensify human vulnerabilities. We become more *deeply, variably* and *selectively* vulnerable to the action of the particular others and the particular institutions on whom we come to depend for specific and often for unavoidable purposes. The social fabric that creates capabilities which strengthen and protect also creates further vulnerabilities; the natural and man-made systems which sustain lives also render them dependent, often asymmetrically dependent. Affections engaged *both* secure others' support *and* expose to cruelty and rejection; dependence on the action of particular officials *both* secures support *and* exposes to the results of their corruption or inefficiency; marriage and family ties *both* support *and* demand; food aid that supplements subsistence agriculture and local markets *both* improves nutrition *and* creates dependence on suppliers.[4] Connected lives become selectively, variably and sometimes acutely vulnerable lives.

---

[4] This has been the theme of intense debates about food aid and its impact on subsistence agriculture. See Amartya Sen, *Poverty and Famine: An Essay on Entitlement and Deprivation* (Oxford, Clarendon Press, 1981); Drèze and Sen, *Hunger and Public Action*; O'Neill, *Faces Of Hunger*; Dasgupta *An Inquiry into Well-being and Destitution*.

While principles of justice take due account of the plurality of lives, they take minimal and formal account of their connectedness,[5] hence none of the *specific* ways in which *specific* sorts of vulnerability are created and heightened by *specific* connections.[6] Yet connection (which like plurality is constitutive of circumstances in which ethical concern has a locus) is always connection of a specific sort, to specific others, with specific power relations and expectations. So an account of ethical principles that focuses *only* on what it takes to sustain plurality, and takes too a limited view of the implications of connection and finitude, is likely to say far too little about inclusive requirements for those who are mutually vulnerable and connected in specific and variable ways that not merely mitigate but restructure, alter and heighten vulnerability. The suspicion that many friends of the virtues voice about writing that invokes 'idealized' images of independence and self-sufficiency (about 'atomistic', 'abstract', 'autonomous' and 'deontological' selves) is well-founded in this context, even if their fantasies that these suspicions provide reason or possibility to shun abstraction or principles are not.

Principles of justice can be derived from the requirement of rejecting inclusive principles of injuring, which are not universalizable across the domain of connected others. An analogous pattern of derivation shows that *inclusive principles of indifference to and neglect of others also cannot be universalized.* The underlying principles of a range of more specific required social virtues that are relevant to particular situations and at particular times can then be derived from the fact that agents have reason to reject principles of indifference or neglect.

---

[5] For example, political and economic theories often view individuals just as *voters* or as *consumers*, but bracket the specific asymmetries which give some great power over others. A conception of justice takes incomplete account of connectedness if it brackets the realities of dependence and vulnerability.

[6] Yet the theme is a classical one. Rousseau describes with pellucid clarity how society itself creates vulnerabilities: see in particular the end of Part I and beginning of Part II of *A Discourse on Inequality*, trans. Maurice Cranston (Harmondsworth, Penguin Books, 1984). Kant notes darkly that different sorts of vulnerability might arise for different sorts of beings, observing that even a nation of devils needs a state, hence justice, with the hint that they need no more. Perhaps there could be non-human beings for whom justice was more or less enough, for whom social virtues would have no place. *Perpetual Peace*, trans. H. B Nisbet, in H. Reiss, ed., *Kant: Political Writings* (Cambridge University Press, 1991), p. 112.

Indifference and neglect are not unjust. Nobody can avoid being indifferent to and neglecting many, if not most, others to whom they are connected. Nevertheless justice is not enough. Those who make indifference or neglect an *inclusive* principle are committed not to help or to care for any others within the domain of ethical consideration to which they are committed. They could think of their principles of indifference and neglect as universalizable, only if indifference and neglect could be inclusive principles for all. Yet no vulnerable agent can coherently accept that indifference and neglect should be universalized, for if they were nobody could rely on others' help; joint projects would tend to fail; vulnerable characters would be undermined; capacities and capabilities that need assistance and nurturing would not emerge; personal relationships would wither; education and cultural life would decline. It follows that those with plans and projects, even of the most minimal sort, cannot regard indifference and neglect as universalizable. Since human beings can foresee their own and others' variable and selective vulnerability and dependence, they could view indifference and neglect as universalizable *only* if they were willing to take it that all relationships and action, indeed all life, including their own, were bound to fail.[7] If, on the other hand, they intend to continue living and acting, they must (as a matter of instrumental rationality) take means required for that continuation, so cannot will that principles of indifference and neglect be universally adopted. Those with limited and variable capacities and capabilities *must* plan to rely in various ways on one another's capacities and capabilities for action, so *must* (if committed to universalizable inclusive principles) be committed to doing at least something to sustain one another's capacities and capabilities, hence committed to rejecting inclusive principles of indifference and neglect.

---

[7] Indifference and neglect are then non-universalizable if connected lives are to continue, while injury is non-universalizable *sans phrase*. Universal nihilism is a coherent but doomsday possibility. Most supposed nihilists embrace nihilism for themselves but assume life as usual for others, whose habits and virtues their own indifference and neglect is to exploit. Free riding nihilism is often sustainable, since others will be good-natured or unsuspecting, even virtuous (Thrasymachus was right up to a point); but nihilism is not universalizable in a world where action is to continue. Cf. chapter 5, note 23.

7.3. SELECTIVE CARE AND CONCERN

Those who reject indifference and neglect must meet demanding standards; but what those standards demand is inevitably variable and selective. Although many ethical traditions extol universal benevolence, love for all mankind, or concern for all, their rhetoric misleads. Justice can be observed in relations with all others; social virtues cannot. Since nobody can provide help or care for all others, or even for some others at every time, the rejection of indifference and neglect cannot be expressed in action for all others. Those who reject indifference must rather take *some* care to sustain *some* others in *some* ways; they must seek to support *some* others by sustaining at least *some* of their capacities and capabilities, their plans and their projects, where and how they can. Systematic indifference to others' plans and projects must be avoided, but gratuitous indifference to some, indeed many, others and to many of their capacities and capabilities, and of their plans and projects, is unavoidable and not wrong.[8] The social virtues make selective demands: they leave open to whom, or when or in what ways virtue is to be expressed. They do not require generalized or maximal benevolence or beneficence, or any set amount of either, but only *selective* and *feasible* help, care, love, generosity, support or solidarity. Consequently acts of virtue will be unclaimable, unwaivable and unenforceable, and there will be no universal rights to others' virtuous action.

If the social virtues leave so much open, they may seem to demand too little. In fact they are hugely demanding, because trivial and sporadic instances of care and concern are not enough to show that principles of indifference and neglect are rejected. Trivial politeness or sporadic 'charity', for example, might be read as evidence of bad conscience or of concern for reputation, but taken in isolation they will hardly be read as evidence of the rejection of principled indifference or neglect. The rejection of indifference and neglect which certain social virtues demand will be appropriately expressed only through patterns of action that,

---

[8] By this is meant only that indifference for which there is no particular reason is not wrong. Sometimes action is spoken of as *gratuitous* with the implication that the contrary was in fact required, or that the action was in some ways spiteful or wrong. In speaking of gratuitous indifference as permissible, such ironic uses of the term are set aside.

although selective, go considerably further to sustain others' lives and their capacities and capabilities for action.

Social virtues can often be fluently expressed within *specific* ways of life and *particular* relationships that sustain others across long periods; they can also be expressed in contexts where destitution and oppression, need and danger, heighten vulnerability. A central context for attitudes and action that express certain social virtues is often provided by the daily, ordered and constraining lives of family and household, school and work, friendship and locality. At their best these provide organizing structures for sustained love, care and solidarity; those who live with and through these patterns of life may develop deep feelings and complex expectations of one another, and with them stably internalized traits of character that enable them to sustain one another. As is well known, at their worst these same constraining structures also deepen vulnerabilities and so enhance opportunities for the ordinary social vices such as cruelty, exploitation, disdain, snobbery and coldness, including their harshest manifestations such as bullying and abuse, even slavery and torture, and for the devastating emotional and even physical stunting and paralysis, neurosis and inhibition which these can produce.[9]

Even when certain social virtues are formed by these sorts of special relationship, and flourish within them, they will not replicate the structures or the tasks of special duties of justice. Special duties of justice arise where contractual or other institutional structures establish enforceable rights and obligations between specified parties. However, when occasions and recipients of action are not fully defined, principles have to be embedded in more flexible ways. This is the basic reason why certain social virtues are better embodied in the characters of agents, in the ethos of institutions and in social practices and traditions, as 'portable', or at least 'semi-portable', ethical attitudes and characteristics, rather than in structures that define precise claims between agents and recipients.

---

[9] The point is not exaggerated. Certain time-honoured ways of life and forms of family have denied some intimates all independence, or condemned them to endless work that supports others' leisure, or allowed them to eat only others' left-overs, and have even mutilated them routinely. For more ordinary ways in which certain social vices are expressed see Judith N. Shklar, *Ordinary Vices* (Cambridge Mass., Harvard University Press, 1984).

The rejection of indifference and neglect are therefore properly expressed not only by the formation of appropriate characters but also in part through the construction and cultivation of *special* relationships which normally *channel* and *focus* certain social virtues. Intimacy, family and friendship can provide privileged contexts for love, concern and generosity; shared work and shared activities for lesser yet still for demanding patterns of help, support and concern. More generally, some patterns of protected dependence and interdependence can create special opportunity and special urgency for quite specific forms of help, care and concern. The genuine rejection of indifference and neglect can therefore be achieved in part through the construction of these sorts of special relationships and associations, which can foster special (if still imperfect) obligations and define special contexts for care and help.

Social virtues are not, however, bound to those daily contexts of social life in which they can flourish. Although special relationships, above all intimate and local relationships, provide a preeminent setting for certain social virtues, and a correspondingly revealing context for certain social vices, they can also be expressed in many other contexts, and in particular through acts of *solidarity* and of *rescue*.

Solidarity can be expressed across large spatial and social distances, to others who are neither near nor dear, through forms of help and support for distant strangers, especially to those who are destitute or oppressed. The efforts of the anti-apartheid movement and of many charities which try to bring aid to parts of the developing world provide instances of care and concern which is not limited to the near or dear. Acts of *rescue* are more dramatic expressions of care and concern, directed towards others in present danger and misfortune, who may also be neither near nor dear. Here too social virtues cannot take over the tasks of social justice, and inevitably offer only indeterminate guidance for acts of solidarity and of rescue: their principles do not determine to whom solidarity should be shown in which ways or at what cost, or who should be rescued from what dangers or at what risk. There are no rights to solidarity, and no rights to be rescued from danger. Like other social virtues, duties of solidarity and duties to rescue are imperfect duties.

The indeterminacy of principles of imperfect obligation may

seem worrying. Will not imperfect obligations sanction arbitrary
action if they fail to determine *to whom* virtuous action is owed, or
how much is owed, or *just what* is owed? A *general* concern about
indeterminacy is unnecessary. Not everything that is left undetermined need be arbitrary in any worrying sense: if it seems so, this
may once again reflect a tacit assumption that ethical reasoning
ought to lead to some practical algorithm. Indeterminacy is in
fact an unavoidable feature of all principles of action, and of all
reasoning about action, hence also of obligations, whether of justice
or of virtue; if it is not a disaster in one case, it need not be one in
the other.

However, a more focused worry about the indeterminacy of social
virtues may be more plausible. This worry concedes that principles
of virtue could not and need not offer complete guidance, but
complains that they offer *too little* guidance: can it be enough to
know that some help and concern are required in some contexts,
such as those defined by special relationships, by distant need and
oppression and by present danger? If social virtues determine too
little, it will seemingly not much matter who gets helped or for
whom care is shown, or which special relationships are cultivated
and which neglected. Can selective helpfulness or care that
addresses the expectations or needs of some, but wholly neglects
those of others, be all that social virtues demand? If it is, will they
not sanction a careless indifference to some who are near or dear,
or a complete neglect of others who are neither near nor dear, but
who are in direct need or present danger?

The hard answer is that no degree of cultivation of social virtues
can avoid some indifference and some neglect both to those near or
dear and to those in distant or present need. Special relationships
never make it possible to offer even those others with whom
connections are closest all possible forms of help and concern.
Acute need never makes all forms of solidarity and rescue
possible.

Nevertheless, some guidance for the allocation of care and
concern is discernible. The patterns of enhanced vulnerability and
dependence created by intimacy and association and other sorts of
special relationship bring with them compelling (if inevitably
incomplete) reasons for directing much care and concern to those
who have become dear or near. Even when special relationships do
not give rise to the special claim rights which just institutions

create,[10] they create broad and deep expectations of support and need for care. A life in which helpfulness and concern were directed *only* at distant strangers, for example, or which was lived *only* for good causes or public service at the expense of family and friends, would be askew in its rejection of indifference; so would a life which burns to rescue others from present danger but neglects them whenever danger is past.

Solidarity and rescue, by which certain social virtues address others' oppression and danger, must be limited for similar reasons. Help and care for the oppressed is all too evidently selective; so are efforts to rescue those in present danger. Nobody can, or can have an obligation to, help all the needy of the earth; nobody can, or can have an obligation to, help or rescue all those in danger. The direction and channelling of such help must be a matter of choice and opportunity; its allocation cannot be antecedently determined; its demands cannot invariably trump those of special relationships.

The indeterminacy of principles of virtue need not, however, be any sort of disaster. The virtuous life will not be undone by lack of conclusive reasons or instructions when there are none; it will be furthered by taking certain social virtues most seriously in the contexts where they can be most powerfully channelled and felt. There is no general reason to worry that there are no fuller instructions. It does not matter that the social virtues do not tell us whether we should rescue one rather than another indistinguishable drowning stranger. If such cases arise, we will have done well if we rescue either, and excellently if we rescue both.[11] Nor is there any general problem if one of those in danger is near or dear to the potential rescuer and the other is not: universal obligations to help others are never obligations to help all in danger, which will often exceed any rescuer's powers. Where only one can be rescued, help and care will have been better expressed in rescuing the near or

---

[10] Often there will also be special rights within special relationships, in particular where relationships also have contractual aspects, or where roles are legally defined, as in the case of marriage or parental roles. Meeting these special rights is not a matter of virtue. See sections 5.2, 5.5.

[11] See Marcus on Buridan cases, 'Moral Dilemmas and Consistency'. Those who feel short-changed by lack of complete ethical guidance for such predicaments hanker for an ethical algorithm; they may have to choose between giving up their craving and the consolations of utilitarianism.

dear, and less well expressed in rescuing a stranger rather than one with whom the rescuer has close bonds (because bonds of dependence and expectations of help and support will have failed in neglecting the near or dear, but not in neglecting strangers). Where more than one can be rescued, help and concern will be excellently expressed in rescuing both the near or dear and strangers. The virtuous life is lived not only by general (and highly indeterminate) commitments to help and care, but among and through relationships and bonds that guide and direct at least some special (rather more determinate) obligations of virtue, although they too do not totally direct it and leave room enough for some help and concern for some others with whom there is no antecedent bond or relationship.

7.4 VARIETIES OF SOCIAL VIRTUE

No complete taxonomy of social virtues is possible. Like principles of justice, any principle of virtue can take an amazing range of more determinate forms. However, three *constellations* of social virtues can usefully be distinguished. Each of these constellations of social virtues bears particularly on one aspect of the lives of pluralities of connected but finite beings that are oriented by inclusive and universalizable principles. Many social virtues may be expressed either *directly* in forms of care or concern for individuals, or *indirectly* through care or concern for shared social worlds or for shared natural and man-made environments.

The central constellation of social virtues includes traits expressed by giving and showing concern and care directly to others in ways that go beyond justice: most of the examples in the previous section fall within this range of social virtues. These central social virtues demand not that direct injury but that *directly expressed indifference* to others be rejected. In a world of vulnerable beings who rejected only principles of injury in their dealings, yet were wholly indifferent to one another, many capacities and capabilities for action would falter and fail. It is a misleading idealization to premise action on the assumption that all have so high a degree of independence, rationality or self-sufficiency that they can always sustain their capacities and capabilities for action, provided only that they are not injured. On the contrary, capacities and capabilities for action are always fragile; even the seemingly autonomous may be so only because they are secure in others' care and concern. Hence systematic indifference to others cannot be a principle for all, and the rejection of systematic indifference is correspondingly required of all. Nevertheless, the allocation of types of care and concern (material support that goes beyond entitlement, beneficence, solidarity and sympathy, generosity, love or friendship) remains a matter of discretion both in general and within special relationships and associations. Systematic indifference to others is vicious, but gratuitous indifference is often unavoidable, and although not virtuous will also not be vicious.[12]

The directly expressed social virtues are particularly important, and their neglect peculiarly undermining, when public institutions are bitterly unjust or destitution extreme. Although no amount of virtuous action can compensate for the injuries of injustice, it can make some difference. Although nobody can care for and help all others, so that any obligation to do so must be selective, and more selective still under the yoke of unjust or corrupt institutions, or in harsh poverty, the very fact that virtue can best be embodied in individual character, and hence exercised in dispersed forms, means that at times it survives when justice does not. Then, as in easier times, nobody can show concern or care for everybody, but some people may be able to show some care or concern for some others, and so forge and sustain forms of solidarity or friendship which ease the pain of poverty and injustice, even if neither can be mitigated. Sometimes dispersed acts of solidarity and support also have cumulative public effects: this is the power of the powerless even in hard times.[13] Histories of solidarity among the oppressed – the early Church, the Jews at Masada, resistance to modern totalitarian powers – reveal the significance of certain social virtues where justice is defective. So in lesser form does solidarity *with* rather than *among* the oppressed, offered by the more fortunate. On a smaller scale, the contrasting records of families and friends who support and who desert one another when times are hard provide evidence enough of the importance of love and kindness when

---

[12] Noting once again that gratuitous indifference (cf gratuitous injury) is simply indifference for which no reason is or need be given; it need not be malicious indifference, let alone vicious.

[13] Havel, *The Power of the Powerless*, pp. 36–122.

justice is unachievable. Of course, no social virtues are redundant in easier times; but their practice will be eased when unjust institutions no longer injure or intimidate.

A second constellation of social virtues expresses the rejection of indifference and neglect less directly by sustaining and supporting social trust and connection, so indirectly sustaining capabilities for action, communication and interaction. Even when unjust institutions or action do not destroy or damage trust, and when support and care for particular others is well expressed, indifference to the social fabric which connects agents will not be universalizable. The fabric of feeling, culture and convention which sustains trust and communication is always fragile and vulnerable. It not only has to be preserved from damage and destruction, but to be shielded from mere indifference or neglect. It has constantly to be created and sustained, recreated and renewed, to preserve 'the food of future generations'; and of the present generation.[14] That 'food' will be reduced, and capacities and capabilities will fail at least for some, when nobody maintains and contributes to sustainable practices of communication, of toleration and confidence-building, of loyalty and engagement, of educating and encouraging, that will enable action, interaction and the development of human potential and culture. The social conditions for human life and interaction can be sustained and supported among connected agents only by attitudes and action that educate new generations, that develop individual characters and their capacities and capabilities and that foster and seek to improve civilizing institutions. To sustain and build confidence and trust, and with them the social fabric, we must not merely act justly, so refrain from destroying them, but help to breathe life both into current and into new practices and ways of life.

The virtues that will help sustain the social fabric include a huge range of practices and attitudes. At most times they will include toleration and trust, openness and patience, and a readiness to cooperate, to participate, to join in, to engage with others. They will also include *both* loyalty to others and support for achieved practices, cultures and traditions *and* a readiness to seek and support new ways of living and new forms of connection. They will

---

[14] Weil, *The Need for Roots*.

be expressed both in personal life and through social practices that form both character and culture. They will be most copiously expressed by forming and sustaining, by reforming and renewing special relationships, shared cultures and shared community, but they may also be expressed (and needed) in relations between strangers and between communities. Although their demands may and must vary, and although their expression must be selective, this constellation of social virtues too is highly demanding.

A third constellation of social virtues also expresses the rejection of indifference and neglect less directly, in action that sustains natural and man-made environments on which both individual lives and the social fabric depend. Universal indifference to the care and preservation of natural and man-made environments undermines and withers human life and capacities and capabilities for action.[15] Refraining from destroying or damaging environments which provide the material basis for socially connected lives constitutes environmental justice. Yet lives and cultures will remain vulnerable if they depend on environments which, although not damaged, are also not cherished. Vulnerabilities multiply for those who find themselves drawing bare subsistence and shelter from environments they do not understand or care for. They are lessened and limited for those who inhabit a natural and man-made world that flourishes and supports them both materially and spiritually. An ethically sound relation to the environment must then go beyond avoiding systematic and gratuitous damage that injures others' lives; it must also be expressed in care and concern to sustain and conserve at least some parts or aspects of that environment in a flourishing condition.

Action that rejects indifference to natural and man-made environments must, once again, be selective; once again it is demanding. Systematic indifference might have slight effects where populations are scattered or technologies small-scale, but in an era of leaping populations and transforming technological powers, systematic indifference to natural and man-made environments has huge effects. In these conditions mere indifference, if systematic, can blight sustainable systems of agriculture, land-

---

[15] Once again the anthropocentric limitations of this account of green virtues is evident: no more proved vindicable without perfectionist starting points; more might not be liveable even by those who help themselves liberally to those starting points.

scapes and ecosystems, and degrade towns and villages that shelter and enrich lives. It can even erode the possibilities of clean air and water. At the limit it may inflict permanent damage on climates and on the ozone layer, or may blight biodiversity. Here, more than anywhere else, the boundaries between just rejection of damage and destruction that injure and virtuous care and concern that express the rejection of indifference and neglect are often blurred. As we come to understand the overwhelming environmental implications of the unintended consequences of universal – or even of widespread – indifference to and neglect of natural and man-made environments, we may come to view patterns of action that were formerly seen only as manifesting systematic indifference as evidence of systematic injury.

Although this boundary is faint in particular cases, the conceptual distinction between environmental justice and care for the environment that goes beyond justice is a clear one. Concern and care for natural and man-made environments, like concern and care for other individuals and for the social fabric of life, is not merely inevitably selective, but quite particular. Not every way in which it can be expressed will be possible, or even resonate for all. Some will express care that goes beyond justice through patient cultivation of fields or care for herds, others by seeking to preserve familiar landscapes and townscapes, yet others by conserving uncultivated wilderness, by protecting endangered species or by restoring them to ancestral habitats. Yet others will express them through scientific work that increases understanding of processes that sustain and that degrade environments, by working for greener industries or greener politics, or by searching for and adopting greener lifestyles. These 'green virtues' are not to be identified with a determinate set of highly specific policies, projects or activities, but rather with the rejection of policies or attitudes that express indifference to natural and man-made environments in ways that are realistic rather than sentimental for actual situations.

The parallels and connections between these three constellations of required social virtues and the three ranges of obligations of justice can be summarized diagrammatically. In each case justice forbids systematic and gratuitous action that injures, whether directly or indirectly, while certain social virtues forbid systematic but not gratuitous indifference or neglect, whose effects may be either direct or indirect.

Obligations of justice: rejection of injury

– Rejection of direct injury to others: no systematic or gratuitous violence, coercion etc.

– Rejection of indirect injury
  (a) Rejection of damage to the social fabric: no systematic or gratuitous deceit, fraud, incitement to hatred etc.
  (b) Rejection of damage to the material basis of life: no systematic or gratuitous damage to natural or man-made environments

Obligations of virtue: rejection of indifference and neglect

– Rejection of direct indifference to others: sympathy, beneficence, love, help, care and concern, solidarity, acts of rescue etc.

– Rejection of indirect indifference to others
  (a) Rejection of indifference to the social fabric: selective care and support for social life and culture, expressed in toleration, participation, loyalty, social reform etc.
  (b) Rejection of indifference to the material basis of life: selective care and concern for natural and man-made environments, expressed in cultivation, preservation and conservation etc.

In working from these sparse principles towards more specific obligations, and towards a conception of the institutions and characters which might embody justice and certain social virtues for a particular time and place, with its particular population and their existing and potential relationships, resources and technologies, we should never expect to find complete instructions for either. The best ways of constructing institutions and practices, characters and cultures, that express justice and certain social virtues will vary; their complete realization is an illusory aim. The most that can be aimed for is then to work *towards* constitutions and institutions, practices and activities which are good enough embodiments of justice for that time and place, and *towards* characters and practices, ways of acting and of feeling, relationships and communities, that are good enough embodiments of certain social virtues for that same time and place. The rejection both of systematic injury and indifference and of gratuitous injury, in their many manifestations, can lead *towards* just institutions and virtuous characters, but there is no point or moment of arrival at which perfect justice or complete virtue will have been achieved.

7.5 SUPEREROGATION AND OPTIONAL EXCELLENCES

Justice and certain social virtues are linked because both are required. Even if all their requirements were reasonably well satisfied much remains open. The fears voiced by friends of the virtues that an ethic of principles and in particular of obligations would convert the whole of life into a moral *gulag* of requirements is groundless, since ethical constraints are indeterminate, so (if not intrinsically inconsistent) open to varied realizations, as well as compatible with the pursuit of sundry other objectives, concerns and 'life projects'.

Yet a focus on required virtues, on required character and required action, and nothing else, is narrow. It says nothing about unrequired excellences of human life which are not a matter of duty. It offers no account either of action which goes beyond duty, such as saintly or heroic action, which is often spoken of as supererogatory, or of unrequired excellences which are other than saintly or heroic.

Many accounts of ethics are unavoidably silent about supererogation. Both their proponents and their opponents sometimes worry about this silence, of which they offer varying explanations. This is not surprising. Supererogatory action is action that exceeds the demands of duty, yet is ethically admirable. A number of ethical positions cannot even allow for this possibility. Utilitarians, for example, cannot allow for supererogatory action, because they hold that in any given situation some act will be optimal, so a matter of duty. For utilitarians there is always one more duty to be done, and the time for going 'beyond duty' never arrives. Anything that is not a matter of duty will neglect duty, so is forbidden: only the best will do. The notorious 'overload of obligations' problem is simply a structural feature of utilitarianism.[16] Other views of ethics cannot account for supererogatory action for quite different reasons. For example, those who wish to rid ethics of the category

[16] James S. Fishkin, *The Limits of Obligation* (New Haven, Conn., Yale University Press, 1982).

of obligation (as some friends of the virtues hope to) will inevitably have difficulty in classifying any sort of action as lying 'beyond obligation'. On the other hand, those who think, as libertarians do, that obligations are unproblematic, provided they are perfect obligations with corresponding rights, will have difficulty explaining what could make action not required by respect for others' rights admirable. Libertarians claim to prize strong liberty rights in part because they leave room for admirable activities, such as 'voluntary giving' or 'voluntary philanthropy',[17] yet it is quite obscure why they should prize either of these voluntary activities any more than they prize (say) 'voluntary indifference' or 'voluntary stinginess' (cf. section 5.2). A clear-headed libertarian should presumably put all of these on a par, as permitted uses of discretionary space. None of these ethical theories offers any account of special admiration for saintly and heroic action, or for action that tends in these directions even if it does not reach those heights.

Yet the achievements for which we admire saints and heroes are not wholly alien. Saints and heroes are admired because they fulfil quite ordinary ethical requirements, but do so with superabundance. Love, help, care and concern for others are matters of ordinary, imperfect obligation, which need elude nobody: but Father Kolbe's act of giving his life for another's at Auschwitz went far beyond meeting the bare demands of love – and of courage. So too do many unknown parents and health-workers whose lives are attentively devoted to caring for others across weary and difficult years. Sustaining and building trust among people is a matter of ordinary if imperfect obligation: but Nelson Mandela's exemplary approach to doing so goes far beyond those ordinary demands. So too do the lives of countless less public figures, who work in ways that reconcile rather than embitter. Care for the environment may be an imperfect obligation, and may so far lack its official saints or heroes: but the work of those individuals and groups who do most to protect and rescue natural and man-made environments from brutal damage and destruction goes far beyond ordinary demands.

In a sense the clue to the notion of supererogation lies in its etymology. Supererogatory action is indeed not required, but it is measured by that which is required: *in supererogatory action the*

---

[17] The scare quotes merely because the idea of compulsory philanthropy is incoherent.

ordinary measures of duty rather than the categories of duty are exceeded.
When heroes and saints say 'I was only doing my duty' their
thoughts are modestly expressed, but not entirely wrong. The
saintly or heroic act was indeed a token of a required type of action,
but a token that exceeded all expectations and all ordinary
measures of duty.

These thoughts also suggest why examples of supererogatory
action typically exceed the measure of virtues rather than those
of justice. It is hard to see how institutions could achieve superabundant justice: justice is a matter of what is due, and going
beyond justice is not more just (although it may be more virtuous).
However, certain virtues can be exemplified in superabundant
ways. Courage and endurance may be present in ordinary measure
in ordinary lives, but in superabundant measure in the lives of
saints and heroes. The virtues of justice have their ordinary
measures in fair and decent behaviour to others, but may be superabundant in the lives of exemplary peace makers or legislators, or
in resistance to extraordinary temptations to act unjustly. Equally
the social virtues of care, help, trust, and solidarity are ordinarily
displayed in ordinary measures, if at all, but are revealed in superabundance in the lives of saints and heroes.

While supererogatory action can, and if these considerations are
plausible, must be understood by reference to duty, this is not true
of other unrequired excellences. The virtues of many traditional
exemplary 'lives', as well as those of more recent ideals and
'experiments in living', depict and celebrate optional excellences
that are not thought of as exceeding the measures of duty; equally
many cautionary tales tell of licit failings rather than of forbidden
vice. The conventional tally of optional excellences includes many
traits of the classical 'lives' of pleasure, wealth, honour and
contemplation, as well as of more recently promoted 'lives' of
devotion and service, of innovation and autonomy, and of the traits
that are central to specific roles, vocations and activities. 'Lives' and
roles can be mutually exclusive not merely if they are intrinsically
incompatible (no genuine hermit can also be an investigative
reporter), but if the conditions for living them are hard to combine
(as lives of honour and of wealth are notoriously hard to combine).
The characteristic virtues of 'lives' that are hard to combine cannot
easily be energetically pursued within one stretch of a single life.
For example, the conventional excellences of a wife and of a

frontiersman, which centre respectively on domestic and adventurous activity, cannot readily be pursued at the same time. Such society or role-specific virtues are no doubt numberless, as Meno thought, but they will have significance beyond the world whose ways of thought and life they record and manifest only if they happen *also* to exemplify ethical principles which have wider justifications.

These optional, other-than-heroic and other-than-saintly, excellences will often be the excellences of specific traditions or of established ways of living, but they can also be the excellences of dreamed-of and unrealized futures, or even of lives currently despised. A revaluation of values may view traits which were formerly seen as failings, or even as vicious, as virtues: poverty, humility and chastity have all had their day as virtues; so have opulence, pride and sexual prowess. The permanent possibility of revaluation is, however, no reason for thinking either that there is a timelessly correct tally of virtues, or that no virtue is more than the fashion of its times. The reasons which may make virtues of a trait that was formerly derided, and conversely may make a vice of a trait that was formerly prized, are reasons that can be followed at all times. They may lead to differing conclusions when times, conditions and possibilities of life differ. It may be hard to imagine that the ascetic or monkish virtues, or the virtues of codes of honour, should become the reborn virtues of a future time – but less hard to imagine if one begins by imagining a different social fabric and a changed natural and man-made environment.[18]

7.6 TOWARDS JUSTICE WITH VIRTUE

If some of the requirements of justice and of a range of social virtues can be identified, they can provide blueprints for embodying and enacting justice and virtue in institutions and characters at particular times and places. Like other blueprints, they will specify structural requirements, but leave other matters undetermined. They will provide standards by which to assess entrenched

---

[18] It is a merit of much historicist writing in ethics that it has taken optional, contextual excellences seriously; a difficulty that it has taken them so seriously that it often treats them as *constitutive* of ethical excellence, so overlooking the possibility of universally available reasons for thinking some rather than other traits excellent in certain circumstances, while masking these limitations by suggesting that ethical standards only can be recommended to those who already share the relevant traditions and standards.

institutions and traits of characters, and to show whether they implement or obstruct the rejection of injury or of indifference, but do not themselves include instructions for entrenching those standards in one rather than another way. The blueprints for justice and for required virtue also cannot show anything about unrequired traits and characteristics that are (rightly or wrongly) cherished or admired, and often thought of as excellences or virtues. They will neither support nor undercut claims about practical principles which simply exhort and recommend, warn and condemn, although they will leave ample room for taking such principles, or their rejection, seriously.

Principles which exhort and recommend, warn and condemn are not, of course, to be taken lightly; but they are also not to be taken as seriously as those which prescribe and proscribe requirements that are not conditional on particular social structures or practices. Requirements are to be taken the more seriously if reasonably meagre and uncontroversial starting points and methods are enough to fix their focus, their scope, their structure and the core of their content. Such starting points have to be taken seriously because they are indeed merely abstract, rather than assuming, so needing to justify, ideals of human life, or idealized conceptions of human capacities, capabilities or of reason. Ways of building on these starting points have also to be taken seriously if they rely on a conception of practical reason which insists only that acknowledged others can be given no reasons for acting on principles which it is impossible for them to adopt. These meagre starting points and methods, supplemented only by materials available in all contexts (e.g. the results of instrumental reasoning and of empirical inquiry, knowledge of social realities and human abilities), provide enough to construct a capacious account of human obligations which does not assume that whatever is, is right, or that 'ought' can be derived from 'is', and does not identify justice with established power or virtue with established habit. Taken together, strictly abstract starting points and a critical conception of practical reason can show why a certain type of integrated account of justice and of virtue is to be taken seriously, while acknowledging that, even if taken seriously, that account of justice and of virtue will not provide complete instructions for a just social order or for virtuous lives; but it will provide guidelines for moving towards justice and towards virtue.

This constructive account of practical reason and of ethics cannot then rebuild the heavenly city of which so many perfectionists have dreamed. Since it provides no account of the *summum bonum* or of the Good for Man, or of other transcendent or intrinsic values, it cannot provide complete plans for building the Good Life. Nor can it provide complete instructions for building either that timeless Kingdom of Ends whose image resonates in utopian thinking, or the Peaceable Kingdom whose image animates deep ecology. Although it offers no reasons for rejecting these ideals and visions, it provides no account of their details and no reason for accepting them even in outline, or for thinking that any timeless yet detailed account of justice and of virtue is possible. What it offers is a reasoned way of thinking about the planning and construction of earthly cities and of lives that are or could be led and shared in them under various conditions without fantasizing that imaginary foundations are available or that permanent solutions are possible.

A constructivist account of ethics is therefore inevitably down to earth, but may lack neither ambition nor success. Its partial success will not satisfy those who still dream the perfectionist dream; but unlike their dreams its claims are both *vindicable* and *practical*. Its limited but achievable ambitions may then resonate for those who think that ethics must be practical as well as reasoned, and that it cannot be reasoned if based on illusory assumptions. As Kant reminded his readers when he reflected on the illusory ambitions of traditional metaphysics near the end of the *Critique of Pure Reason*, a critical approach to thought and to action will disappoint if measured against the aspirations of those soaring dreams, yet may provide what we need for leading earthly lives:

... although we had in mind a tower that would reach the heavens, yet the stock of materials was only enough for a dwelling house – for our tasks on the plain of experience, and just high enough for us to look across the plain .... Since we have been warned not to risk everything on a favourite but senseless project, which could perhaps exceed our whole means, yet cannot well refrain from building a secure home, we have to plan our building with the supplies we have been given and also to suit our needs.[19]

[19] Immanuel Kant, *Critique of Pure Reason* (1781), A707/B735 (Prussian Academy pagination), trans. O. O'Neill; for commentary on this passage and its significance for a constructivist account of reason, see the discussion in section 2.4 above and the items quoted in chapter 2, note 34, especially 'The Public Use of Reason' in *Constructions of Reason*.

If we cannot attain other-worldly ethical heights, then any rejection of nihilism must find some permanently available this-worldly touchstone for ethical claims. Some have sought this permanent touchstone in the actual psychological propensities of human nature, others in historically achieved ethical standards and practices. Although I have said rather little about the difficulties of naturalistic and historicist ways of making ethics this-worldly, I have, I hope, said enough to show why I doubt whether naturalisms in fact use only 'supplies that we have been given', and whether historicisms can in fact build 'to suit our needs', rather than trapping us in the buildings and boundaries of a given time.

A constructive approach need, I hope, fail in neither of these ways and can point towards both justice and virtue. The touchstones of abstraction and universalizability on which it relies will be available for all: they can provide guide-lines but do not offer complete instructions for building lives or societies. At each time and place, those who hope to move towards justice and towards virtue will have to build, and to rebuild, shaping the institutions, polities and practices which they find around them, and their own attitudes and activities, to meet standards which, they believe, can be standards for all within the domain of their ethical consideration.

Bibliography

Allott, Philip, *Eunomia: New Order for a New World*, New York, Oxford University Press, 1990.

Alston, Philip, 'International Law and the Human Right to Food' in P. Alston and K. Tomasevski, eds., *The Right to Food*, Dordrecht, Nijhoff, 1984, pp. 9–68.

Anscombe, G. E. M., 'Modern Moral Philosophy' in *The Collected Papers of G. E. M. Anscombe*, vol. III, *Ethics, Religion and Politics*, Oxford, Blackwell, 1981, pp. 26–42.

Archard, David, *Children: Rights and Childhood*, London, Routledge, 1993.

Arendt, Hannah, *The Human Condition*, University of Chicago Press, 1958.

    Eichmann in Jerusalem: A Study in the Banality of Evil, London, Faber and Faber, 1963.

Aristotle, *Nichomachean Ethics*, trans. W. D. Ross, in Richard McKeon ed., *Basic Works of Aristotle*, New York, Random House, 1941.

    The Politics, trans. W. D. Ross, revised by J. L. Ackrill, J. O. Urmson and Jonathan Barnes, ed. Stephen Everson, Cambridge University Press, 1988.

Baldwin, Thomas, 'The Territorial State' in Hyman Gross and Ross Harrison, eds., *Jurisprudence: Cambridge Essays*, Oxford, Clarendon Press, 1992, pp. 207–30.

Baron, Marcia, 'Kantian Obligations and Supererogation', *Journal of Philosophy*, 84 (1987), 237–62.

Beardsmore, R., *Moral Reasoning*, London, Routledge and Kegan Paul, 1969.

Behler, Rodger, *Moral Life*, London, Methuen, 1983.

Beitz, Charles, *Political Theory and International Relations*, Princeton University Press, 1979.

Bell, David, 'The Art of Judging', *Mind*, 96 (1987), 221–44.

Benhabib, Seyla and Drucilla Cornell, eds., *Feminism as Critique: Essays on the Politics of Gender in Late Capitalism*, Cambridge, Polity Press, 1987.

Berlin, Isaiah, *The Crooked Timber of Humanity*, London, John Murray, 1990.

Blackburn, Simon, 'Rule Following and Moral Realism' in Steven Holtzmann and Christopher Leach, eds., *Wittgenstein: To Follow a Rule*, London: Routledge and Kegan Paul 1981, pp. 163–87.

Blum, L. W., *Friendship, Altruism and Morality*, London, Routledge and Kegan Paul, 1980.

Brink, David O., 'Rawlsian Constructivism in Moral Theory', *Canadian Journal of Philosophy*, 17 (1987), 71–90.

Brown, C., ed., *Political Restructuring in Europe: Ethical Perspectives*, London, Routledge, 1994.

Buchanan, Alan, 'Justice and Charity', *Ethics*, 97 (1987), 558–75.

Campbell, T. D., 'Perfect and Imperfect Duties', *The Modern Schoolman*, 102 (1975), 185–94.

Carruthers, Peter, *The Animals Issue: Moral Theory in Practice*, Cambridge University Press, 1992.

Cavell, Stanley, *Must We Mean What We Say?*, Cambridge University Press, 1976.

Cicero, Marcus Tullius, *De Republica*; section 3 is not included in some editions and translations but can be found in *On Government*, trans. Michael Grant, Harmondsworth, Middlesex, Penguin Books, 1993.

Cohen, G. A., 'Equality of What? On Welfare, Goods and Capabilities', in Martha Nussbaum and Amartya Sen eds., *Quality Of Life*, Oxford, Clarendon Press, 1993, pp. 9–29.

Coleman, Janet, 'MacIntyre and Aquinas' in John Horton and Susan Mendus, eds., *After MacIntyre: Critical Perspectives on the Work of Alasdair MacIntyre*, Polity Press, 1994, pp. 65–90.

Crisp, Roger, ed., *How Should One Live?*, Oxford University Press, 1996.

Dancy, Jonathan, 'Ethical Particularism and Morally Relevant Properties', *Mind*, 92 (1983), 530–47.

Dasgupta, Partha, *An Inquiry into Well-Being and Destitution*, Oxford, Clarendon Press, 1993.

Diamond, Cora, 'Anything but Argument' and 'Missing the Adventure' in D. Z. Phillips and P. Winch, eds., *Wittgenstein: Attending to the Particular*, London, Macmillan, 1989, pp. 291–308 and 309–18.

The Realistic Spirit: Wittgenstein, Philosophy, and the Mind, Cambridge, Mass., MIT Press, 1991.

Douglas, Mary and Baron Isherwood, *The World of Goods*, Harmondsworth, Middlesex, Penguin Books, 1979.

Drèze, Jean and Amartya Sen, *Hunger and Public Action*, Oxford, Clarendon Press, 1989.

Dworkin, Ronald, *Taking Rights Seriously*, London, Duckworth, 1977.

Law's Empire, London, Fontana, 1986.

Elster, Jon, *The Cement of Society*, London, Routledge, 1989.

Feinberg, Joel, 'The Nature and Value of Rights' in his *Rights, Justice and the Bounds of Liberty*, Princeton University Press, 1980, pp. 143–58.

Fishkin, James, *The Limits of Obligation*, New Haven, Conn., Yale University Press, 1982.

Gadamer, Hans-Georg, *Truth and Method*, trans. Anon., London, Sheed and Ward, 1975.

Reason in the Age of Science, trans. Frederick G. Lawrence, Cambridge, Mass., MIT Press, 1981.

George, Robert P., ed., *Natural Law Theory: Contemporary Essays*, Oxford, Clarendon Press, 1992

Gewirth, Alan, *Human Rights: Essays on Justification and Applications*, University of Chicago Press, 1982.

'Rights and Virtues', *Analyse und Kritik*, 6 (1984), 28–48 and *Review of Metaphysics*, 38 (1985), 739–62.

'Ethical Universalism and Particularism', *Journal of Philosophy*, 85 (1988), 283–302.

Gilligan, Carol, *In a Different Voice: Psychological Theory and Women's Dependence*, Cambridge, Mass., Harvard University Press, 1982, 2nd edition 1993.

Goffman, Erving, *Stigma: Notes on the Management of Spoiled Identity*, Englewood Cliffs, NJ, Prentice Hall, 1963.

Habermas, Jürgen, *The New Conservatism: Cultural Criticism and the Historians' Debate*, trans. Shierry Weber Nicholsen, Cambridge, Polity Press, 1989.

Haksar, Vinit, *Equality, Liberty, and Perfectionism*, Oxford, Clarendon Press, 1979.

Hampshire, Stuart, ed., *Public and Private Morality*, Cambridge Unversity Press, 1978.

Hart, H. L. A., 'Rawls on Liberty and its Priority' in Norman Daniel, ed., *Reading Rawls*, Oxford, Blackwell, 1975, pp. 230–52.

Havel, Vaclav, 'The Power of the Powerless', trans. P. Wilson, in Jan Vladislav, ed., *Living in Truth*, London, Faber and Faber, 1986, pp. 36–122.

Herman, Barbara, *The Practice of Moral Judgement*, Cambridge, Mass., Harvard University Press, 1993.

Hill, Thomas E., Jr, 'Kantian Constructivism in Ethics', *Ethics*, 99 (1989), 752–70 and in his *Dignity and Practical Reason*, Ithaca, NY, Cornell University Press, 1992.

Hirschman, Albert O., *Exit, Voice and Loyalty*, Cambridge, Mass., Harvard University Press, 1970.

The Passions and the Interests: Political Arguments for Capitalism before Its Triumph, Princeton University Press, 1977.

Höffe, Otfried, 'Universalist Ethics and the Faculty of Judgement: An Aristotelian Look at Kant', *Philosophical Forum*, 25 (1993), 55–71.

Holmes, Steven, 'The Permanent Structure of Antiliberal Thought' in Nancy L. Rosenblum, ed., *Liberalism and the Moral Life*, Cambridge, Mass., Harvard University Press, 1989, pp. 225–53.

Honneth, Axel, *The Critique of Power: reflective stages in a critical social theory*, trans. Kenneth Baynes, Cambridge, Mass., MIT Press, 1991.

Horton, John and Susan Mendus, eds., *After MacIntyre: Critical Perspectives on the Work of Alasdair MacIntyre*, Cambridge, Polity Press, 1994.

Hume, David, *A Treatise of Human Nature* (1739), ed. L. A. Selby Bigge, revised edn., Oxford, Clarendon Press, 1958.

Hutcheson, Frances, *Illustrations upon the Moral Sense* (1728), ed. Bernard Peach, Cambridge, Mass., Harvard University Press, 1971.

Kant, Immanuel, *Critique of Pure Reason* (1781), trans. Norman Kemp Smith, London, Macmillan, 1929.

   What is Enlightenment? (1784) in H. Reiss, ed., *Kant: Political Writings*, Cambridge University Press, 2nd edn, 1991, pp. 54–60.

   Groundwork of the Metaphysic of Morals (1785), trans. H. J. Paton as *The Moral Law*, London, Hutchinson, 1953.

   What is Orientation in Thinking? (1786), in H. Reiss, ed., *Kant: Political Writings*, Cambridge University Press, 2nd edn, 1991, pp. 237–49.

   Perpetual Peace (1795) in H. Reiss, ed., *Kant: Political Writings*, Cambridge University Press, 2nd edn, 1991, pp. 93–130.

   On a Supposed Right to Lie out of Benevolent Motives (1797) in *Kant's Critique of Practical Reason and Other Writings on Moral Philosophy*, trans. L. W. Beck, University of Chicago Press, 1949.

Kittay, Eva Feders and Diane Meyers, eds., *Women and Moral Theory*, Totowa, NJ, Rowman and Littlefield, 1987.

Kruschwitz, Robert B. and Robert C. Roberts, eds., *The Virtues: Contemporary Essays in Moral Character*, Belmont, Calif., Wadsworth, 1987.

Kukathas, Chandran and Philip Pettit, *Rawls: 'A Theory of Justice' and its Critics*, Cambridge, Polity Press, 1990.

Laslett, Peter and James S. Fishkin, eds., *Justice Between Age Groups and Generations*, Philosophy Politics and Society, Sixth Series, New Haven, Conn., Yale University Press, 1992.

Lovibond, Sabina, *Realism and Imagination in Ethics*, Oxford, Blackwell, 1983.

Macedo, Stephen, *Liberal Virtues*, Oxford, Clarendon Press, 1990.

MacIntyre, Alasdair, *After Virtue: A Study in Moral Theory*, London, Duckworth, 1981.

   Is Patriotism a Virtue?, Department of Philosophy, University of Kansas, 1984.

Marcus, Ruth Barcan, 'Moral Dilemmas and Consistency', *The Journal of Philosophy*, 77 (1980), 121–36.

McDowell, John, 'Virtue and Reason', *Monist*, 62 (1979), 331–50, reworked as 'Non–Cognitivism and Rule-Following' in Steven Holtzmann and Christopher Leach, eds., *Wittgenstein: To Follow a Rule*, London, Routledge and Kegan Paul, 1981, pp. 141–62.

McMillan, Carol, *Women, Reason and Nature*, London, Routledge and Kegan Paul, 1982.

Milgrim, Stanley, *Obedience to Authority: An Experimental View*, London, Tavistock Publications, 1974.

Mill, J. S., *Utilitarianism* (1861) in *Utilitarianism, On Liberty and Other Essays*, ed. Mary Warnock, London, Fontana, 1962.

The Subjection of Women (1869) in *On Liberty and Other Writings*, ed. Stefan Collini, Cambridge University Press, 1989.

Mulhall, Stephen and Adam Swift, *Liberals and Communitarians*, Oxford, Blackwell, 1992.

Nagel, Thomas, *Equality and Impartiality*, Oxford University Press, 1991.

Nietzsche, Friedrich, *Thus Spoke Zarathustra*, trans. R. J. Hollingdale, Harmondsworth, Middlesex, Penguin Books, 1961.

The Gay Science, trans. Walter Kaufmann, New York, Vintage Press, 1974.

Nozick, Robert, *Anarchy, State, and Utopia*, New York, Columbia University Press, 1974.

Nussbaum, Martha, *The Fragility of Goodness: Luck and Ethics in Greek Tragedy and Philosophy*, Cambridge University Press, 1986.

Nussbaum Martha and Amartya Sen, *Quality of Life*, Oxford, Clarendon Press, 1993.

Okin, Susan, 'Justice and Gender', *Philosophy and Public Affairs*, 16 (1987), 42–72.

O'Neill, Onora, 'The Most Extensive Liberty', *Proceedings of the Aristotelian Society*, New Series 80 (1979–80), 45–59.

Faces of Hunger: An Essay on Poverty, Justice and Development, London, George Allen and Unwin, 1986

'Practical Thinking and Socratic Questions', *Ratio*, 28 (1986), 89–95.

'The Power of Example' in *Philosophy*, 61 (1986), 5–29 and in *Constructions of Reason*, pp. 165–86.

'Abstraction, Idealization and Ideology' in J. D. G. Evans, ed., *Moral Philosophy and Contemporary Problems* (RIP Series), Cambridge University Press, 1988, pp. 55–69.

'Ethical Reasoning and Ideological Pluralism', *Ethics*, 98 (1988), 705–22.

'Children's Rights and Children's Lives', *Ethics*, 99 (1988), 445–63 and in *Constructions of Reason*, pp. 187–205.

Constructions of Reason: Explorations of Kant's Practical Philosophy, Cambridge University Press, 1989.

'The Great Maxims of Justice and of Charity' in Neil MacCormick and Zenon Banowski, eds., *Enlightenment, Rights and Revolution*, University of Aberdeen Press, 1989 and in *Constructions of Reason*, pp. 219–33.

'Enlightenment as Autonomy: Kant's Vindication of Reason' in Peter Hulme and Ludmilla Jordanova, eds., *The Enlightenment and its Shadows*, London, Routledge, 1990, pp. 184–99.

'Autonomy, Coherence and Independence' in David Milligan and William Watts-Miller, eds., *Autonomy, Liberalism and Citizenship*, London, Avebury, 1992, pp. 202–29.

'Vindicating Reason' in Paul Guyer, ed., *The Cambridge Companion to Kant*, Cambridge University Press, 1992, pp. 280–308.

'Justice, Gender and International Boundaries' in Martha Nussbaum and Amartya Sen, eds., *Quality of Life*, Oxford, Clarendon Press, 1993, pp. 303–23.

'Duties and Virtues' in A. Phillips Griffiths, ed., *Ethics* (RIP supplementary volume 35), Cambridge University Press, 1993, pp. 107–20.

'Four Models of Practical Reason' in *Bounds of Justice*, Cambridge University Press forthcoming; German version 'Vier Modelle der praktischen Vernunft' in Hans Friedrich Fulda und Rolf-Peter Horstmann, eds., *Vernunft Begriffe in der Moderne*, Stuttgart, Klett-Cotta, 1994, pp. 586–606.

'Justice and Boundaries' in C. Brown, ed., *Political Restructuring in Europe: Ethical Perspectives*, London, Routledge, 1994, pp. 69–88.

Bounds of Justice, Cambridge University Press, forthcoming.

'Kant's Ethics and Kantian Ethics' in *Bounds of Justice*, Cambridge University Press, forthcoming.

Parfit, Derek, *Reasons and Persons*, Oxford, Clarendon Press, 1984.

Passerin d'Entrèves, Maurizio, *Modernity, Justice and Community*, Milan, Franco Angeli Libri, 1990.

Pateman, Carol, *The Sexual Contract*, Cambridge, Polity Press, 1988.

Paul, Ellen Frankel et al., eds., *Philanthropy and the Public Good*, Oxford, Blackwell, 1987.

Phillips, Derek L., *Looking Backward: A Critical Appraisal of Communitarian Thought*, Princeton University Press, 1933.

Phillips, D. Z. and H. O. Mounce, *Moral Practices*, London, Routledge and Kegan Paul, 1970.

Phillips, D. Z. and P. Winch, eds., *Wittgenstein: Attending to the Particular*, London, Macmillan, 1989.

Piaget, Jean, *The Moral Judgement of the Child*, London, Routledge and Kegan Paul, 1932; Glencoe, Ill., The Free Press, 1950.

Plato, *Meno*, in *Protagoras and Meno*, trans. W. K. C. Guthrie, Harmondsworth, Middlesex, Penguin Books, 1956.

Pocock, J. G. A., *Virtue, Commerce and History*, Cambridge University Press, 1985.

Pogge, Thomas, *Realizing Rawls*, Ithaca, NY, Cornell University Press, 1989.

'Cosmopolitanism and Sovereignty' in C. Brown, ed., *Political Restructuring in Europe: Ethical Perspectives*, London, Routledge, 1994, pp. 89–122.

Putnam, Hilary, *Realism and Reason: Philosophical Papers*, vol. III, Cambridge University Press, 1983.

Rachels, James, *The End of Life*, Oxford University Press, 1986.
Railton, Peter, 'How Thinking about Character and Utilitarianism might Lead to Rethinking the Character of Utilitarianism' in Peter A. French, Theodore E. Uehling and Howard K. Wettstein, eds., *Ethical Theory: Character and Virtue*, Midwest Studies in Philosophy, vol. XIII, University of Notre Dame Press, 1988, pp. 398–416.
Rawls, John, *A Theory of Justice*, Cambridge, Mass., Harvard University Press, 1971.
  'The Basic Structure as Subject', *American Philosophical Quarterly*, 14 (1977), 159–65.
  'Kantian Constructivism in Moral Theory', *Journal of Philosophy*, 77 (1980), 515–72; revised version in his *Political Liberalism*, New York, Columbia University Press, 1993.
  'Justice as Fairness: Political not Metaphysical', *Philosophy and Public Affairs*, 14 (1985), 223–51.
  'The Priority of Right and Ideas of the Good', *Philosophy and Public Affairs*, 17 (1988), 252–60.
  'The Law of Peoples' in Stephen Shute and Susan Hurley, eds., *On Human Rights: The Oxford Amnesty Lectures*, New York, Basic Books, 1993.
  Political Liberalism, New York, Columbia University Press, 1993.
Raz, Joseph, *Morality and Freedom*, Oxford, Clarendon Press, 1986.
Ripstein, Arthur, 'Foundationalism in Political Theory', *Philosophy and Public Affairs*, 16 (1987), 115–37.
Rosenblum, Nancy L., ed., *Liberalism and the Moral Life*, Cambridge, Mass., Harvard University Press, 1989.
Ross, David, *The Right and The Good*, Oxford University Press, 1930.
Rousseau, Jean-Jacques, *A Discourse on Inequality* (1755), trans. Maurice Cranston, Harmondsworth, Middlesex, Penguin Books, 1984.
Ruddick, Sara, *Maternal Thinking: Towards a Politics of Peace*, Boston, Mass., Beacon Press, 1987.
Sandel, Michael J., *Liberalism and the Limits of Justice*, Cambridge University Press, 1982.
Sartre, Jean-Paul, *Existentialism is a Humanism* in W. Kaufmann, ed., *Existentialism from Dostoevsky to Sartre*, Cleveland, World Publishing, 1956, pp. 287–311.
Schneewind, J. B., 'The Misfortunes of Virtue', *Ethics*, 101 (1990), 42–63.
Sen, Amartya, 'Behavior and the Concept of Preference', *Economica*, 40 (1973), 241–59; reprinted in his *Choice, Welfare and Measurement*, Oxford, Blackwell, 1982.
  'Rational Fools: A Critique of the Behavioral Foundations of Economic Theory', *Philosophy and Public Affairs*, 6 (1977),317–44.; reprinted in his *Choice, Welfare and Measurement*, Oxford, Blackwell, 1982.
  'Equality of What?' in S. McMurrin, ed., *Tanner Lectures on Human Values*, vol. I, Cambridge University Press, 1980.

Poverty and Famines: An Essay on Entitlement and Deprivation, Oxford, Clarendon Press, 1981.

'Capability and Well-Being' in Martha Nussbaum and Amartya Sen, eds., *Quality Of Life*, Oxford, Clarendon Press, 1993, pp. 30–53.

Sennet, Richard and Jonathan Cobb, *The Hidden Injuries of Class*, Cambridge University Press, 1972.

Sherman, Nancy, *The Fabric of Character: Aristotle's Theory of Virtue*, Oxford, Clarendon Press, 1991.

Shklar, Judith, *Ordinary Vices*, Cambridge, Mass., Harvard University Press, 1984.

Shue, Henry, *Basic Rights: Subsistence, Affluence and US Foreign Policy*, Princeton University Press, 1980.

Singer, Peter, *Animal Liberation: Towards an End to Man's Inhumanity to Animals*, London, Jonathan Cape, 1976.

Practical Ethics, Cambridge University Press, 1979.

Singer, Peter and Helga Kuhse, *Should the Baby Live?*, Oxford University Press, 1985.

Slote, Michael, 'Utilitarian Virtue' in Peter A. French, Theodore E. Uehling and Howard K. Wettstein, eds., *Ethical Theory: Character and Virtue*, Midwest Studies in Philosophy, vol. XIII, Notre Dame University Press, 1988, pp. 384–97.

Smart, J. J. C. and Bernard Williams, *Utilitarianism: For and Against*, Cambridge University Press, 1973.

Steiner, Hillel, 'Individual Liberty', *Proceedings of the Aristotelian Society*, New Series 75 (1974–5), 33–50.

An Essay on Rights, Oxford, Blackwell, 1994.

Stern, Robert, 'MacIntyre and Historicism' in John Horton and Susan Mendus, eds., *After MacIntyre: Critical Perspectives on the Work of Alasdair MacIntyre*, Cambridge, Polity Press, 1994, pp. 146–60.

Stocker, Michael, *Plural and Conflicting Values*, Oxford, Clarendon Press, 1990.

Strauss, David, 'The Liberal Virtues' in John W. Chapman and William A. Galston, eds., *Virtue* (*Nomos*, 34), New York University Press, 1992.

Symposium on Duties Beyond Borders, Ethics, 98 (1988)

Tamir, Yael, *Liberal Nationalism*, Princeton University Press, 1993.

Taylor, Charles, 'What is Human Agency?' in his *Human Agency and Language: Philosophical Papers*, vols. I and II respectively, Cambridge University Press, 1985, pp. 15–44.

'Atomism' and 'What's Wrong with Negative Liberty?' in his *Philosophy and the Human Sciences: Philosophical Papers*, vol. II, Cambridge University Press, 1985, respectively pp. 187–210 and 211–29.

Sources of the Self: The Making of Modern Identity, Cambridge, Mass., Harvard University Press, 1989.

Taylor, Charles et al., *Multiculturalism and 'The Politics of Recognition'*, Princeton University Press, 1992.

Thomson, Judith Jarvis, *Rights, Restitution and Risk: Essays in Moral Theory*, Cambridge, Mass., Harvard University Press, 1986.

Tooley, Michael, 'Abortion and Infanticide', *Philosophy and Public Affairs*, 2 (1972), 37–63.

Abortion and Infanticide, Oxford University Press, 1983.

Trianosky, Gregory, 'What Is Virtue Ethics All About?', *American Philosophical Quarterly*, 27 (1990), 335–44.

Trilling, Lionel, *Sincerity and Authenticity*, Oxford University Press, 1972.

Waide, John, 'Virtues and Principles', *Philosophy and Phenomenological Research*, 48 (1988), 455–72.

Walzer, Michael, 'The Distribution of Membership' in Peter Brown and Henry Shue, eds., *Boundaries*, Totowa, NJ, Rowman and Littlefield, 1981.

Spheres of Justice: A Defence of Pluralism and Equality, Oxford, Martin Robertson, 1983.

Interpretation and Social Criticism, Cambridge, Mass., Harvard University Press, 1987.

Weil, Simone, *The Need for Roots: Prelude to a Declaration of Duties towards Mankind*, trans. A. F. Wills, London, Routledge and Kegan Paul, 1952.

Wiggins, David, 'Deliberation and Practical Reason' in his *Needs, Values and Truth: Essays in the Philosophy of Value*, Aristotelian Society Series, 6, Oxford, Blackwell, 1987.

Williams, Bernard, 'Morality and the Emotions' in *The Problems of the Self: Philosophical Papers 1956–72*, Cambridge University Press, 1973.

Moral Luck: Philosophical Essays 1973–80, Cambridge University Press, 1981.

Ethics and the Limits of Philosophy, London, Fontana, 1985.

Winch, Peter, *Ethics and Action*, London, Routledge and Kegan Paul, 1972.

Wittgenstein, Ludwig, *Philosophical Investigations*, ed. G. E. M. Anscombe and R. Rhees, Oxford, Blackwell, 1953.

Remarks on the Foundations of Mathematics, trans. G. E. M. Anscombe, ed. G. H. von Wright, R. Rhees and G. E. M. Anscombe, Oxford, Blackwell, 1965.

Lectures on the Foundations of Mathematics, ed. Cora Diamond, Sussex, Harvester, 1976.

Index

abortion 95–6, 100; *see also* bioethics
abstraction 2, 3, 18, 23, 38–44, 56, 59ff, 67–9, 72–8, 90, 122, 154–7, 182–3, 210; *see also* idealization; principles; thick concepts
act descriptions *see* action
act-centred ethics 71, 73–90, 122–3, 145ff, 154ff, 180
act-oriented conceptions of practical reason *see* practical reason
action 66–90; act descriptions 66–71, 74–90, 138, 154; act-tokens 159, 208; act-types 66–7, 127, 143, 159, 208; ends of action 66–7; preference-oriented conceptions of action 47; sources of action 66–7, 72–3, 89; *see also* intelligibility; presuppositions of activity; principles
action-guiding ethics 2, 51–2, 57, 59, 70, 85, 87–90, 211
agent-centred ethics 71–3; *see also* virtue ethics
agents 64, 91–121, 127; agency 4, 44, 82; solitary agents 103–4; proto-agents 112; *see also* conceptions of the self; metaphysics, of the person; scope of ethical consideration; subjects
agreement and disagreement, ethical 86–9; *on* agreement *see* intelligibility; rule-following; thick concepts; *on* disagreement *see* cross-cultural reasoning; ethical pluralism
agriculture 177–8, 192, 203–4; *see also* environment; justice, environmental
algorithms 75, 78–81, 85, 123, 182; quasi-algorithms 75, 82
anarchy 166
antagonism between justice and virtue *see* justice and virtue
anthropocentrism in ethics 8, 177, 203; *see also* justice, environmental; virtues, green
Aquinas 138

Aristotelian ethics 12, 14–17, 27, 33, 86
Aristotle 14, 15, 17, 27, 67, 103, 108, 138
asylum *see* borders
atomistic conception of self *see* conceptions of the self
attachments and relationships 12, 17, 20–1, 36–7, 49, 96–7, 168, 185–6, 194–7, 200–3; *see also* commitments; love; loyalty; 'near and dear'
attention, attentiveness *see* judgement, as perception; virtues, social
attitudes 58, 66, 186, 188, 202ff; *see also* commitments, reflexive attitudes; remainders
authority of reason *see* constructivism; practical reason
autonomy and independence 26, 42–4, 94, 158, 187, 193, 201; *see also* connection; dependents and dependence; finitude; virtues, executive; vulnerability

basic structure *see* Rawls
biodiversity 178, 204; *see also* environment; justice, environmental
bioethics 42, 94–5, 110–11
blame 40, 83; *see also* remainders
borders 5, 19, 22, 29, 53–5; of communities 123; porous 20, 54, 173; of private life 123, 186; of states 113, 123, 172–3; *see also* cross-cultural reasoning; scope of ethical consideration; states

capacities and capabilities 8, 41, 56, 62–5, 100, 102, 105–6, 108–11, 120–1, 124, 168–73, 191, 200, 210; to act 111, 125, 171; incipient 111; lack of 110–11; to experience 111; *see also* agents; connection; finitude; idealization; self-sufficiency; vulnerabilities
care and concern 141, 149, 151, 195–201, 207–8; *see also* virtues, social